For our mothers,
Adelle Frenzel Schnabel and Laura Shauman Bailey

# ADOLESCENT FEMALE PORTRAITS IN THE AMERICAN NOVEL 1961–1981

GARLAND REFERENCE LIBRARY
OF THE HUMANITIES
(VOL. 405)

## Editors
Jane S. Bakerman    Mary Jean DeMarr

## Assistants
Mary Lu McFall    Justyn Moulds    Louise W. Richards

## Contributors

Martha Alderson
Virginia Anderson
Barbara J. Asay
Marilyn J. Atlas
Catherine A. Baker
Jane S. Bakerman
Sarah D. Beckley
Lonnie Paul Beene
Evonne Burdison
Vera G. Channels
Neysa Chouteau
Carol Cleveland
Le Anne Daniels
Mary Jean DeMarr
Donna Dunbar-Odom
Sarah B. Greenburg
Susan Lee Hoffman
Shirley L. Jones
Nancy Carol Joyner

Valda Kester
Sara Kixmiller
Mary Lu McFall
Constance H. McLaren
Teresa Mangum
Justyn Moulds
Trudy J. Newmister
Anda Olsen
Charlene B. Pierard
Louise W. Richards
Faye Sanders
William C. Schnabel
Michael Shelden
Susan Lynn Smith
Karen Chittick Stabler
Carol Sutherland
Bonnie J. Wallace
Elizabeth Weller
W. Tasker Witham

# ADOLESCENT FEMALE PORTRAITS IN THE AMERICAN NOVEL 1961–1981

Jane S. Bakerman
Mary Jean DeMarr

GARLAND PUBLISHING, INC. · NEW YORK & LONDON
1983

**Library of Congress Cataloging in Publication Data**

Bakerman, Jane S., 1931–
    Adolescent female portraits in the American novel, 1961–1981.

    (Garland reference library of the humanities ;
v. 405)
    Includes index.
    1. American fiction—20th century—Bibliography.
2. Adolescent girls—United States—Fiction—
Bibliography.  3. Children's stories, American—
Bibliography.  4. Adolescent girls in literature—
Handbooks, manuals, etc.  I. DeMarr, Mary Jean,
1932–   .  II. Title.  III. Series.
    Z1231.F4B354  1983      813'.54'09352042      82-49139
    [PS374.A3]
    ISBN  0-8240-9136-1

Cover design by Laurence Walczak

Printed on acid-free, 250-year-life paper
Manufactured in the United States of America

# CONTENTS

# PREFACE

During the past decade, as the social awareness of many Americans has deepened, literary critics, librarians, teachers, and other readers have begun to make new demands upon authors of reference books and upon the reference materials themselves. Many of these demands arose from changing views of the roles of women in American society. As readers searched for reference sources which would help them select primary materials useful in studies of the literary portraits of women and their societal roles, it became increasingly clearer that few such sources were available. This problem became especially evident to us in the late seventies when we planned and conducted sessions for a Modern Language Association convention. These seminars dealt with portraits of adolescent females in novels, and we discovered that, for the most part, personal knowledge of primary works was the chief means of locating such portraits. We were also struck by the great number of proposed papers which arrived in our offices as well as by the large attendance at the sessions. These factors indicated that interest in literary treatments of young women was very high. The plan for this bibliography arose, then, from a sense of the need for such a reference work and from our own interest in and knowledge of the subject and of the genre.

The years 1961 to 1981 were set as boundaries for this volume because our initial research revealed that a twenty-year span was a manageable unit, because the novels published between those dates yielded abundant materials for such a reference work, and because significant changes in the way portraits of adolescent females were being drawn took place during the period—for example, sex-role stereotyping became a shade less prevalent, young women's sexuality was discussed more forthrightly, and some topics (such as single women's pregnancies and lesbianism) were treated more overtly, sometimes less judgmentally. The annotations for the novels discussed in this volume, however, do not comment upon those changes, for doing so is not the proper function of this book. Instead, the annotations convey an idea of plots and themes and indicate the significance of adolescent female characters to the structures, themes, or theses of the novels. The bibliography is intended as a reference tool for scholars, librarians, teachers, and other readers, as a means of locating fictional treatments of female adolescents. The task of fully identifying and evaluating changing or developing trends falls more properly to works of analytical discourse than to annotated bibliography, and we hope that this book will lay a useful foundation for such work. Bibliographical data refer to the first American editions.

Novels published between 1961 and 1981 were selected for inclusion if the roles of the female adolescent characters had genuine importance to the plots or theses. Novels with significant female characters between the ages of approximately twelve and twenty-two are included, although occasionally slightly younger characters—as in the case of Bruce Jay Friedman's *The Dick* (#135), which features an "uncommonly mature" ten year old—qualified a novel for this bibliography. Of necessity, all of the annotations are brief but designed to point out the functions of the female adolescent characters. Entries for such works as John Ashmead's *The Mountain and the Feather* (#14) and Anton Myrer's *The Last Convertible* (#331), for instance, are examples of inclusions which depict young female characters only in subplots or depict adolescent females as adjuncts (often motivations for the behavior) of male protagonists. These portraits are significant, for they reveal important attitudes toward women.

Novels listed are about American girls in American settings and were written by American authors; thus, *Now Ameriky* (#96) by Betty Sue Cummings which deals with the Americanization of an adolescent female appears in the listing whereas some other popular favorites such as May Sarton's *Mrs. Stevens Hears the Mermaids Singing*, Norma Klein's *Sunshine*, and Bette Greene's *Morning Is a Long Time Coming* do not appear because they are set, wholly or primarily, in other countries; Richard Jessup's *A Quiet Voyage Home* (#224), set on the high seas, is included because the ship is a microcosm of the United States in the period; similarly, Ursula LeGuin's *The Beginning Place*, (#268), although not set entirely in the United States, is included (as are several other fantasies) because of the novel's comment upon American adolescent alienation. Books in both "high" and "popular" culture are listed as are some young adult and juvenile novels which also appeal to reasonably sophisticated adult readers. In the interest of uniformity, however, these titles are not singled out within the entries. A very few paperback originals have been included.

During the process of selecting novels for inclusion, approximately two thousand novels were read and evaluated. Principal sources of likely titles were *Book Review Digest* (1960–1982), *Adolescence in Literature* by Thomas West Gregory (New York and London: Longman, 1978), and a list developed by Professor W. Tasker Witham for use in his own teaching and research. For many years, Dr. Witham has been a valued fellow student, colleague, and mentor to us, and we thank him for his constant support and friendship. Friends, colleagues and contributors were also quick to suggest titles which would be useful but which did not appear in our source materials.

As editors of this volume, we owe great thanks not only to Tasker Witham but also to many others—most particularly to our contributors for their work, for their suggestions, and, very importantly, for the warmth and moral support which many of them so generously offered. Contributors were selected on the basis of their interest in contemporary fiction, their skills as readers and critics—and their willingness to do a great deal of very hard work; all read many titles which did not prove to be acceptable for inclusion; all have been amenable to the demands made on their time. Though most are teachers, librarians, and graduate students known to us through our own earlier work, some were recommended by friends, associates, and other contributors as a network of dedicated participants developed. Both contributors and editors also owe not only thanks but applause to librarians in towns and cities widely separated geographically yet closely united on this project. Locating the novels was a massive task, and we much appreciate the work of all the librarians who accomplished it.

    We are grateful to the Indiana State University Research Committee for the grant which enabled us to organize the original concept into a workable plan. And, here at Indiana State, a very special group of people gave aid and encouragement as this book developed from idea to manuscript, from two-woman undertaking to a team project. The splendid Interlibrary Loan staff at Cunningham Memorial Library, particularly Karen Chittick Stabler, Mary Ann Phillips, and Carol Chapman, as well as the extraordinarily able secretarial personnel in the Department of English, Sonia Martin, Mary Ann Wallace, and Betty Harstad, were all unfailingly patient and helpful. To Justyn Moulds, Mary Lu McFall and Louise Richards, our warm thanks and deep gratitude for their special contributions of time, talent, and skills in the organizational work and in the preparation of the manuscript. Of course, we take responsibility for any errors which may appear.

    We appreciate the efforts of all who believed in and helped create this book.

Jane S. Bakerman, Mary Jean DeMarr
*Indiana State University*

# INTRODUCTION

Despite the wide variety of techniques, styles, and plots employed by the 477 authors of the 579 subject-novels covered in our study, four strong elements unify this annotated bibliography. The first of these factors, the subject matter (the adolescent female), is obvious and was, of course, a given from the outset. Second, most of these fictions are *Bildungsromane* and are devoted to the portrayal of adolescents entering and accommodating to the "real," adult world. This second unifying element was not surprising and revealed itself almost immediately.

From the first, we also presupposed the eventual emergence of a third unifying element which, we assumed, would arise from the preponderance of certain images. Its form, however, was a bit different from what we had anticipated (or feared). Because "teenager," "adolescent," and "juvenile" (like such terms as "housewife," "libber," "old folks," and "career woman") are often perceived as pejoratively "loaded" words, we speculated that negative stereotypes might occur in abundance. We wondered if images of infuriatingly peppy cheerleaders, grimy hippies, bespectacled grinds, infatuated gigglers, thoughtless rebels, and sultry Lolitas would dominate these pages.

Some of these stereotypical figures do, of course, appear. These characters are used almost solely to serve various plot devices (they often trigger subplots) or to motivate male characters. Books which depict such examples are *Hammett* (#152), *The Long Gainer* (#294), and *The Mountain and the Feather* (#14). Other fairly stereotypical characters, as in *Valley of the Dolls* (#500), serve their authors' themes (in *Valley*, that the pressures of the actor's life can destroy young women). Another stereotype, the talented young black who escapes from the ghetto and into show business, appears only once—in *The Soul Brothers and Sister Lou* (#213), but even then, the escape motif is more suggested than fully realized, and one old stereotypical standby, the "tomboy," also appears fairly infrequently. Even these limited examples indicate, then, that the *dominant* images authors use to characterize these young females are not stereotypes, and this perception helps lay to rest a dated, unappealing myth. Fictional adolescents are no more often stereotypical than are their "real-life" counterparts.

However, in place of the tomboys and the gigglers, certain patterns did appear. As we read, contemplated, evaluated, and wrote, it became evident that whereas each portrait discussed in this bibliography is, in itself, a separate, individual image, numbers of them also fall into useful "group" images which stem from specific areas of continuing auctorial interest. Fourteen of these important, powerful female images emerged, constituting the third element of unity for the bibliography. They are (in alphabetical order):

1. *Aspiring Artists/Gifted Girls.* These characters have special talents or abilities and wish to use them in pursuit of creative, scholarly, or artistic careers in order to establish their self-definitions.

2. *Beauty Queens/Stars.* These characters also aspire; they wish for recognition (rather than for achievement), and they perceive their bodies and their personalities as primary tools for reaching their goals.

3. *Friends.* These characters are examined through their relationships as comrades; they may be friends of either males or females, but friendship and their reactions to it are central to the revelation of their personalities.

4. *Heroes.* These characters engage in some remarkable act of courage, endurance, commitment; some show surprising stability or even maturity within their particular, trying circumstances.

5. *Love-Struck Girls.* These characters are intent upon seeking, acquiring, or being found by a love object; either heterosexual or lesbian relationships may be involved.

6. *Mates.* These characters are seen primarily within their relationships with husbands, cohabitors, or long-term lovers.

7. *Mothers.* These characters are seen primarily as parents; a smaller number of young women are seen in this light because of

the young age of the subjects and because this topic is almost always treated in conjunction with *Mates*.

8. *Protesters*. These characters reject the values of the culture; their rejections may lead to action or to withdrawal and alienation.

9. *Rebellious Daughters*. These characters are seen primarily through their rejection of family, and they are often also *Protesters*.

10. *Sirens*. These characters define themselves primarily in terms of their sexuality which they use to achieve power and control over others; their portraits tend to be negative.

11. *Sisters*. These characters are examined through their sibling relationships; they may be sisters of either males or females, but the family tie is central to the revelation of the girls' personalities.

12. *Students*. These characters are all shown as secondary school or college pupils; their responses to the academic and social demands of their schools are central to their development. This group is a shade more miscellaneous than most of the others because most adolescents *are* students; also, the novels tend to vary in tone—social criticism, satire, analysis of the academic scene, for example.

13. *Victims*. These characters are depicted as vulnerable to circumstance; they suffer from crime, poverty, illness, or child abuse, and they are characterized by their fates. Some appear only briefly (or even not at all), but their victimization is crucial to the novel.

14. *Villains/Tricksters*. These characters, either through mischief or malice, consciously harm others. Frequently, their machinations set the plot rolling and they, perhaps, tend to serve the plot more than to be characterized in their own rights.

These are the dominant images; they do not appear in every novel included in the bibliography, but each appears frequently enough to indicate that they are objects of primary interest not only to writers but also to readers.

Within this more limited diversity lies the fourth and final element unifying the titles annotated here, a factor which serves almost every title included and which lends extraordinary power to many of the fourteen key images: the theme of the female adolescent striving to establish an acceptable identity (one of our editors at Garland called it "the image of females straining for self-realization") is, indeed, pervasive.

In *The Cherry in the Martini* (#220), Rona Jaffe describes adolescence as

> less than a country; it is an island . . . a wild, dark place with moments of blinding white light, where the landscape stretches forever and the markers are few. The people who inhabit it are half savage and full of the beginning of tenderness. They drink blood. They huddle together without understanding why they like whom they think they love, and they break apart without explanation because the smallest thing is reason enough.

Such words as "acceptable," "self-realization," "markers," and "huddle" are crucial, coloring the important fictional images of adolescent females.

The *Love-Struck Girls*, *Mothers*, *Mates*, many *Sirens*, and most *Friends* and *Sisters* tend to be examples of those who "huddle together," seeking, in varying ways and in varying degrees, to achieve maturation through unity with "significant others" who help them to define themselves. Sometimes, these relationships function well temporarily but must later be dissolved, as in *The Friends* (#174), or must be redefined, as in *Entering Ephesus* (#16). In other novels, the huddling never works effectively, and the young women are forced to realize that alternate means of self-realization are necessary; *Baby Love* (#300) is one example.

Of primary importance in growth toward full selfhood is the identification of "markers," as Jaffe suggests, and the young women in these categories believe, at least initially, that their huddles converge at signposts which will guide them. When the huddles "break apart" (with or without explanation), as in *The Girls from the Five Great Valleys* (#441), the youngsters continue their searches, usually having learned how better to identify useful markers. The dissolution of the huddles and the abandonment of the original markers are almost always painful, and these characters, like nearly every female adolescent in every group, suffer as they strain for maturity, demonstrating that neither achieving nor losing true self-realization can be considered a comfortable, easy process.

By virtue of their preoccupation with school, one of society's approved institutions, *Students* frequently initiate their maturation experiences by embracing established markers, and for them, also, huddling sometimes seems to be a useful method of coping with life. Very often, however, neither the established markers nor their relationships with their peers prove adequate for successful development, and they must redefine their landmarks as they define their self-images. Characters in *The Cheerleader* (#286) and *Masquerade* (#55) display this pattern of growth.

The *Protesters* and the *Rebellious Daughters*, in a sometimes wry, often ironic, and usually interesting twist, progress by rejecting the obvious, traditional markers which have been useful to the "establishment" or to parents. These girls' acts of rejection generally force them to invent, erect, and rely upon their own markers, their own standards and values. Some of these social insurgents prevail, establishing workable, effective new markers; others fail and are forced to reevaluate the recommendations they once scorned. Sample titles for these patterns are *The Weedkiller's Daughter* (#13) and *Dinky Hocker Shoots Smack* (#308). Success or failure depends, generally, upon another of the crucial words—"acceptable." To the *Protesters* and *Rebellious Daughters*, "acceptable" means one thing; to their would-be mentors, it means another.

Acceptability of one's self-definition, one's mature identity, is also a problem for another important image group. The *Aspiring Artists/Gifted Girls*, such as Janey Hurdle of *Lessons* (#573) and Jane Seaman of *The Small Room* (#440), seek identities for which few (if any) viable markers exist. Because they wish to penetrate fields widely regarded as male preserves, they must chart unmarked courses while rejecting markers traditionally approved for female use. Self-actualization is often particularly painful for the young women characters in this group, but though some of them, as in *The Edge* (#316), fail, a gratifying number do manage to achieve it.

Less successful, generally, are the *Beauty Queens/Stars*, for most rely upon false or misleading markers. Too frequently, these girls embrace the tawdry or demeaning standards of their desired professions (such as film stardom) without much attempt at self-definition. By allowing others' markers to define their lives, they often fail and are sometimes destroyed. *Miss Rhode Island* (#249) and *Tinsel* (#150) illustrate these patterns.

This image group shares a problem with many of the *Victims*: others identify their markers for them. In the cases of victims of various crimes, illness and disability, or racism, for instance, victimization is forced upon them. Some examples are *Outrun the Dark* (#26), *The Bluest Eye* (#326), and *Waiting for Johnny Miracle* (#18). In other cases, the *Victims* themselves mistakenly embrace false and destructive markers. *Early Disorder* (#232) is a good example here.

Quite frequently, however, intended *Victims* summon enough energy and wisdom to refuse others' definitions of themselves, to define their own identities, and to claim useful markers. In doing so, they help, along with hosts of other female characters depicted in the books treated in this bibliography, to lay to rest one final stereotypical myth—the myth that the fictional female is essentially unthinking or passive. Most of the characters in the novels examined during this study are young women of physical action or people who lead examined lives. Of course, this pattern is in keeping with the *Bildungsroman* structure, a structure organized around some sort of physical or emotional maturation journey, but some of the characters discussed in these pages are even more than voyagers and actors.

Some are *Heroes*. As examplified in *The Last Year of the War* (#335), *Grandpa and Frank* (#290), *Leafy Rivers* (#543), and *After the First Death* (#87), these young women engage in great feats of bravery, defining themselves in terms of moral or spiritual courage, strength, and will. Generally, they, too, must invent and establish their own markers, and they are competent to do so.

In contrast with the *Heroes*, who usually emerge as admirable characters, the *Villains/Tricksters* are certainly less than admirable, often downright despicable. These females use deceit, fakery, and lies to achieve their ends or simply to "have fun," sometimes because of false markers (such as selfishness) or, even more sadly, from a sense that destructiveness is their only option. As a rule, they, too, avoid passivity, but their actions are outrageous and disruptive. Though some persist in this behavior throughout their stories, others learn and mature enough to abandon their childish, willful pranks. Pertinent examples are *Angel of Light* (#341), *Let's Go Play at the Adams'* (#226), and *The Fires of Arcadia* (#185).

It is notable, perhaps, that these last two images, the *Heroes* and the *Villains/Tricksters*, are not identifiable in the subject index of this bibliography, as are, for example, *Mothers*, *Mates*, *Students*, or even *Sirens* (who appear under "Sexual Activity"). This fact may be a final and telling example of the unity within diversity evident throughout this study. Those *Villains/Tricksters*, disquietingly, and those *Heroes*, happily, are apt to turn up anywhere! To facilitate our readers' examination of all fourteen major images, the following checklist of important images cites titles typical of each group; only one important image is identified for any novel.

*Jane S. Bakerman, Mary Jean DeMarr*
*Indiana State University*

# CHECKLIST OF IMPORTANT IMAGES

Adolescent Female Portraits
in the American Novel
1961–1981

1. Abbey, Edward. *Black Sun*. New York: Simon and
   Schuster, 1971. 159pp.

   Disenchanted with academe, marriage, and society,
   Will Gatlin, thirty-seven, has become a fire
   watcher in the Southwest. His redemptive summer
   affair with nineteen-year-old Sandy MacKenzie is
   contrasted with a friend's failing marriage.

2. Abrams, Linsey. *Charting by the Stars*. New York:
   Harmony Books, 1979. 256pp.

   This episodic first-person novel traces Angela's
   life from childhood, when her father deserts the
   family to go to sea, through boarding school, a
   liberal college in the sixties, first love affairs,
   and first, and wildly inappropriate, job. Told
   as a series of anecdotes, some of which are fantasy, some straightforward narrative, the story
   is intense and witty.

3. Adams, Alice. *Rich Rewards*. New York: Alfred A.
   Knopf, 1980. 205pp.

   Adams focuses on the freedoms and neuroses of
   an independent middle-aged woman of the 70s and
   80s and uses flashbacks to traces her protagonist's
   development from a boy-crazy childhood and adolescence to an enthusiastically heterosexual adulthood. The survivor of multiple affairs, Daphne
   Matthieson vividly recalls her first act of adultery at the age of twenty with Jean-Paul, a French
   socialist and economist. Recalling her time with
   him as intense and wonderful, she becomes mildly
   obsessed with him after twenty-plus years apart.
   At the same time, she becomes embroiled with the
   problems of a San Francisco family, the Houstons,
   and, more specifically, Caroline Houston, a
   young woman seeking her own sexual identity.
   Caroline chooses homosexuality, and Daphne, reunited with Jean-Paul, reasserts her heterosex-
   uality.

4. Adleman, Robert H. *The Bloody Benders*. New
   York: Stein & Day Publishers, 1970. 225pp.

   In his first novel, Adleman details the activities of an actual family who used their road-
   side inn as a means to murder and rob travelers
   in 1870 Kansas. Bradley Fisher is the first-

person narrator who falls in love with Kate Bender,
the overpoweringly beautiful and seductive ring-
leader of this family of killers.  The lovely,
young Kate seduces a number of gullible and infatuated men including Bradley and uses her
sexuality to convince them to help her family
dispose of stolen goods.  After killing an un-
known number of travelers and burying eleven of
their victims on their property, the Benders
disappear, fearing disclosure of and execution
for their deeds.  Adleman claims to have discovered the actual fate of the family: Bradley and
several more of Kate's suitors track down and
murder the fleeing family.  The author's use of
Kansas dialect brings this novel a step above
mere historical gore.

5.   Albert, Mimi.  *The Second Story Man*.  New York:
        Fiction Collective, 1975.  106pp.

     Anna, a student, recounts the disintegration
of her friend, Mary, college dropout and refugee
from her parents' middle-class life.  Mary's
involvement with Florian Rando,undercutting her
independence and sense of self, sets her roaming
from one grim job to another to support him.
Highly episodic, told in the present tense, the
novel evokes the lives of these contemporary
New York City nomads.

6.   Allen, Elizabeth.  *The Loser*.  New York: E.P.
        Dutton & Company, Inc., 1965.  128pp.

     This novel portrays the development of Deitz
and Lee Ames, sixteen and fifteen.  Denny Hawks,
a twenty-year-old Harvard dropout, affects the
lives of both sisters.  Deitz, the protagonist,
dates Denny and learns some hard lessons when
she discovers he is a liar and a poseur.  Lee,
a blossoming writer, conquers her disappointment
when he steals one of her poems.  Both girls
gain insight and maturity as a result of this
painful relationship.

7.   Alther, Lisa.  *Kinflicks*.  New York: Alfred A.
        Knopf, 1976.  503pp.

     Virginia Babcock Bliss remembers her youth in
extensive flashbacks.  Her memories are marked
with humor and insight and document her rebellion
against parental domination, her sexual activity

during high school and college as well as some
of the major influences of her college years.

8. Alther, Lisa. *Original Sins*. New York: Alfred
   A. Knopf, 1981. 592pp.

   Emily and Sally Prince, privileged daughters of
   the mill-owner in the small town of Newland,
   Tennessee, are part of The Five, close friends
   who innocently feel they are in control of their
   own glorious destinies. Since their class, opportunity, and abilities vary, The Five follow destinies of their own making but not necessarily
   of their own choosing. Sally, the popular princess, marries so early that she rushes prematurely
   into adulthood, parenthood, and resentful boredom. Emily, who always did well in school but
   was uncomfortable with being plain and unpopular,
   has a more difficult adolescence but finds a non-
   conforming niche of her own after moving to New
   York City. Sally and Emily face many of the same
   crises--racism, political activism, classism,
   sexual conflict, confusion over their relationships with their parents--with quite different
   defenses and accommodations.

9. Andrews, V.C. [Virginia]. *Flowers in the Attic*.
   New York: Pocket Books, 1979. 411pp.

   In this paperback bestseller, young Cathy
   Dollanganger, her older brother Chris, and their
   younger siblings Carrie and Cory, are locked in
   a room adjacent to a huge attic at the home of
   their maternal grandparents after the sudden death
   of their father. By imprisoning them, their Momma
   seeks to inherit millions from her father who
   disapproved of her marriage to his brother's
   son. During their imprisonment Cathy dreams
   of becoming a ballerina and enters a fearful
   adolescence after being raped by her brother.
   After Cory's death from eating doughnuts laced
   with arsenic, Cathy and Chris effect their escape with the surviving twin, Carrie.

10. Andrews, V.C. [Virginia]. *Petals on the Wind*.
    New York: Pocket Books, 1980. 439pp.

    The sequel to *Flowers in the Attic* relates the
    further adventures of Cathy Dollanganger, her
    brother Chris, and Carrie who enters her adoles-
    cence scarred by the events in the previous book.
    The novel concentrates on Cathy's development,

her marriages, her ballet career, and her eventual
"marriage" to her brother. The subplot traces
the adolescence of Carrie and relates her inability
to grow either physically or emotionally.

11. Applewhite, Cynthia. *Sundays.* New York: Avon
    Books, 1979. 204pp.

    Puzzled by the separation of her parents, offend-
    ed by the patronizing attitude of her aunts with
    whom she, her mother, and brother have taken
    refuge, Charlotte Louella Moonlight enters puberty
    torn by conflicting influences. The aunts' outward
    devoutness pulls Cha'Lou toward Bible Belt Chris-
    tianity; dim awareness of her adored uncle's sen-
    suality and the overt efforts of another teenager,
    Irma Renner, to introduce her to sexuality (Irma
    is both seductress and fumbling madam) generate
    guilt and tension. Everyone tells Cha'Lou how to
    behave; no one gives her real attention or an
    honest set of values. The result is a troubled,
    tormented adolescent.

12. Armstrong, Charlotte. *The Turret Room.* New York:
    Coward-McCann, 1965. 253pp.

    A writer of mystery and suspense novels based
    on solid characterizations, Armstrong creates
    here a complex situation involving a wealthy
    and powerful California family, its spoiled daugh-
    ter and her brief marriage at sixteen, her deaf
    baby, and a distantly related social worker who
    perceives the thoughtless cruelty of the family.
    Nineteen-year-old Wendy is concerned only with her
    own freedom and gratification, and she is perfectly
    willing to victimize once again her naive but
    responsible former husband. Although not sym-
    pathetic to Wendy, the author implies that she
    has been caught in an environment which has warped
    her. Though the novel's taut suspense primarily
    concerns others, the portrait of Wendy is very
    important.

13. Arnow, Harriett Simpson. *The Weedkiller's Daughter.*
    New York: Alfred A. Knopf, 1970. 372pp.

    At fifteen, Susan Schnitzer leads a double life.
    Most of the year she resides with her immediate
    family, sternly ruled by her excessively patriotic,
    racist father. During vacations, Susan lives hap-

pily with her mother's relatives whose attitudes
oppose those of her parents. Susan's secret adventures with two boys and the growing disaffection of
her friends dramatize the great gap between young
people and adults in the sixties.

14. Ashmead, John. *The Mountain and the Feather*.
    Boston: Houghton Mifflin Company, 1961. 397pp.

    At nineteen, Leilani Kim, a Japanese-Korean
    resident of Hawaii, is completing her nursing
    training during World War II. Her difficult
    romance with Montgomery Classen, a serviceman
    from the mainland, is the important subplot to
    the story of his wartime experiences.

15. Astor, Mary. *The Image of Kate*. Garden City,
    N.Y.: Doubleday & Company, Inc., 1962. 331pp.

    Though Kate Martin's life to age sixty is relat-
    ed, the novel focuses at length on her adolescence.
    Her mother dies in childbirth and Kate is reared
    by her father, adult brothers and a sister-in-law.
    Among these busy people, Kate feels unwanted and
    guilty; she copes with these emotions by per-
    fectionism in her school work, aloofness, and
    self-imposed exile from the California ranch she
    loves. Her tangled relationships with her one
    good friend, Vivian, a school chum, and her
    husband, Douglas, are the complications in the
    plot.

16. Athos, Daphne. *Entering Esphesus*. New York:
    The Viking Press, 1971. 442pp.

    The gifted and precocious daughters of eccentric
    parents, Irene, Urania, and Sylvia Bishop come
    to Ephesus, Georgia, where their father hopes to
    recoup resources lost in the Depression. The
    girls must reconcile the high standards and un-
    usual behavior of their family to the middle-
    class values of their classmates. Some of the
    detailed characterizations of Urie, the protagonist,
    and Sylvia (Loco Poco) are conveyed through their
    relationships with Zebulon Whalley, a boy befriended
    by the entire family. Urie's strength of mind
    and ambition are contrasted with Loco's lack of
    purpose; the girls' discoveries of sensuality are
    compared; and elements of the American Dream are
    examined.

17. Auchincloss, Louis. *Portrait in Brownstone.*
    Boston: Houghton Mifflin Company, 1962.  371pp.

    A long flashback reports the strained adoles-
    cent relationship of two cousins, Ida Trask and
    Geraldine Denison.  Geraldine, pretty and flir-
    tatious, and Ida, serious and insecure, react
    differently to the Victorian standards of their
    influential and interfering Denison relatives.
    These adolescent years shape the cousins' entire
    lives.

18. Bach, Alice. *Waiting for Johnny Miracle.* New
    York: Harper & Row, Publishers, 1981.  240pp.

    Becky and Theo Maitland are twins, sports stars,
    and all-round talented and promising high school
    students.  They are suddenly forced to carry the
    very heavy burden of knowing that Becky has ·cancer.
    Their lives now diverge as Theo must continue to
    lead a normal life yet understand Becky's new one.
    Hospital life, the desperate need for honesty and
    empathy (much more than sympathy), and the im-
    portant lives of other children both living with
    and dying from cancer now of necessity occupy
    nearly all of Becky's consciousness and much of
    Theo's.  Both young women have humorous and
    sensitive ways of absorbing the situation.

19. Baldwin, James. *If Beale Street Could Talk.* New
    York: The Dial Press, 1974.  197pp.

    Life for a young black couple in New York is
    anything but pleasant.  Fonny, a sculptor, is in
    jail falsely accused of raping a Puerto Rican
    woman.  He had planned to marry his nineteen-
    year-old girlfriend Tish, but before they could
    find a place to live, Fonny had been arrested
    and sent to prison.  Told through the eyes of
    Tish, this is a story both of young love with
    its hopes and sorrows and of the attempts of the
    two families to locate evidence that will clear
    Fonny.

20. Ballard, Phoebe, and Todhunter Ballard. *The Man
    Who Stole a University.*  Garden City, N.Y.:
    Doubleday & Company, Inc., 1967. 348pp.

    This satire of the university scene in the late
    1960s touches on many phenomena of the time and

contains characters representing varied facets
of university life. Among them is Martha Yates,
an undergraduate leader in a student protest
movement. Partly a comic character, she is nonetheless treated sympathetically, and the novel
parodies much that was and remains recognizable
in college life.

Ballard, Todhunter--*see* Ballard, Phoebe.

21. Bambara, Toni Cade. *The Salt Eaters*. New York:
Random House, 1980. 295pp.

Bambara's first novel is centered around the life
of a woman named Velma Henry, an attempted suicide.
Velma considers her experiences, examining her
childhood and adolescence, her friends, her husband, her son and the black movement, and considers whether she indeed does want the responsibility of wholeness. Around her revolve other
female characters attempting to come to terms
with their own lives. Minnie Ransom, a faith
healer, frustrated by the difficulty of healing
Velma, recalls her own adolescence and with it
her relationship with her spiritual guide, Old
Wife. Nadeen, a high school student, watching
Velma, decides that she will choose to slip
from childhood to adulthood and keep the infant
forming in her womb.

22. Barker, Shirley. *Strange Wives*. New York: Crown
Publishers, Inc., 1963. 377pp.

An historical novel set during the American
Revolution, this book deals with the marriage of
a Christian servant girl into the Sephardic Jewish
community of Newport, Rhode Island. Her bigoted
father had taught her to distrust and fear Jews,
but while still a child, she became infatuated
with the Jewish boy she was later to marry. The
novel portrays Jenny Tupper's evolution from naive
and ignorant girl to mature and loving wife.

23. Barrett, B.L. *Love in Atlantis*. Boston: Houghton
Mifflin Company, 1969. 182pp.

A long flashback to a California beach town in
the 1930s constitutes the bulk of this novel about
sexual initiation. At fourteen and fifteen,

Virginia achieves popularity, becomes involved
with several boys at different times, learns of
the bearing of illegitimate twins by another
girl, and discovers her own sexuality. This view
of awakening girlhood is narrated by the adult
Virginia, anticipating what her own daughter is
soon to experience.

24. Barrett, Mary Ellin. *Castle Ugly*. New York:
    E.P. Dutton & Co., Inc., 1966. 255pp.

    Several interlocking families, their adulteries,
    and three violent deaths form the substance of
    Sally Courtland's memories of the summer she was
    eleven and of her first brief love affair less
    than ten years later. Only partly understood
    then, these episodes are fully explained (but
    even this explanation is open to interpretation).
    The effect on Sally of these girlhood experiences,
    while damaging, has not been incapacitating.
    Sally's suspenseful narration blends the adult
    and the girlish viewpoints.

25. Barry, Jane. *A Time in the Sun*. Garden City,
    N.Y.: Doubleday & Company, Inc., 1962. 384pp.

    Kidnaped by Apaches while traveling to join her
    soldier-fiancé, Anna Stillman learns to love a
    half-breed and chooses to stay with him rather
    than return to the white world. Always spirited
    and determined, she grows in strength and toler-
    ance as she struggles to become part of "The
    People," and as she comes to feel completely at
    home in neither world. Her happiness is doomed
    by warfare between whites and Indians. Her life
    with the Apaches and her white fiancé's attempts
    to "free" her are portrayed with equal sympathy.
    sympathy.

26. Bartholomew, Cecelia. *Outrun the Dark*. New York:
    G.P. Putnam's Sons, 1977. 318pp.

    Billyjean has returned home after thirteen years
    in a mental asylum and now must adjust to a life
    completely foreign to her. She confessed to the
    murder of her four-year-old brother when she was
    eight, but the entire event has been blocked from
    her memory. Once she is home, Billyjean realizes
    she must try desperately to recall the events of her
    brother's death as she becomes more and more certain

that someone is trying to kill her or drive
her back to the mental institution.

27. Baumbach, Jonathan. *What Comes Next*. New York:
    Harper & Row, Publishers, 1968. 176pp.

    Rosemary Byrd, a college student, is one of
    three central characters. She initiates an affair
    with her history professor and eventually becomes
    involved with an emotionally disturbed male student.
    Less clearly characterized than the male characters,
    she is used primarily as a device in motivating and
    explaining the strange relationship between them
    in this experimental novel set against the back-
    ground of the Vietnam War and urban violence.

28. Beattie, Ann. *Falling in Place*. New York: Random
    House, 1980. 342pp.

    This book depicts a floundering suburban Connecti-
    cut family and the equally confused people around
    them. The characters share only their discontent
    and their inability to communicate with each other.
    The teenaged daughter Mary, forced to attend summer
    school because she has failed English, is the cent-
    ral character in one of the novel's many subplots.
    It is she who gives the books its title. Her
    required reading of the "dumb" old classics intro-
    duces her to the idea that in the normal course of
    events, life just falls into place. Mary's father
    has a mistress not too much older than she is,
    and her too-fat kid brother John Joel requires
    psychiatric treatment after he shoots and injures
    her. They are typical of the disturbed characters
    drifting through this novel.

29. Benchley, Nathaniel. *Welcome to Xanadu*. New York:
    Atheneum, 1968. 304pp.

    The story of the relationship that develops
    between a kidnaper and his victim is told in this
    half-comic, half-serious novel. Doris Mae Winter,
    an ignorant, foul-mouthed, clever girl of six-
    teen, is abducted by Leonard Hatch, an escapee from
    a mental hospital who loves poetry and is sexually
    impotent. They are both changed by their en-
    counter, and Doris Mae's growing involvement with
    her captor is clearly drawn.

30. Berkley, Sandra. *Coming Attractions*. New York:
    E.P. Dutton & Co., Inc., 1971. 212pp.

    This satiric novel of Hollywood in the 1930s
    and 1940s follows Cassandra Keen from the age
    of four (when her mother prompts her to be a
    Shirley-Temple-like moppet) to her marriage at
    seventeen. Her growth from childhood, through
    pubescence and into young womanhood is depicted,
    with particular stress on her sexuality. This
    humorous novel appropriates some film techniques
    to comment on Hollywood's dream world and on
    those, like Cassie, who are infatuated with it.

31. Bernays, Anne. *Growing Up Rich*. Boston: Little,
    Brown, 1975. 343pp.

    Upon the death of her German-Jewish mother, Sally
    Stern is sent from New York City to live with a
    middle-class Russian-Jewish family in Brookline,
    MA. The adjustments she must make to a totally
    unfamiliar lifestyle are challenging and often
    devastating to this witty thirteen-year-old.
    Her acceptance of her new family is vacillating
    and tentative since she half-expects to live
    with her own father. However, his remarriage to a
    woman Sally cannot accept and the hurtful betrayal
    by her first boyfriend help her to appreciate the
    support of her foster parents. Sally and her
    new mother help each other develop in significant
    ways as they become mother and daughter in the
    deepest sense of the words.

32. Berriault, Gina. *Conference of Victims*. New
    York: Atheneum, 1962. 248pp.

    After being seen with Dolores Lenci, his seven-
    teen-year-old mistress, a young candidate for
    Congress commits suicide. The novel follows
    the lives of Dolores and several members of
    her family in the ensuing six years. Dolores
    continues to have affairs with men who are older
    and married, searching for renewed evidence that
    she is "desirable beyond reason." The novel
    evokes a number of drab lives, Dolores' story
    being only one among several.

33. Betts, Doris. *The Scarlet Thread*. New York:
    Harper & Row, Publishers, 1964. 405pp.

Three children, two boys and a girl, growing
up in North Carolina around 1900, are the subjects of this novel. The oldest, Esther Allen,
is shown facing such experiences as first men-
struation, the deaths of her grandfather and a
cotton mill worker, and her infatuation and then
love affair with a professional young man temporarily in town. Though she is strong and
assertive, a combination of misapprehensions
leads her to run away when she is fifteen. Both
comic and serious, the novel evokes its time and
place and depicts a potentially crippling though
outwardly normal adolescence.

34. Blackwood, Caroline. *The Stepdaughter*. New
    York: Charles Scribner's Sons, 1977. 96pp.

    Renatta, a fat and silent thirteen-year-old,
becomes the focus of blame for her stepmother's
alienation from her husband and from life itself.
Through self-confessional letters, the stepmother
portrays for the reader her perceptions of the
shortcomings of her stepdaughter. The sometimes
comic vision of the changing nature of their
relationship illustrates the complexity of human
emotions.

35. Blake, Katherine. *My Sister, My Friend*. New
    York: Reynal & Company, 1965. 115pp.

    Nineteen-year-old Liz Barclay has failed at
marriage and at work; she desperately wants
something to love. Liz's narrative details one
painful and eventful day and includes flashbacks
to crucial experiences of the past. This terse,
suspenseful story enables the reader to enter
her desperate world.

36. Blake, Sally [as Sara, pseud.]. *Where Mist Clothes
    Dream and Song Runs Naked*. New York: McGraw-
    Hill, 1965. 200pp.

    Libby Stoler, precocious eleven-year-old daughter
of Russian-Jewish immigrants in a lower-middle-class
section of Boston, is puzzled that her nineteen-
year-old brother Abe feels compelled to have sex
with an older woman whom he strongly resists
marrying when he learns that she is pregnant. In
a deserted garage at night, Libby offers her
body to Squint, a sixteen-year-old albino with

a record of juvenile delinquency. At his sub-
sequent trial for statutory rape, he tries to
take the blame completely on himself, whereas
she insists on testifying that she "let him."
At an age when most girls have scarcely begun
adolescence, Libby is forced, by her environment
and her precocity, to face facts and make decisions
which would be challenging to a mature woman.

37. Blanton, Margaret Gray. *The White Unicorn*. New
    York: Rudo S. Globus, Inc., 1961. 424pp.

    A semi-comic, semi-nostalgic story of life in
    Tennessee from 1897 to 1904, this novel takes
    Maidie Chapman through two major stages in her
    life: manipulating her father into a suitable
    marriage after her mother's death in childbirth
    and then growing into love with a young reporter,
    her older sister's hopeless suitor. Maidie, her
    family, and their black servants interact as the
    novel dramatizes Maidie's maturation.

38. Blatty, William Peter. *The Exorcist*. New York:
    Harper & Row, Publishers, 1971. 340pp.

    A novel of suspense, this bestseller tells the
    story of satanic possession of eleven-year-old
    Regan MacNeil as seen by her horrified mother.
    While Regan's experiences may be related to her
    vulnerable stage of life, the fact of actual
    possession is assumed by the novel, with the reso-
    lution occurring through the traditional Roman
    Catholic rite of exorcism. Explicit in depicting
    Regan's bizarre behavior while controlled by her
    demon, the novel has been praised for its authen-
    ticity of detail and gripping suspense and damned
    as a pretentious and tasteless exercise in sensa-
    tionalism.

39. Blume, Judy. *Forever*. Scarsdale, N.Y.: Bradbury
    Press, Inc., 1975. 199pp.

    By one of the best-known authors of books for
    young people, this book explores the fragility of
    first love. Katherine Danziger is a high school
    senior when she meets Michael Wagner at a New
    Year's Eve party, and for the next six months,
    they share what they are certain is a love that
    will last forever. It is only when they are sep-

arated for the summer and Katherine is working at
a camp for gifted children in New Hampshire that
she discovers she is capable of caring for someone
else.

40. Blume, Judy. *Tiger Eyes*. Scarsdale, N.Y.: Bradbury
    Press, 1981. 206pp.

    When Adam Wexler is shot and killed during a
    robbery of his 7-Eleven store, fifteen-year-old
    Davey Wexler and her mother Gwendolyn are so
    overwhelmed that they are unable to adjust to
    their new roles of orphan and widow. Gwendolyn
    Wexler arranges for her family to visit Adam's
    sister in Los Alamos, New Mexico. Although Davey
    begins to mend in Los Alamos, through friendships
    as well as change of place, she is frustrated
    by her mother's continuing incapacitation and
    by the assumption of responsibility by other
    family members for herself and her little brother,
    Jason. *Tiger Eyes* deals with the fear of violent
    death and with the anger and grief that ensue
    when a loved one dies.

41. Borland, Barbara Dodge. *The Greater Hunger*.
    New York: Appleton-Century-Crofts, Inc., 1962.
    406pp.

    A love story set in Massachusetts in 1629-30,
    this novel has as its central character a young
    woman of great courage and independence. Hetty
    Downing accompanies her father, an expert on
    gardening, to America, and when he dies on ship-
    board, she takes over his work. Crossed in her
    love, she builds a life for herself and soon be-
    comes an accepted leader in the community.

42. Boyd, Shylah. *American Made*. New York: Farrar
    Straus and Giroux, 1975. 409pp.

    Shylah Dale's relationship with her father and
    stepmother, her efforts to adjust to life in the
    Florida Keys, her sexual initiation, and her ad-
    ventures with her friends comprise a major portion
    of this account of a supposedly typical American
    life. Sexually explicit scenes and language
    attempt to convey adolescent efforts to seem ma-
    ture; later sections depicting Shylah's marriage
    and its effect on her indicate that her maturation
    process is far from complete. Important passages

deal with Shylah's sexual exploitation by an older
man and with her father's abusive behavior.

43. Boyle, Kay. *The Underground Woman*. Garden City,
    N.Y.: Doubleday & Company, Inc., 1975. 264pp.

   Melanie Gregory, twice a mother by nineteen,
is a member of Pete the Redeemer's commune, a
cluster of young people united by their fear and
hatred of society and their renunciation of their
families. Her story is told by her mother, Athena
the protagonist, who is preoccupied with understanding the reasons for her daughter's estrangement as well as with her own attempts at self-
definition.

44. Boylen, Margaret. *A Moveable Feast*. New York:
    Random House, 1961. 269pp.

   Orphaned by a tragic double accident, the Mor-
trudes (two girls and three boys) are adopted by a
bachelor newspaperman and their entire village.
The two girls are both talented and creative.
Jessica (elder girl and second child) is the
strongest of the five; she becomes a surrogate
mother and gives the family its stability. Eleanor, the more active and imaginative, seems
more perceptive about the family and its situation.
All the surviving children leave the town as soon
as they are old enough, and this comic novel, in
some deft plot twists, reveals them as successful adults (Jessica as an actress and Eleanor
as a writer), less seriously harmed by the gradually revealed dark truths of their youth than one
might expect.

45. Bradbury, Bianca. *A New Penny*. Boston: Houghton
    Mifflin Company, 1971. 188pp.

   At seventeen, Carey Carter is far removed from
the carefree teenager's life she led a year before.
She is now a high school dropout who is married,
has a small baby and lives in a two-room trailer
while Hank, her young husband, attends college.
Carey feels lonely, trapped, and bored and is resentful of Hank's determination to complete his
education, of his family which opposed the marriage, and of her own parents who insist that her
home is now with Hank and the baby. This book

deals with the problems of a young couple's first
year of marriage as well as with Carey's growth as
a wife and mother.  As she matures, she realizes
she must make changes herself for their life to
be better and for their marriage to survive. She
decides that completing high school is the first
step.

46. Bradford, Richard. *Red Sky at Morning*. Phila-
    delphia: J.B. Lippincott Company, 1968.  256pp.

    Marcia Davidson, though a subsidiary character,
    is a realistically depicted seventeen-year-old
    girl, daughter of an Episcopal rector, uninhibited
    in speech if not in action.  She and two male
    schoolmates, one of them the protagonist and nar-
    rator of the novel, become  close friends.  They
    aid and support each other in times of trouble as
    well as strive together to solve many of the
    mysteries confronting them in their world and
    in their own changing bodies and emotions.  Marcia
    is honest and open, and her ironic amusement at
    herself and others, as well as her basic stability
    of character, are among the helpful influences on
    the protagonist.  This novel is a comic and tender
    story of growing up in a rural but ethnically
    mixed area of New Mexico during World War II.

47. Brancato, Robin F. *Blinded by the Light*.  New
    York: Alfred A. Knopf, 1978.  215pp.

    Gail Brower, a college·student, becomes concerned
    about her brother, Jim, when she learns he has
    cut all his ties and joined a religious cult called
    the Light of the World.  Learning that her parents
    are planning a rescue attempt set up by a de-
    programmer, Gail is afraid they will do more harm
    than good and decides to try herself to convince
    Jim to leave the organization.  By keeping her
    identity a secret, Gail moves into the inner circle
    of the cult at a rally in Philadelphia where
    she is able to observe Jim and the other members
    and their activities.  In the end, however, Gail
    must decide if freeing her brother is her decision
    to make.

48. Brautigan, Richard. *The Abortion: An Historical
    Romance 1966*.  New York: Simon and Schuster,
    1971.  226pp.

The warm and gentle protagonist, who lives
almost a hermit's existence, becomes the lover
of Vida Kramar, a nineteen-year-old beauty. Vida
has hated her body because of the effect its
spectacular endowments have on others, but through
this affair she learns to accept it. Her pregnancy and abortion seem just incidents in the
development of what is a sustaining and strength-
ening relationship for both of them. The semi-
comic novel is quite short, and it is made up of a
succession of brief chapters which often break continuous action into small segments.

49. Breslin, Jimmy. *The Gang That Couldn't Shoot
    Straight.* New York: The Viking Press, 1969.
    249pp.

A comic and satiric depiction of the Mafia in
Brooklyn, this novel uses Angela Palumbo to show
how innocent relatives of Mafiosi may be drawn into
its net. Angela is brought in for questioning
by the police about her brother, a minor criminal.
As a result she loses her Irish lover, drops out
of college, and finally gives her allegiance to
the gang. She is the only character not treated
ironically or as a butt for satire; however, her
characterization is sketchy.

50. Breuer, Bessie. *Take Care of My Roses.* New York:
    Atheneum, 1961. 184pp.

This sentimental account of the Salter family
is narrated by an embittered friend and housekeeper who feels unrewarded for the years she has
nurtured Mr. Salter and his children after the
death of his first wife. Although the novel's
main conflict is the hatred between the housekeeper
and the second Mrs. Salter, there is some depiction
of Via, the teenaged daughter, and the difficulties
she faces growing up with a stepmother in an unstable family.

51. Bristow, Gwen. *Calico Palace.* New York: Thomas
    Y. Crowell Company, 1970. 589pp.

An unwanted daughter of a still-young and attractive Army wife, Kendra marries in haste--from
passionate love and from a wish to escape home and
to be loved and wanted. Her husband proves to be a
bigamist and deserts her. Frightened but deter-

mined, she builds a new life for herself and her
infant son among loyal friends.  This romantic adventure novel is set in Northern California during
Gold Rush days, and Kendra's misadventures enable
the author to depict the mining camps, the growing
city of San Francisco, and the wide variety of people who inhabited them.  Her development from an im-
petuous nineteen-year-old to a mature young woman
who finds a new love is the central theme of the
novel.

52. Brown, Kenneth. *The Narrows*. New York: The
     Dial Press, 1970.  277pp.

    This novel of adolescence in Brooklyn in the
early 1950s centers mainly on a group of boys
during their high school years.  For their girlfriends, the stress is on sexuality--their respon-
siveness to the boys' sexual overtures and their
maintenance of at least technical virginity.
They participate in some of the boys' pranks,
showing daring in reckless games and even in some
criminal activity.  They are important to the boys
but are kept on the fringes of much of the group
behavior.

53. Buchan, Perdita. *Girl with a Zebra*. New York:
     Charles Scribner's Sons, 1966.  208pp.

    This novel of college life develops the three-
way relationship between Emily Ames, the zebra for
whose care she is given responsibility by the
Harvard Biology Department, and Blaise (he is not
given a last name), who seeks to use Emily to
achieve social standing on campus.  Emily is portrayed both as an actual girl and as a maiden whose
existence may be real only in her own special world.
There are many parallels with and allusions to
classical and medieval lore, but this mythic novel
remains a comic rendering of undergraduate life.

54. Busch, Niven. *The San Franciscans*. New York:
     Simon and Schuster, 1962.  349pp.

    Laura Yarnum is the central figure in this
novel of power and wealth in San Francisco in
1949.  Recently widowed, she fights to maintain
her husband's reputation when a lawsuit charging

fraud is brought against the bank which her husband
and his family controlled. Legal and financial man-
euverings make up much of the novel; however, a shor
section describes Laura's impoverished girlhood
in a motherless home and her first serious relationship with a man, significantly, a rich
man. It is this affair which illustrates her
fascination with the acquisition and control of
wealth.

55. Butters, Dorothy Gilman. *Masquerade.* Philadel-
    phia: Macrae Smith Company, 1961. 189pp.

    Four new students in a Philadelphia art school,
    each with her own problem to overcome, live
    together. Liz Gordon has just been jilted by
    her fiancé; Cara Jamison, a light-skinned black,
    is passing for white out of her desperate desire
    to attend the school; Melanie Prill, the only one
    unaware of having a problem, is a shallow and some-
    times malicious snob; and Penny Saunders is gauche
    and painfully shy. With Liz as the catalyst, Penny
    comes out of her shell, and the revelation of Cara's
    race is faced without catastrophe; even Melanie
    begins to see what she really is.

56. Cahill, Susan. *Earth Angels.* New York: Harper
    & Row, Publishers, 1976. 213pp.

    Martha Girlinghausen fights a running battle
    with the rules and restrictions of her Roman
    Catholic schooling from grade school through
    college until she enters a convent. Intelligent
    and independent, Martha survives conflict with
    her parents, sexual experimentation, and voca-
    tional uncertainty without impairing her sense of
    self.

57. Caidin, Martin. *Devil Take All.* New York: E.P.
    Dutton & Co., Inc., 1966. 382pp.

    This crime novel tells of the kidnapping, rape,
    and further abuse of Terri Bradshaw, nineteen.
    The elements for an atomic bomb are the ransom, and
    the intricacies of the scheme form the plot.

58. Calisher, Hortense. *Queenie.* New York: Arbor
    House, 1971. 282pp.

    Reared by an "Aunt" who is mistress to her
    guardian "Uncle," Alexandra Dauphin Raphael

(Queenie) tries to evade the traditional calling of
her female ancestors by going to college at sixteen.  A virgin, she bands together with her
college roommates to find a social cause and to
lose her virginity, only to discover that she is
unconventionally conventional.  She unites with
her true love, and they work toward a revolutionized
world.  Told as if spoken aloud in a surrealistic,
stream-of-consciousness style, the novel is marked
by humor and wordplay.

59. Calisher, Hortense. *Textures of Life*.  Boston:
    Little, Brown, 1963.  249pp.

    The novel opens with the marriage of nineteen-
year-old would-be artist-sculptor Elizabeth
Jacobson, daughter of widowed Margot ( a mater-
ialistic, well-to-do, practical woman), to David
Pagani, a maker of experimental films.  Over half
of the novel centers on the first year of their
marriage, on their rebellion against the possess-
ory values of Elizabeth's mother, and on their
routines as artists-bohemians moving from one New
York loft to another.  Elizabeth adopts a phil-
osophy which prevents her from owning anything
but the most basic worldly good.  As the novel
closes, the couple prepare for a move. Elizabeth,
now herself a mother, accepts a gift, a possession, from her mother, a blue watch that has
caught the eye of her young daughter.

60. Carleton, Jetta. *The Moonflower Vine*.  New York:
    Simon and Schuster, 1962.  351pp.

    The lives of the Soames family are portrayed
in long flashbacks, some reporting the same
events from different points of view.  Especially
important are the accounts of Jessica's and Mathy's
adolescent romances which are both joyous and
tragic, altering all the Soames' attitudes
forever.  The loving, good-humored voice of Mary Jo,
the first person narrator, informs this story of
rural Missouri life.

61. Carpenter, Don. *Blade of Light*.  New York: Har-
    court, Brace & World, Inc., 1968.  181pp.

    The details of Carole Weigandt's tragic high
school affair with Harold Hunt, a local tough,

dominate a long flashback. Determined to control her own life, Carole resists intercourse, per-
ceiving it as a symbol of his potential dominance
over her. When she becomes aware of Harold's long,
exploitative, sexual relationship with Marjorie
Butts, Carole's scorn and anger cost her her
self-control and her life.

62. Carrighar, Sally. *The Glass Dove*. Garden City,
    N.Y.: Doubleday & Doubleday, Inc., 1962. 347pp.

    During the 1860s Sylvia MacIntosh spends her
    late adolescence helping run the family farm and
    underground railway station. As she learns about
    herself and her capabilities, she also learns to
    interpret the characters of the young men who are
    her suitors. This novel about a young woman's
    maturation incorporates details of everyday life,
    the tragic drama of the escaping slaves' ex-
    periences, and the clash between abolitionists
    and Federal law.

63. Carroll, Gladys Hasty. *Next of Kin*. Boston:
    Little, Brown and Company, 1974. 248pp.

    In her eighteenth year, Lisa Gallico Sturtevant
    becomes a wife and a mother and acquires several
    generations of family memories as she and her
    husband, Larry, learn the Sturtevant family his-
    tory from old William Crowley who becomes a fos-
    ter father to them both. Flashbacks tell the
    stories of Lisa's and Larry's barren child-
    hoods and reveal why this new relationship means
    so much to them both.

64. Carter, Mary. *A Fortune in Dimes*. Boston: Little,
    Brown and Company, 1963. 338pp.

    Jane Murdoch is in love with her college class-
    mate, Decker Wells, the protagonist of this novel.
    Her affection survives a serious sexual mis-
    understanding, but her acceptance of Decker crum-
    bles when he behaves ignobly during a tragic event.

65. Cassill, Ronald Verlin. *The Goss Women*. Garden
    City, N.Y.: Doubleday & Company, Inc., 1974.
    464pp.

    Dean Goss is a modern artist in his seventies

whose life story is being written by Susan Vail,
a divorcée and mother of Tamisan, the central
adolescent woman in this novel. Tamisan is having
an affair with Jason, Goss's youngest son, whom
she consumes with her passion. At twelve and
thirteen years of age, Tamisan aspired to be a
"legend" and then an "adventuress." She is a
beautiful young woman who attracts older men,
including Dean Goss, and her life is a search for
meaning through her promiscuous sexual activities.
Although Tamisan learns from an older woman that
there are many ways to be feminine, she, like
all the Goss women, becomes a "thing"; in the es-
timation of Dean Goss, all she is good for is
sex. Throughout the novel sensuality and the de-
gradation of women as sex objects are predominant
themes.

66. Chappell, Fred. *Dagon*. New York: Harcourt, Brace
    & World, Inc., 1968. 177pp.

    Mina Morgan, about sixteen, represents the
decay of contemporary culture in this allegory.
After protagonist Peter Leland's veneer of civilization has been damaged by self-indulgence, he
falls into Mina's hands and through her debasing
ministrations believes himself transformed into
the god Dagon.

67. Chappell, Fred. *The Gaudy Place*. New York:
    Harcourt Brace Jovanovich, Inc., 1973. 178pp.

    At nineteen, seemingly tough but actually
insecure Clemmie has been a prostitute for three
years. Her lies, designed to counter her fear
of being without protection, motivate the humorous
climax of this novel about the various kinds and
levels of con games operating in contemporary
Braceboro, North Carolina.

68. Chappell, Fred. *The Inkling*. New York: Harcourt,
    Brace & World, 1965. 153pp.

    Timmie Anderson is a retarded girl who adores
her brother, Jan, who devotes most of his time and
energy to protecting her. Their widowed mother
is preoccupied by the job with which she supports
the family. Lora Bowen, nineteen, becomes the
family's housekeeper and entices both Jan, the
protagonist, and their alcoholic uncle.

69. Cheatham, K. Follis. *Bring Home the Ghost*.
    New York: Harcourt Brace Jovanovich, 1980.  288pp.

    In this story of male friendship, a young woman
    plays an important motivational role.  In August,
    1827, Jason, a ten-year-old slave, saves young
    Tolin Cobb's life.  He becomes Tolin's personal
    slave and best friend.  By the time Jason is
    nineteen, he is in love with fifteen-year-old
    Louisa, who disappears while the young men are
    fighting in the Seminole wars.  Tolin and Jason
    head west, encountering many adventures which help
    Jason become his own man even before he knows
    Tolin has freed him.  After several years, Jason
    finds Louisa, and she persuades him to become
    even more independent by leaving Tolin.

70. Childress, Alice. *Rainbow Jordan*.  New York:
    Coward, McCann & Geoghegan, Inc., 1981.  142pp.

    Fourteen-year-old Rainbow Jordan is almost
    more mature than her twenty-nine-year-old mother,
    Kathie, who has abandoned her several times.  Now
    Kathie is gone again, there is an eviction notice
    on the apartment door, and Mayola the social worker
    is coming to take Rainbow to Miss Josephine's for
    the third time.  Rainbow is trying to make ex-
    cuses for Kathie and to keep Kathie's behavior
    secret from friends, teachers, and others.
    Miss Josephine is trying to appear younger and
    stronger and more securely married than she really
    is.  Rainbow and Miss Josephine help each other
    to look at life more realistically and look for-
    ward to building a stronger relationship with
    each other.

71. Childress. Alice. *A Short Walk*.  New York: Coward,
    McCann & Geoghegan, Inc., 1979.  333pp.

    According to her father, it's just a short walk
    from the cradle to the grave, but in her walk,
    Cora sees her people change from niggers to Negroes
    to blacks and begin to assume their rightful place
    in the mainstream of American life.  Born of a dy-
    ing mother and ignored by her white father's
    family, Cora is reared by child-hungry Etta and
    Bill James in the Charleston, SC, of 1900.  She
    is only five when she discovers the tragedy of
    being black in a white-oriented society, and for

the rest of her life she chafes against the restrictions of being both black and female. But
she is not a passive victim of circumstances;
she matures, marries, escapes to New York City,
remarries, and sees that her own daughter not
only goes to college but joins the Navy in World
War II. She is involved in early struggles
against discrimination, and her teenaged daughter
echoes her mother's dreams as she actively faces
the challenge to make the world a better place.
Cora does not live to see this new world, as she
ends her walk much too soon, but she carries with
her the vision of true liberation.

72. Christman, Elizabeth. *A Nice Italian Girl*. New
    York: Dodd Mead & Company, 1976. 139pp.

    At twenty, Anne Macarino, sedate and dignified,
seems too mature for most of her male college
classmates. Inexperienced, she is easy prey for
Steve Albright who deliberately seduces her as
part of a complicated, illegal adoption con-
spiracy. Pregnant and alone, Anne fights to keep
her baby.

73. Chute, B.J. *The Moon and the Thorn*. New York:
    E.P. Dutton & Co., Inc., 1961. 190pp.

    As this novel opens, Henrietta returns to the
island where her family traditionally spends the
summer. Thirty years before, she had stolen away
in the fog with her lover, who has recently died.
Familiar places and faces awaken memories of her
girlhood as she deals with her grief over his death
and seeks acceptance from the villagers and reconciliation with her sister. She encounters
an ironic repetition of her youth's passion in
her niece, Lucy, a girl who must also choose
between the man she loves and her family.

74. Chute, B.J. *The Story of a Small Life*. New York:
    E.P. Dutton & Co., Inc., 1971. 208pp.

    The story of Mig and Anna, a teenaged New York
slum couple, is alternated with the story of the
narrator, a social worker. Tiny, weak, impoverished,
illiterate, and deeply in love with and dependent
upon Mig, a street kid, Anna feebly tries to cope
with an unwanted pregnancy.

Clark, Dorothy Pace--*see* McMeekin, Isabella Mc-
Lennan.

75.  Clarke, Mary Stetson. *The Iron Peacock*. New
     York: The Viking Press, 1966.  251pp.

     This book compares and contrasts the lives of
     Joanna Sprague, sixteen, and her Indian friend,
     Yaweta. Joanna, once a young woman of means,
     is sold as a bond servant to pay for her passage
     to the New World and through her strength, cour-
     age and skill, wins the respect and affection of
     her master and mistress. Yaweta's father con-
     fuses his newly adopted Christianity with white
     customs and insists his daughter follow white
     ways. Interest centers on numerous details of
     Bay Colony life and on the girls' romances.

76.  Clarke, Mary Stetson. *The Limer's Daughter*.
     New York: The Viking Press, 1967.  255pp.

     At sixteen Amity Lyte is the chief support and
     head of her family. She finds employment and
     confronts the hatred of the community who believe
     her family to have been Tories. The fictional
     story of Amity's adventures plays itself out
     within a factual setting as the girl discovers
     economic security, family love, and romance in
     the Massachusetts of 1805.

77.  Cleaver, Bill, and Vera Cleaver. *Where the
     Lilies Bloom*. Philadelphia: J.B. Lippincott
     Company, 1969.  174pp.

     At the age of fourteen, Mary Call Luther
     becomes the surrogate parent of her three sib-
     lings, including her older sister, Devola,
     eighteen. Strong and able, Mary Call neverthe-
     less understands that she is being forced to
     cope with too many economic and emotional pres-
     sures. Her most severe pressure stems from her
     determination to keep the promise to her dying
     father, that she will head the family. Ultimate-
     ly, she comes to interpret her promise wisely and
     practically.

     Cleaver, Bill--*see also* Cleaver, Vera.

78. Cleaver, Vera, and Bill Cleaver. *Lady Ellen
    Grae*. Philadelphia: J.B. Lippincott Co., 1968.
    124pp.

    Eleven-year-old Ellen Grae is pushed pre-
maturely into adolescence when her parents
decide to send her to her aunt in Seattle to
become a "lady." Ellen resents and fears the
move, which she perceives as the loss of
identity, freedom, security, and friends. A
precocious, highly imaginative girl, she ini-
tiates several plans to convince her parents
to change their minds and allow her to remain
in her small-town Florida home. They eventually
relent, but not until Ellen Grae's uninhibited
spirit has effected changes in a number of
people, including her sophisticated teenaged
cousin.

79. Cleaver, Vera, and Bill Cleaver. *Trial Valley*.
    New York: J.B. Lippincott Co., 1977. 158pp.

    In this sequel to *Where the Lilies Bloom*,
Mary Call Luther, sixteen, is caring for her
younger brother and sister in the Appalachian
mountains after the death of their parents. When
she finds an abandoned five-year-old boy who
attaches himself to her and refuses to live with
her married sister, Mary Call sees him as just
one more obstacle to tie her down and delay
the pursuit of her own dreams. However, the
child, Jack Parsons, matches Mary Call with her
own kind of strength and fierce determination.
When he runs away, this sparks an adventurous
search through the mountains and teaches Mary
Call, strong-willed and independent, new lessons about love and commitment.

    Cleaver, Vera--*see also* Cleaver, Bill.

80. Coffey, Marilyn. *Marcella*. New York: Charter-
    house, 1973. 240pp.

    Because she has been "saved" at twelve, Mar-
cella Colby expects prayer and devotion to
help her refrain from masturbating. This ex-
pectation imposes severe strains upon her self-
concept and ultimately upon her faith.

81.   Coleman, Lonnie. *Orphan Jim*. Garden City, N.Y.:
      Doubleday & Company, Inc., 1975. 204pp.

      At thirteen, Trudy Maynard finds herself
      solely responsible for her younger brother.
      By her fourteenth birthday, Trudy has been brow-
      beaten by vicious relatives, raped by a passing
      stranger, informally adopted by a black ex-
      prostitute, and accepted as an able clerk in
      a general store. As narrator, Trudy reports
      these facts in an even tone, revealing herself
      as a strong, admirable survivor, if not a
      lovable child.

82.   Colter, Cyrus. *The Rivers of Eros*. Chicago:
      The Swallow Press Incorporated, 1972. 219pp.

      Addie, sixteen, is the chief motivating force
      in this story of a middleclass Chicago black
      family headed by the matriarch Clotilda, the
      protagonist. Rebelling against the placidity
      of her life and sensing that she can dominate
      Clotilda because of some secret buried in the
      past, Addie has an affair with an older, married
      man. The conflict between the two women cul-
      minates in tragedy.

83.   Connell, Evan S. *Mr. Bridge*. New York: Alfred
      A. Knopf, 1969. 369pp.

      Walter Bridge is a successful, middle-aged
      lawyer in 1930s Kansas City who prizes order
      and is easily mystified by the unpredictability
      of the world around him. By his own admission,
      he has never experienced joy even though he
      has attained almost everything he ever wanted.
      He finds communication with his teenaged child-
      ren--alluring Ruth, intelligent Carol, and
      obstinate Douglas--especially trying because he
      recognizes his own headstrong nature in them.
      The story, which covers years and unfolds in
      short episodes, focuses mostly upon Mr. Bridge's
      interactions with his children as they grow
      into young adults and prepare to leave home.
      This book is a plotless, elaborately detailed
      character study, not a conventionally structured
      novel.

84.   Connolly, Edward. *Deer Run*. New York: Charles
      Scribner's Sons, 1971. 186pp.

Christine drops out of college to join a
newly established Vermont commune. Her love
for Josh, the group's founder, cannot survive
the violence of the local people toward the
commune.

85. Corbett, Elizabeth F. *Hidden Island*. New York:
    Appleton-Century-Crofts, 1961. 274pp.

    This novel follows Edith Sewell, a pampered
    darling from a rich New York family, from her
    coming-out in 1930 to her coming-of-age birthday
    party in New York City with a wealthy crowd only
    vaguely aware of the Depression. She spends sum-
    mers and one winter on a family-owned island off
    the coast of Maine. Gradually, she gains a mea-
    sure of maturity through her relationships with
    three men: an English nobleman who cannot par-
    don her careless floutings of conventions and
    laws, the island steward with a scandal in his
    past which prevents their marriage, and a boat
    designer whom she marries.

86. Cores, Lucy. *The Misty Curtain*. New York:
    Harper & Row, Publishers, Incorporated, 1964.
    214pp.

    The sudden death of Anna Gregor, retired film
    star married to an Eastern prince, turns her
    daughter of an earlier marriage into an amateur
    detective. Strangely immature for twenty,
    Elizabeth must learn to cope with the realities
    of her mother's life, facts far different from
    the idealizations in which she has indulged.
    Elizabeth's own budding romance forms a subplot
    and dramatizes her maturation.

87. Cormier, Robert. *After the First Death*. New
    York: Pantheon Books, Inc., 1979. 233pp.

    Kate Forrester, about eighteen, substitutes
    as driver on a bus taking a group of small
    children to camp. When terrorists hijack the bus,
    Kate undertakes an inner battle for courage even
    as she seeks means of escape and ways to under-
    mine one of her captors, himself a teenager.

88.   Cormier, Robert.  *I Am the Cheese*.  New York:
        Pantheon Books, Inc., 1977.  234pp.

        Amy Hertz represents a slim chance for nor-
      malcy in the mystery-shadowed life of protagonist
      Adam Farmer.  Adam's only friend, she shares
      his passion for reading and his tentative sexual
      explorations.  Her sense of humor and prankish-
      ness balance, to some degree, his shyness and
      introversion.  Though Amy is a relatively
      minor figure, she is important in Adam's devel-
      opment.

89.   Cormier, Robert.  *Take Me Where the Good Times
        Are*.  New York: Macmillan Publishing Co., Inc.,
        1965.  213pp.

        Although she is fourteen years old, Annabel
      Lee Jones has--and always will have--the mind
      of a child of eight.  The only surviving child
      of the superintendent of a home for the aged
      and infirm, she is a good friend of seventy-year-
      old Tommy Barton, the protagonist.  Sketchily
      drawn, Annabel Lee is only one of a troop of
      acquaintances whose lives touch Tommy's in his
      fight against age and dependence, but though her
      role is small, it is important.  Her fascination
      with a motorcycle gang leads her into danger
      and Tommy into serious trouble.

90.   Covert, Paul.  *Cages*.  New York: Liveright
        Publishing Corporation, 1971.  181pp.

        Alice Hemmingway and Barbara Garret are the
      first loves of Eric Mathews and Bob Ward, the
      central characters.  Alice is the object of
      Eric's sexual initiation, and Barbara is the
      motivation for the novel's final tragedy.  Her
      reaction to Bob's impotence during their first
      attempt at intercourse is to accuse him first
      of rape and then of homosexuality.

91.   Crawford, Joanna.  *Birch Interval*.  Boston:
        Houghton Mifflin Company, 1964.  183pp.

        Jesse, the narrator-protagonist, matures early
      because of the trouble that befalls her ex-
      tended family.  An uncle is branded as "crazy,"
      and his son is considered a "bad boy" by the
      community and by some members of the family

itself. When the family disintegrates, Jesse
is separated from her beloved cousins. She
faces loneliness bravely and maturely evaluates
the behavior of the adults who have ended her
childhood so abruptly.

92.  Crews, Harry. *A Feast of Snakes*. New York:
     Atheneum, 1976. 177pp.

An orgy of sex and violence explodes in this
Southern Gothic novel during an annual Rattle-
snake Festival, pushing protagonist Joe Lon
Mackey into madness. Contributing to his breakdown are Berenice Sweet, a college cheerleader
who is his sometime mistress; Lottie May, black
and about twenty, who emasculates Joe Lon's
buddy, the sheriff, who has raped her; and
Joe Lon's insane sister, Beeder.

93.  Crews, Harry. *The Hawk Is Dying*. New York:
     Alfred A. Knopf, 1973. 226pp.

The most important minor character in this
Southern Gothic novel, Betty is the college-aged
mistress of protagonist George, a middle-aged
amateur falconer. Tough and cold, Betty is
at first scornful of George's efforts to train
a chicken hawk. Eventually she becomes entranced
with the process, which is an initiation rite.

94.  Culin, Charlotte. *Cages of Glass, Flowers of
     Time*. Scarsdale, N.Y.: Bradbury Press, 1979.
     316pp.

Fourteen-year-old Claire is the victim of
the court which removes her from the care of
a drunken but loving father and delivers her
into the hands of an alcoholic and physically
abusive mother. Her awakening sensibilities
are stirred by young romantic love, friendship
with a caring old black musician, her developing
artistic talent, and fear of continued battering.
Nature, poetically described as ephemerally
"green," is not neglected in this book as Claire
attempts to sketch the beauty she sees about her.
At last her drunken mother beats her so badly
she is hospitalized, and the authorities place
her in the care of friends who love her enough
to fight for her best interests.

95. Culp, John H. *A Whistle in the Wind*. New
    York: Holt, Rinehart and Winston, 1968.  281pp.

    Cesre is a white girl who grows up in an
    Indian camp in Texas Comanche country during the
    middle of the nineteenth century. The other
    whites in the camp are also the Indians' cap-
    tives. Cesre loves Roderick Chafin, and the two
    court and marry against the wishes of a power-
    ful chief. Rich in Indian lore, the novel traces
    the youths' grim fates.

96. Cummings, Betty Sue. *Now Ameriky*. New York:
    Atheneum, 1979.  175pp.

    The Great Potato Famine of Ireland drives
    spunky Brigid Ni Clery, nineteen years old, to
    "Ameriky" in the late 1840s. Dispossessed from
    the land they have rented for seven generations,
    the family plans to follow Brigid to America to
    obtain land of its own as soon as possible.
    Leaving behind her fiancé Padraic, her family,
    and her beloved country, Brigid faces hunger,
    threatened prostitution, sexual frustration,
    crooked employers, and a rival for Padraic's
    love before Padraic and her brother William join
    her from Ireland. Proud at discovering herself
    a resourceful, self-reliant person, who has not
    only supported herself for several years but
    also sent money home, Brigid is shocked to learn
    that Padraic considers her a mere female and
    scoffs at her dream of land ownership. Jilting
    him, she sets off with her brother to earn the
    desired land. A chastened Padraic follows; the
    priest is summoned, and we see the probable
    fulfillment of the Great American Dream.

97. Cuomo, George. *Bright Day, Dark Runner*. Garden
    City, N.Y.: Doubleday & Company, Inc., 1964.
    421pp.

    The romantic entanglements of Sandra Miller's
    summer spent working at a Cape Cod resort are
    pivotal to a subplot in this complex novel.
    Sandra is primarily characterized by descriptions
    of her alluring appearance and by discussions of
    her concern for her virtue.

98. Curtiss, Ursula. *Out of the Dark*. New York:
    Dodd, Mead & Co., 1964.  183pp.

Libby Mannering, fourteen, is a normal teenager who vacillates between responsible and irresponsible behavior. Her friend, Kit Austen, also fourteen, is a model of behavior on the surface but is actually a willful, destructive personality. The girls' prank phone calls incite murder and eventually grave danger to themselves in this suspense story.

99.  Daniels, Sally. *The Inconstant Season.* New York: Atheneum, 1962. 244pp.

This highly episodic novel depicts the girl-hood of Peggy Dillon, as nostalgically related by Peggy many years later. Though she faced such typical problems of adolescence as curiosity about sex, first true awareness of death, first infatuation, and so on, her growing up was comparatively painless. The book lacks clear narrative structure and its focus is blurred, but Peggy and her family and friends are likable. It is a pleasant and readable presentation of fortunate adolescence.

100.  Davis, Christopher. *First Family.* New York: Coward-McCann, Inc., 1961. 253pp.

This novel deals with the first black family to move into a middle-class white neighborhood and centers around Kate Charles, a white of thirteen, and Scotty McKinley, a black of twelve. Scotty is the central figure (the novel's British title is *Scotty*), but Kate is also important. She is bright, tolerant, and good-hearted. Her relationship with Scotty is complex and fluid; she tries to behave well but sometimes is frightened or frustrated by forces and attitudes (not all of them related to race) which are beyond her understanding.

101.  Davis, Mildred [B.]. *Three Minutes to Midnight.* New York: Random House, 1971. 213pp.

Four girls, ranging in age from twenty-one to five, are left to fend for themselves when a Ferris wheel "accident" kills their mother and so seriously injures their father that he must be institutionalized. The eldest, Blair Procter, is the protagonist of this suspense novel, and she is portayed as a

serious and reliable but inexperienced young
woman who does her best in an extremely difficult
situation. The sinister meaning of the "accident" is ultimately revealed after much terror
and anguish.

102.   Deal, Babs H. *It's Always Three O'Clock*. New
       York: David McKay Company, Inc., 1961. 334pp.

       Approximately the first third of this novel
       deals with the adolescences of a group of small-
       town Alabama boys and girls in the 1920s. Eileen
       Holder, the protagonist, is a vital, life-loving
       girl who marries, while still in high school, a
       doomed young veteran of World War I whom she
       has loved since childhood. Still only about
       seventeen when he dies, she has matured through
       caring for him and their child. While her high
       school friends generally find little happiness,
       her strength and wisdom make her a prop for
       them to lean on. The story covers overs thirty
       years, showing Eileen at the end still a sur-
       vivor, still giving her strength to others.

103.   Deal, Babs H. *The Reason for Roses*. Garden
       City, N.Y.: Doubleday & Company, Inc., 1974.
       276pp.

       Nostalgia for girlhood is the ostensible
       subject of this narrative, as the adult narrator,
       Spencer Howard, remembers a pivotal summer she
       and her cousins spent in a small Alabama town on
       the eve of World War II. Their activities,
       projects, and observations of romance and scandal
       are depicted, but the reader gradually learns
       that most of the young people have fared badly;
       only Spencer has attained a satisfying adult
       life. She ponders the experiences of that
       summer in her attempts to understand both the
       failures and the success.

104.   De Vries, Peter. *Consenting Adults; or The
       Duchess Will Be Furious*. Boston: Little,
       Brown, 1980. 221pp.

       Columbine is a symbolic force in the life of
       the narrator of this satirical novel. She and
       Peachum are brought together when she is ten
       by her mother who envisions a future match for
       them. During the subsequent years, her image
       as the innocent girl next door is always con-

trasted with the dissolute spirit of Peachum as
he makes his wild way as an actor in New York
City. The circle is completed when the two
marry when Columbine is nineteen.

105. Dew, Robb Forman. *Dale Loves Sophie to Death*.
     New York: Farrar, Straus, Giroux, 1981. 217pp.

     During her annual summer stay in a rented house
in her Ohio hometown, thirty-six-year-old Dinah's
memories return to her life at sixteen. Through
flashbacks and real confrontations with people
from her past, Dinah takes up the unfinished
business of growing up and understanding her
father, mother, older brother, and best friend.
Dinah's adult roles of mother, wife, and entre-
preneur continue to take shape in the light of
her girlhood experiences. The competitiveness
which has affected most of Dinah's relationships
comes to the foreground as she contends with the
power and responsibility of adulthood.

106. Disney, Doris Miles. *The Hospitality of the House*.
     Garden City, N.Y.: Doubleday & Company, Inc.,
     1964. 183pp.

     When eighteen-year-old Mandy O'Brien travels
alone to visit the long-time pen-pal whom she
has never met, she is welcomed cordially by
Janet, her parents, and a cousin of Janet's.
She is surprised to discover that Janet and she
are not so congenial as she had expected, and
then, after they all go to care for Janet's aged
grandmother, she gradually becomes more and more
suspicious that things are not what they seem.
This suspense novel reveals Mandy as a decent
and courageous young woman who comes through her
ordeal because of her intelligence and bravery.

107. Dizenzo, Patricia. *An American Girl*. New York:
     Holt, Rinehart & Winston, 1971. 148pp.

     A loosely structured collection of sketches
of the unnamed narrator's daily life, this novel
recreates the 1950s as seen by a New Jersey
high school girl. Her home situation is bad
(an alcoholic mother and a frustrated father),
but she seems to cope reasonably well. Family
fights, her mother's erratic behavior, her

relationships with her older sister and younger
brother, her attempts at cleaning and redecorating
the house, homework, shopping trips, movies, library books, and school activities--all are described with similar understatement and, usually,
with objectivity. An unexpected climactic event
sharply underscores the dangers to her emotional
well-being inherent in her family situation.

108.  Dizenzo, Patricia. *Phoebe.* New York: McGraw-
      Hill Book Company, 1970. 120pp.

      This novelette examines a middle-class high
      school senior during the brief span of time
      in which she is forced to accept the fact of
      her pregnancy. Phoebe's inability to confide
      in either her parents or her boyfriend and her
      attempts to find a course of action are treated
      in some detail. A good deal of information
      about the early stages of pregnancy is given,
      but the choices Phoebe faces are not very
      fully examined. Her story ends as she finally
      reveals her condition to the boy and her parents.

109.  Doctorow, E.L. *The Book of Daniel.* New York:
      Random House, 1971. 303pp.

      This political, historical, and psychological
      novel, inspired by the Rosenberg case, involves
      Phyllis, a nineteen-year-old woman, the wife of
      Daniel and the mother of young Paul, and Susan,
      Daniel's sister, a twenty-year-old college stu-
      dent. It is, however, primarily the story of
      Daniel, a graduate student at Columbia, who
      spends his days in the library writing his novel
      while neglecting his dissertation. He and Susan
      are the children of communist parents imprisoned
      for stealing atomic secrets for the Soviets during
      the fifties. The story takes place in the late
      sixties when both children are caught up in
      the turmoil and dissension of the times as they
      suffer the traumatic effects of the long
      separation from and ultimate execution of their
      parents. Phyllis allows herself to be treated
      in a demeaning and sometimes cruel way by
      Daniel, but when he is overcome with bitterness
      and helplessness, she is compassionate, support-
      ive, and strong. Unable to handle the complex-
      ities and stresses of her life, Susan is dependent
      on Daniel and is used by many men. Both women
      are necessary to Daniel: Phyllis because of her
      stability, and Susan because Daniel comes to

understand loving relationships by caring
for her.

110. Dornfield, Iris. *Jeeney Ray*. New York: The
     Viking Press, 1962. 188pp.

     Naively told by its protagonist who uses only
     the present tense and generally relies on simple
     sentences, this is the story of a spastic in
     her early teens who is thought to be a half-wit.
     Her people are ignorant, and except for the
     grandmother whose death opens the novelette, they
     are ashamed of her. She is put to menial work
     but luckily is befriended by a man who takes the
     time to understand her slurred speech and re-
     cognizes her intelligence. In its apparent
     simplicity, this is a compassionate presentation
     of a character who once would have been con-
     sidered a "blessed innocent."

111. Doty, Carolyn. *A Day Late*. New York: The
     Viking Press, 1980. 232pp.

     It is Sam Batinovich's forty-first birth-
     day, and he is on the homeward leg of his
     regular several-state sales run. He is almost
     mad with grief from the death, two months earlier,
     of his fourteen-year-old daughter. Seventeen-
     year-old Katy Daniels is hitchhiking home to her
     wealthy, intellectual family in Berkeley and
     dreading the moment she must announce that she
     is pregnant. In Wendover, Nevada, she hitches
     a ride with Sam. During the long, healing ride
     across the desert, they help each other deal
     with their feelings of guilt, anger, and pain.

112. Douglas, Ellen. *A Family's Affairs*. Boston:
     Houghton Mifflin Company, 1962. 442pp.

     This long chronicle deals with three generations
     of women--only the youngest is an adolescent.
     The novel's central theme is the impermanence
     and fragility of love, a lesson young Anna
     McGovern learns through two relationships: one
     with a sexually exploitative high school teacher
     and one with her first sweetheart, Taylor Kelly.
     She succeeds in ending the upsetting relation-
     ship with the teacher; her relationship with
     Taylor lasts several years, breaking off when

she is in college and leaving her embittered.
Through these episodes and others, the novel
illustrates some difficulties of love and of
human understanding.

113.   Downey, Harris.  *The Key to My Prison*.  New
       York: Delacorte Press, 1964.  192pp.

       The poetic journal of a young woman who has
determined to kill herself, this novel describes
a one-sided romance of schoolmates, the for-
mation and destruction of a relationship with
a surrogate mother, and a purely sexual affair
with a crude laborer.  Delia Wright, protagonist
and narrator, values freedom and personal
identity above all else and is never able to
form lasting relationships (nor does she perhaps really wish to).  She drifts ever deeper
into isolation and even toward insanity.  Compelled by her need to record her motivations,
Delia muses on time, identity, and death.

114.   Drexler, Rosalyn.  *I Am the Beautiful Stranger*.
       New York: Grossman Publishers, 1965.  185pp.

       Growing up in New York City in the late 1930s,
Selma Silver keeps a diary from the time she
is thirteen until she is sixteen.  A Jewish girl
from an unloving, volatile family, she has a poor
concept of herself.  A major preoccupation is
her physical maturation and early sexual career.
She goes from a chaste correspondence with a
young car thief, through a period of sexual
promiscuity to, finally, the possibility of
a relationship with a young man she really cares
about.

115.   Duncan, Lois.  *Daughters of Eve*.  Boston: Little,
       Brown & Company, 1979.  252pp.

       Irene Stark, faculty adviser to a high school
service club, wants to punish all males for the
injustices which she has suffered since childhood.  Irene's subtle power over these ten students affects not only the girls but also their
families and school.  The novel's message is
think for yourself and be true to your own values
instead of blindly accepting direction because
of loyalty and admiration.  Awareness and response vary with the individual students.

116.  Duncan, Lois.  *I Know What You Did Last Summer*.
      Boston: Little, Brown and Co., 1973.  199pp.

      Julie James, seventeen years old, receives
a letter informing her she has been accepted at
Smith, a matter of great happiness for her.  In
the same mail there is a note which starkly
states, "I know what you did last summer."  Julie
has cause for terror because the previous summer
she and three friends were involved in a hit-
and-run accident in which a small boy was fatally
injured.  Against her will, Julie has agreed to
a pact in which all four friends vow never to
reveal their shameful secret.  Now, however, their
vengeful stalker begins an insidious campaign of
terror.  Ultimately, Julie and her boyfriend
Ray, plagued by guilty consciences, make a
clean breast of their guilt and in doing so
realize that they have found the strength to
face the consequences with courage.

117.  Dunn, Katherine.  *Truck*.  New York: Harper &
      Row, Publishers, 1971.  217pp.

      Jean Gillis, known as Dutch, is fifteen and
describes herself as boyish, inept, and stupid.
Actually a clever shoplifter and ingenious
plotter, she runs away from a life she hates
(with only a few regretful thoughts for her
mother) to join a drifter who is her closest
friend.  Her planning for escape and the journey itself, told in present tense and through her
stream of consciousness, form the substance of
this novel.  Dutch's sense of alienation and
her confused attempts to deal with it are
clearly communicated.

118.  Echard, Margaret.  *I Met Murder on the Way*.
      Garden City, N.Y.: Doubleday & Company, Inc.,
      1965.  240pp.

      This mystery story compares and contrasts the
personalities and development of Betsy Foster,
fourteen, and her aunt, Bryn Pomeroy, fifteen.
Betsy is plain, shy, and uncertain of her position in the Pomeroy clan whereas Bryn is beautiful, alluring, and manipulative.  Each reacts
differently to her crush on Dr. Phillip Grieg,
who is suspected of murdering Pomeroy relatives,
and each is in grave danger.

119.   Eclov, Shirley. *My Father's House*. New York:
       Harper & Brothers, Publishers, 1962.   181pp.

       At nearly eighteen, Lydia Morrison is in
       love with a boy her family finds unsuitable and
       is at odds with her mother, Rena.  These ten-
       sions culminate in an attempted elopement.
       The focus is on Rena and her efforts to under-
       stand both her daughter and her own father, but
       the mother-daughter relationship affords the
       plot its main complication.

120.   Ehle, John. *The Land Breakers*. New York:
       Harper & Row, Publishers, 1964.   407pp.

       In this tale of pioneer life in the post-
       Revolutionary-War Carolinas, Ehle presents
       strong yet necessarily dependent young women.
       Lorrey Harrison, abandoned by her husband,
       Lacey, takes up with Mooney Wright, a former in-
       dentured servant, in order that she and her
       sons might survive.  Belle, the child-bride of
       Lorrey's father, endures her marriage to an
       old man.  Mina Plover, Lorrey's cousin, fights
       her attractions for both Mooney and Lacey.
       She finally reaches maturity after an ordeal
       in which she saves the life of a young German,
       Felix, who will become her husband.

121.   Epstein, Jacob. *Wild Oats*. Boston: Little,
       Brown, 1979.   267pp.

       Of the many people contributing to Billy
       Williams' chaotic adolescence, Elizabeth
       ("Zizi") Zannzibar plays a minor but significant
       role.  The two meet while their families are
       vacationing on the East Coast, and they become
       involved in a brief, intense summer romance.
       Their paths cross again at Beachum College
       where Zizi exploits Billy's rekindled affection
       after she becomes pregnant by her English pro-
       fessor.  Epstein personifies facets of the
       turbulent 1970s in his characters.

122.   Eyerly, Jeannette. *Bonnie Jo, Go Home*. New
       York: J.B. Lippincott Company, 1972.   141pp.

       On the rebound from a broken romance with a
       very popular boy, Bonnie Jo Jackson becomes
       pregnant by an unsavory teenager she doesn't

even like. She travels from her midwestern town
to New York City only to learn that her pregnancy
is too far advanced for an abortion. The confusion of the city symbolizes Bonnie Jo's emotional
state as she searches for and finally finds a
doctor who will perform a "salting-out process."
The simple style underscores Bonnie Jo's loneliness and alienation.

123.  Faasen, Neal. *The Toyfair*. New York: Simon,
      and Schuster, 1963. 186pp.

      Ace and Worm, two girls who accompany William
      Noone when he runs away from Michigan to Chicago
      in search of his father, are subordinate but
      useful characters. Ace's father is a wealthy
      and drunken physician, while Worm is from a
      poor, immigrant family; Ace is pretty, while
      Worm emphatically is not. But both are loyal
      to William, and they are inventive companions
      on his odyssey. The novel portrays the three
      as angry and bitter young people whose rebellion
      against school and adult society is justified.

124.  Fall, Thomas. *The Ordeal of Running Standing*.
      New York: The McCall Publishing Company, 1970.
      312pp.

      Crosses-the-River, also known by her Christian
      name of Sara Cross, meets Running Standing of f
      the Kiowa tribe when both are adolescents in
      Oklahoma territory at the turn of the century.
      Joe (as Sara calls him) follows Sara to the
      Carlisle Indian School in Pennsylvania. They
      separate on their wedding day because Joe is
      seduced by the white man's promises of wealth
      and fame; Sara returns to her family and applies
      her education toward improving her father's
      land. Joe's naive involvement with unscrupulous
      oil explorers reunites him with Sara, but their
      values and attitudes remain divergent. Fall
      depicts the American Indian in his struggle
      to preserve traditional customs and beliefs in
      a white-dominated society.

125.  Farrell, James T. *What Time Collects*. Garden
      City, N.Y.: Doubleday & Company, Inc., 1964.
      421pp.

The second volume of Farrell's tetralogy
depicts the disastrous marriage of two confused adolescents, Ann Duncan and Zeke Daniel.
Ann, a nineteen-year-old high school dropout,
wants to become somebody important. After a
few brief confrontations, she elopes with Zeke
an immature self-seeking individual. For two
years, Ann desperately tries to make the loveles
marriage work; however, it finally ends in
divorce. The novel portrays the banality of
life of Anglo-Saxon Protestant families in a
midwestern city in the 1920s.

126.  Fast, Howard. *Second Generation*. Boston:
      Houghton Mifflin, 1978. 441pp.

In this second novel of the Lavette trilogy,
covering the years 1934 to 1946, Barbara, at
twenty the soon-to-be heiress and daughter of
Jean and Daniel Lavette, abruptly ends her education at Sarah Lawrence to return to her
home in San Francisco. There she joins a long-
shoremen's strike against her stepfather's ship-
ping interests. In the years preceding the
Second World War, she grows rapidly into a
compassionate and self-sufficient woman and
eventually writes a novel about her experiences
in Paris and Berlin during that decade of turmoil. Another adolescent, Sally Levy, the precocious thirteen-year-old daughter of a wine-
maker in the Napa Valley, is infatuated with Joe
Lavette, Barbara's half-brother. She pursues
him until, at the age of twenty, she marries
him. Her eagerness for adult experiences is
apparent, but her character is marked by
impetuosity.

127.  Faulkner, William. *The Reivers: A Reminiscence*.
      New York: Random House, 1962. 305pp.

In this comic novel, Everbe Corinthia, famil-
iarly known as Corrie, is a prostitute in a
Memphis brothel where Boon Hogganbeck and
eleven-year-old Lucius Priest stop off during
their joy-ride in Boss Priest's automobile.
Lucius, the protagonist-narrator, does not give
her age but describes her as a "young girl."
A typically kind-hearted woman of ill repute,
Corrie mothers Lucius, washes his clothes, and

tends his wounds after his fight with a
young boy who impugns her character. She prom-
ises Lucius that she will quit her profession
and she does; she marries Boon. Lucius' feelings
for Corrie are important motivating factors
in his maturation.

128.  Fikso, Eunice [Cleland] [as C.G. Griffin, pseud.]
      *The Impermanence of Heroes*. Philadelphia:
      Chilton Company Publishers, 1965. 185pp.

      Jessica Brewer, eleven, discovers the com-
      plexity of human relationships when her loving
      friendship with Korean veteran Joe St. George
      is complicated by his animosity toward the
      New England townspeople and by his murder of
      a despicable stranger. The novel focuses on
      Jessica's growth rather than on the crime she
      witnesses, which initiates her into adult res-
      ponsibility.

129.  Finch, Phillip. *Haulin'*. Garden City, N.Y.:
      Doubleday & Company, Inc., 1975. 225pp.

      Mynette Hancock at eighteen is beautiful and
      bored with small-town life. Seeking romance
      and excitement she leaves home, hitching a ride
      from Kansas to Boston with the protagonist,
      J.W. Pickett, and his relief man, Lenny Lewis,
      two long-distance truck drivers. Mynette and
      Lenny have a brief but passionate affair. When
      their short but intense relationship ends,
      each seems to have benefited. Mynette is a
      secondary character, however, and seems more
      mature than her stated age.

130.  Flagg, Fannie. *Coming Attractions: A Wonderful
      Novel*. New York: William Morrow and Company,
      1981. 320pp.

      Between the ages of eleven and eighteen,
      Daisy Fay Harper keeps the diary which con-
      stitutes this *Bildungsroman* of southern girl-
      hood in the 1950s. Candid, cheerful, spunky,
      and determined to become a movie star, Daisy
      Fay describes her parents' turbulent marriage
      and their intermittent struggle to dominate her
      affections, her father's crazy business ventures,
      the bizarre behavior of the Harpers' eccentric

circle of acquaintances, and her own hap-
hazard school career. Daisy Fay rejects
life in her stultifying towns, where danger
and chicanery undergird surface conformity,
and puzzles over the double standard. Comic
in tone, the novel relies upon the central
device of the "wise innocent."

131.  Forbes, [Delores Florine] Stanton, and Helen
      Rydell [as Forbes Rydell, pseud.]. *They're
      Not Home Yet*. Garden City, N.Y.: Doubleday
      & Company, Inc., 1962. 189pp.

      As the principal figure of the secondary plot,
      Lana, aged twelve, is thrust into a premature
      adulthood when she and four of her school-
      mates are kidnapped. Her actions, and the
      actions of the other captive children,
      are compared to the actions of their parents.

132.  Forman, James. *The Cow Neck Rebels*. New York:
      Farrar, Straus & Giroux, 1969. 272pp.

      Although Rachel Campbell is subsidiary
      to Bruce and Malcolm Cameron, her change from
      a lighthearted girl to a strong young woman
      is important, and she is central to several
      dramatic scenes in this novel of the American
      Revolutionary War.

133.  Freely, Maureen. *Mother's Helper*. New York:
      Delacorte Press, 1979. 369pp.

      Because the only thing she has ever been good
      at is being a child, college freshman Laura
      takes a job as a mother's helper. The open
      household is a caricature of liberal attitudes
      toward child raising, sex, feminism, and other
      causes of the early 1970s. We see Laura drawn
      into the sexual and emotional tangle of the par-
      ents, their lovers, and their friends, and we
      watch as the children, who are privy to all that
      goes on in the household, disintegrate into
      tragedy.

134.  Friedman, Alan. *Hermaphrodeity: The Autobio-
      graphy of a Poet*. New York: Alfred A. Knopf,
      1972. 426pp.

      The protagonist of this novel is Millie/Willie

Niemann, a poet and true hermaphrodite who
spends the first sixteen years of life as a
girl and the next three as a boy before finally
deciding to settle into life as a woman. This
decision is reached only after an awkward attempt at making love to a woman results in
Millie/Willie's self-impregnation. A study
of the relationships between sexuality and
art, this novel uses the situation of the
hermaphrodite to poke fun at our sexist notions
about the characteristics that make artists or
lovers great.

135.   Friedman, Bruce Jay. *The Dick*. New York:
       Alfred A. Knopf, 1970. 310pp.

Although her character is not fully developed,
ten-year-old Jamie LePeters plays a significant
part in this comic novel about her father's
life as a public relations representative for
a large police department on the East Coast.
A white student at a tough, mostly black grade
school, Jamie is uncommonly mature for her age.
When her father's job and marriage turn sour,
she is able not only to take these setbacks in
stride but also to provide her father with important emotional support. Eventually, her
father abandons both his job and his marriage,
and Jamie decides to run off with him to start
a new life.

136.   Friedman, Bruce Jay. *A Mother's Kisses*. New
       York: Simon and Schuster, 1964. 286pp.

Seventeen-year-old Joseph, the novel's hero,
encounters a variety of girls as he leaves high
school and prepares for college, but predictably,
he is mainly interested in sex. Eileen Fast-
ner is a neighborhood girl, known to Joseph as
"Fasty," who, after one semester in college,
has sophisticated and wanton ways that appeal
to him. When Joseph works as a waiter in a
summer camp, a girl nicknamed "Droshkula" attracts him. He meets her under the trees at
night for teasing and petting. As a freshman
at a Kansas agricultural college, he partici-
pates in a "gang-scrub" of a nude coed. The
girls in the novel function as objects of sexual exploitation and fantasy.

137.  Fumento, Rocco. *Tree of Dark Reflection*.
      New York: Alfred A. Knopf, 1962. 528pp.

      A secondary character, Miriam Stern has a
      pivotal relationship with Danny Faustino, the
      protagonist. Danny is Catholic, and Miriam
      is Jewish, though she observes religious holi-
      days and ceremonies only for the sake of her
      brother. Her relationship with Danny is
      always close and briefly sexual. The opening
      and closing of the novel are addressed to her,
      for she has given Danny the impetus to write
      it and thus to come to terms with the religious
      and sexual tensions of growing up.

138.  Gagarin, Nicholas. *Windsong*. New York: William
      Morrow and Company, 1970. 275pp.

      Flo Brown is the symbol of protagonist Harold
      Mettleson's adolescence and is seen only through
      his perceptions. All during his college days,
      their lives twine and cross, and although they
      are close friends, they never become lovers--
      as he would like. They do, however, share im-
      portant experiences and serve as touchstones
      for one another. Eventually each falls in love
      with someone else. This resolution seems to
      them the appropriate, happy ending.

139.  Gallagher, Patricia. *All for Love*. New York:
      Avon Books, 1981. 391pp.

      Beautiful Jacintha Howard is left alone in
      the world at seventeen when her impoverished
      grandfather dies, leaving her with only a
      large home and a faithful housekeeper-friend.
      Her guardian, Earl Britton, is a wealthy and
      unhappily married banker. Despite her love
      for him, Jacintha refuses to become his mistress
      and stubbornly maintains her independence until,
      in desperation, she marries an immoral and crude
      businessman who considers her only a piece of
      property. This historical novel, set in New
      York City in Civil War times, is full of action
      and romance. Its strong-willed young heroine
      not only matures, but eventually finds happiness
      with her former guardian and the son she has
      borne him while still married to her brutal
      husband.

140.  Gallagher, Patricia.  *The Sons and the Daughters*.
      New York: J. Messner, 1961.  348pp.

      A small town in west Texas is the background
      for seventeen-year-old Jill Turner's thwarted
      yearnings for romance and education.  Denied
      the chance to go to college, she is thrilled
      when the son of a wealthy and prominent family
      takes notice of her.  But through her experiences
      with him and her observations of the ugliness
      and emptiness of the lives of other inhabitants
      of the ironically named Shady Bend, she comes
      to value a more solid, though less exciting,
      young man and to face life more realistically.
      In the tradition of the romantic exposé, the
      novel reveals the sordidness and cruelty of
      life in a stifling small town.

141.  Gallagher, Patricia.  *Summer of Sighs*.  New York:
      Avon, 1971.  288pp.

      Thomas Courtland, a southern minister, has
      for years carried on a passionate affair with
      a wealthy and socially prominent widow, Grace
      Bradley.  His son Christopher, a college student,
      was embittered by his discovery at thirteen of
      his father's infidelity.  Nina Bradley, Grace's
      seventeen-year-old daughter, becomes the victim
      of this complex net of relationships.  The
      summer of the title is that between her gradua-
      tion from high school and her entrance into
      college: she is seduced by Christopher and
      falls deeply in love with him.  She becomes
      pregnant despite their precautions and then
      is devastated to learn of her mother's liaison
      with her minister, leading to a final catas-
      trophe.

142.  Gallagher, Patricia.  *The Thicket*.  New York:
      Avon, 1973.  256pp.

      Two ill-fated interracial love affairs are
      examined in this novel: one between a wealthy
      white widow and a man who discovers near the
      end of the novel that he is a quadroon, and the
      other between her sixteen-year-old daughter
      and a young Indian.  The mother's social and
      racial snobbery contrasts with Beth's some-
      times naive and very fashionable tolerance and

concern for such causes as ecology. When Beth,
her sweetheart, and her mother's lover become
lost in the wild area that gives the book its
title, she shows remarkable courage, and the
end of the novel ironically sets her grief
for the Indian who has given his life for her
against her mother's repugnance at learning
that her lover is black.

143.  Gardner, John. *Nickel Mountain*. New York:
      Alfred A. Knopf, 1973. 312pp.

      Henry Soames is a fat, kind-hearted, middle-
aged introvert who runs a truck stop in the
Catskill Mountains during the early 1950s.
Callie Wells, an attractive and naive girl of
sixteen, goes to work for Henry and soon becomes
pregnant by a local boy who deserts her. Henry
falls in love with Callie, and though they both
know the love between them is one-sided, they
marry, mostly out of loneliness. The plot
revolves, for the most part, around the gradual
changes in Henry's and Callie's relationship.
Their son, their eccentric friends, and the
haunting landscape lead them through alternate
periods of despair and joy until, finally, the
purpose of their lives becomes clear to them.
Gardner subtitled this book "A Pastoral Novel"
and stressed the rural New York setting, with
its rustic charms and its spirit-soothing
qualities.

144.  Gasner, Beverly. *Girls' Rules*. New York:
      Alfred A. Knopf, 1968. 208pp.

      Celia St. Clair Dobbs is transformed from
pudgy awkwardness to beauty during her first
year in college. Though she loves school, she
marries at the end of her freshman year, plunging
once again into uncertainty. These stages and
the furious tension between the young Celia
and her mother are presented in flashbacks
during the story of Celia's young matronhood,
which is contrasted with the life of her friend,
Marina.

145.  Gates, Natalie. *Hush, Hush Johnson*. New York:
      Holt, Rinehart and Winston, 1967. 175pp.

When Mindy Johnson, eighteen, drops out of
college to take a job in a missile plant, she
becomes the target of Russian spies. This
adolescent girl functions primarily as a genera-
tor of action and suspense.

146.  Gerber, Merrill Joan. *An Antique Man*. Boston:
      Houghton Mifflin Company, 1967. 278pp.

At twenty, Carol Goldman has her first love
affair. Bard, her lover, introduces her to
people, places, and ideas far outside her
parents' value system. The differences between
them place great strains on their relationship.
All these factors complicate the main plot of
the novel, the family's reaction to the death
of Carol's father.

147.  Gerber, Merrill Joan. *Now Molly Knows*. New
      York: Arbor House, 1974. 263pp.

This book is basically the story of one girl
growing up in the 1950s. The focus is on
Molly's life from her early teens until her
wedding day and on her relationship with her
boyfriend, Joshua, whose parents disapprove of
her, of her friends and of her family. Although
her own parents are unhappy with each other
most of the time and are always having financial
problems, they are devoted to Molly and give her
the very best they have to offer. Molly often
fights with them, resents their authority, and
questions their rules, yet comes to understand
and appreciate all they have done for her.

148.  Gilbert, Julie Goldsmith. *Umbrella Steps*.
      New York: Random House, Inc., 1972. 181pp.

Prudence Goodrich is a modern New York teenager who, at sixteen, attends a progressive
private school, sees a psychiatrist, and is
having an affair with Nate Spitz, the father
of her best friend Lolly. Prudence is bright
and funny with a sharp wit and a tongue to
match, but beneath her caustic exterior, she is
vulnerable and a little sad. Prudence and
Nate have a surprisingly solid relationship
and in him she finds a friend, confidant, and
teacher who helps her cope bravely with her

mother's mental illness, with the rejection of
her best friend, and with the discovery that
Lolly has had a two-year affair with Prudence's
own father.

149.   Giles, Janice Holt. *Savanna*. Boston: Houghton
       Mifflin Company, 1961. 312pp.

       Though she was first widowed at nineteen,
       supported herself for several years by running
       trading posts, bore twins, and survived a second
       husband, Savanna Fowler Brook Lathrop prolongs
       her adolescence until her early twenties. She
       matures only when, faced with personal tragedy
       and financial ruin, she assumes full intellectual
       as well as economic responsibility for her fami-
       ly. The book depicts army life on the Arkansas
       frontier in the second quarter of the nineteenth
       century.

150.   Goldman, William. *Tinsel*. New York: Delacorte
       Press, 1979. 344pp.

       This novel of the ways in which Hollywood
       ruins people has among its major characters
       three women who unknowingly compete for the
       lead in a major film, *Tinsel*. The adolescence
       of Dixie, a not-terribly-talented middle-aged
       star of an old television series, is described;
       and Pig, a relatively talented young actress
       who has no cinematic experience but a busy
       record of sexual liaisons with industry figures,
       is another element of the plot. The third
       woman is Ginger, a brilliant doctoral student
       with a beautiful body and spotty success as a
       movie star. Most of Ginger's story centers
       upon her adolescence--as a bright, popular,
       pretty teenaged victim of *anorexia nervosa*.
       All of the characters are hurt by *Tinsel*, and
       the women probably suffer most. Ginger, though,
       who had the most problems reaching adulthood is
       perhaps least affected by the final events of
       the novel.

151.   Gordon, R.L. *The Lady Who Loved New York*. New
       York: Thomas Y. Crowell Company, 1977. 277pp.

       Brief but significant flashbacks to aged

Alice Barrington Melville's youth depict the
life of upper-class New York City society in
the late nineteen and early twentieth centuries.
Alice's restrained but affectionate relationship
with her mother and her struggle, at nineteen,
against the dominance of her mother-in-law
prepare her to become the formidable symbol
of a vanished era.

152.  Gores, Joe. *Hammett.* New York: G.P. Putnam's
      Sons, 1975. 251pp.

Goodie Owens, twenty, and Crystal Tam, fifteen,
both flat characters, are contrasted in this
conventional "hard-boiled" detective story,
an imaginary episode in the life of Dashiell
Hammett. Goodie is a small-town girl facing
"real" life for the first time in the wide open
San Francisco of 1928; her initiation is harsh,
causing her to reject the lure of the city
in favor of home and marriage. Crystal is
a Chinese-American so corrupted by her experiences as a child-mistress of wealthy men
that she becomes the genesis of all evil in
the plot.

153.  Gorham, Charles. *McCaffrey.* New York: The
      Dial Press, 1961. 245pp.

Doreen, the major female character in this
study of a male teenager's tormented sexual
coming of age, has been transformed from a poor,
Alabama "cracker" into a polished, poised New
York prostitute by the time she has reached
her late teens. She helps Vincent McCaffrey,
the protagonist, make what adjustment he can
to becoming a male prostitute; they are colleagues, and they are also lovers. Desperation
and fury drive them into the calculation and
manipulation necessary to escape the Life for a
few idyllic days, an adventure which precipitates
the novel's violent climax. Doreen's major
functions in the novel are to contrast with
Vincent and to articulate her theory that
the prostitute finds the world ugly and de-
ceitful and strikes back through the Life.

154.  Gould, Lois. *Necessary Objects.* New York:
      Random House, 1972. 275pp.

Jill Landau and Cathy Rossbach, cousins, are centers of important subplots. The girls are the children of two of the four Lowen sisters, who are the daughters of a department store magnate whose oppressive training and overprotectiveness have rendered them incapable of love or trust--instead, they are the ultimate consumers. At fourteen, Jill is afraid that she will "get frigid," that she will become like her mother. At eighteen, Cathy, the divorced mother of an infant, is addicted to drugs and alcohol, often unable to care for herself or her child. The fumbling though well-intended efforts of the oldest Lowen sister's newest husband affect both Jill and Cathy briefly, but the Lowen dominance prevails-- and there is little hope for the youngest generation.

155.   Gould, Lois. *A Sea-Change*. New York: Simon and Schuster, 1976. 163pp.

At thirteen, Diane Waterman watches her stepmother undergo a mythic change--from former model and submissive wife into androgynous leader (Gould draws parallels between Jessie Waterman's transformation and the life patterns of *labroides dimidiatus*; another variety of these fish is called "sea wives"). Jessie's example is not lost upon her stepdaughter, and it helps give Diane the strength and courage to undergo her own rebirth during a fierce storm, a transformation which parallels that of her stepmother.

156.   Gover, Robert. *Here Goes Kitten*. New York: Grove Press, Inc., 1964. 184pp.

In this sequel to *One Hundred Dollar Misunderstanding,* a seventeen-year-old black woman is living in a commune and supplementing her income from prostitution by singing in a nightclub. When her white friend, J.C. Holland, sets her up with a new client, a cheap political boss, the pair are in for trouble, for they must hide the fact that the client succumbs to a heart attack during intercourse. J.C. and Kitten both report the events, and their accounts clash wildly.

157.  Gover, Robert.  *J C Saves.*  New York: Trident
      Press, 1968.  190pp.

      In a serio-comic sequel to *One Hundred Dollar
      Misunderstanding* and *Here Goes Kitten*, Kitten,
      now twenty, and J.C. Holland, a young white
      man, encounter one another again during a race
      riot.  He abducts her to transform her into
      a traditional black maid so as to "save" her
      from a "career" as a prostitute.  Instead, her
      vigor and attraction overcome him, and they
      develop a vaguely satisfying relationship.

158.  Gover, Robert.  *One Hundred Dollar Misunder-
      standing.*  New York: Grove Press, Inc., 1961.
      192pp.

      At fourteen, Kitten is a prostitute who
      mistakes a college sophomore client (investing
      a windfall in "experience") for a wealthy man.
      She pursues their relationship to earn more
      money; he takes her interest as praise of
      his performance.  Kitten, who is black, and
      J.C., who is white, take turns narrating their
      wild, comic adventures.

159.  Grau, Shirley Ann.  *The House on Coliseum Street.*
      New York: Alfred A. Knopf, Inc., 1961.  242pp.

      Joan Mitchell leads a quiet, rather settled
      life in an unsettled and somewhat eccentric
      New Orleans household, headed by her mother
      who has had four daughters by four husbands.
      Joan seems to be drifting slowly into marriage
      with sedate Fred Aleman, when she impulsively
      has a few dates with exploitative Michael Kern.
      When Joan becomes pregnant by Michael, her
      mother arranges for an abortion.  There is no
      fuss, no recrimination, but Joan is shaken out
      of her routine and into a solitary, almost
      unnoticed, emotional turmoil.

160.  Grau, Shirley Ann.  *The Keepers of the House.*
      New York: Alfred A. Knopf, 1964.  309pp.

      The substantial episodes recording the
      adolescences of Margaret Carmichael and Abigail
      Howland provide explication and motivation for
      the climax of this southern family saga.  At
      eighteen, Margaret, of mixed black, Indian, and

white blood, leaves her extended black family
to embrace her white heritage as mistress of
Will Howland, a much older white planter.
Eventually, she becomes foster mother to
Will's granddaughter, Abigail, whose adolescence
is a study of the art of ignoring what one
chooses not to know; that pattern defines all
of Abigail's important decisions until, as a
grown woman, she is forced to face reality and
to confront bigotry. At the novel's climax,
the stories of Margaret and Abigail, always
intertwined, explode into violence and hatred.

161.   Graves, Wallace. *Trixie*. New York: Alfred
       A. Knopf, 1969. 333pp.

Trixie Mae Smith keeps her diary for almost
five years, recording major changes in her own
life as well as the Watts riots and the assas-
sinations of John F. Kennedy and Martin Luther
King. Each of these events affects Trixie
profoundly as she is transformed from an
illiterate kitchen worker into a literate, poised
college senior. Almost everyone she meets
during her college career---Woody, her Watts
lover; professors; a roommate; and Dicky Atwater,
a wealthy white youth--exploits Trixie sexually,
and as the novel closes, she is about to bear
Dicky's child. But Trixie's most serious
problems are those of identity; she is torn
between Woody's beliefs and the seeming
liberalism of her white friends. The latter,
true to Woody's predictions, accept her only
conditionally. There are no easy answers to
Trixie's problems, and the novel ends as it
begins, with a death.

Green, Hannah--*see* Greenberg, Joanne.

162.   Greenan, Russell H. *The Queen of America*.
       New York: Random House, 1972. 214pp.

When Betsy March, sixteen, a runaway and a
killer, joins the loosely knit, eccentric
circle of Ignacio Never, protagonist, one
hideous event follows another. The novel is a
horror story set in contemporary Boston.

163. Greenberg, Joanne [as Hannah Green, pseud.].
*The Dead of the House.* New York: Doubleday
& Company, Inc., 1972. 180pp.

Vanessa Nye reflects on her life and development from childhood to early maturity as she
tells the story of her family, early Ohio
pioneers. Though her grandfather is the central
character of this account, the long middle
section depicts Vanessa's adolescence against
the background of stable family relationships
and the onset of World War II.

164. Greenberg, Joanne [as Hannah Green, pseud.].
*I Never Promised You a Rose Garden.* New York:
Holt, Rinehart and Winston, 1964. 300pp.

Between the ages of sixteen and nineteen,
Deborah Blau is confined to an institution
for the insane. Greenberg's account of
Deborah's slow return to health dramatizes the
tension and agony of the wards and the painful
but healing sessions with her therapist. Both
the "real" worlds of the institution and of
Deborah's family are contrasted with the alluring
and devastating imaginary world Deborah has
created.

165. Greene, Bette. *Summer of My German Soldier.*
New York: The Dial Press, 1973. 230pp.

During Patty Bergen's twelfth year, she
offers aid and shelter to a young German prison-
er-of-war escapee. This act not only exacer-
bates Patty's alienation from family and com-
munity--she is seriously at odds with her
parents and is the only Jewish girl in her small
Arkansas town--but also leads to punishment by
the law. Yet the experience is not a destructive one, for Patty learns the values of
sacrificial love, of friendship, and of self-
reliance. This story depicts prejudice and
hatred lightened by Patty's decency and growing
strength. (In a sequel, *Morning Is a Long Time
Coming,* 1978, Patty searches for "her" soldier
in Germany, her final attempt to resolve the
problems generated in *Summer of My German Soldier.*)

Griffin, C.G.--*see* Fikso, Eunice [Cleland].

166.   Grossman, Alfred. *Marie Beginning*. New York:
       Doubleday & Company, Inc., 1965.  216pp.

       Marie Svobodna, an adolescent employee, turns
       a company and her co-workers upside down by her
       outrageous tricks and plots to achieve power in
       this satire of the business and political worlds.

167.   Grubb, Davis. *Shadow of My Brother*. New York:
       Holt, Rinehart and Winston, 1966.  316pp.

       At twenty, Amy Wilson secretly witnesses her
       father, Loy, participate in the lynching of a
       young black man; her initiation into res-
       ponsible adulthood consists of her efforts to
       behave correctly in the face of this horror.
       Flashbacks depict Nelly Wilson's maturation, a
       process twisted and spoiled by Loy, her brother.
       Loy's lack of balance as father and brother (as
       well as his inhumanity) is attributed to the
       racism which colors all his actions and associ-
       ations, particularly his relationships with Amy
       and Nelly.

168.   Grubb, Davis. *The Watchman*. New York: Charles
       Scribner's Sons, 1961.  275pp.

       The citizens of Adena, West Virginia, are
       shocked to discover one morning that Cole
       Blake, a well-liked eighteen-year-old, has been
       murdered in a particularly brutal manner. Sus-
       picion soon falls upon several people, chief
       among them being Sheriff Luther Alt and his two
       teenaged daughters, the seemingly virginal Jill
       and the reckless Cristi.  A series of bizarre
       personal relationships involving the sheriff,
       his family, and his deputy are uncovered, re-
       vealing the murderer's identity and motive.
       As is common in Grubb's work, the novel ex-
       amines the capacity for good and evil within
       us all.

169.   Grumbach, Doris. *The Short Throat, the Tender
       Mouth*.  Garden City, N.Y.: Doubleday & Company,
       Inc., 1964.  184pp.

       Vivian Lefevre is the most clearly drawn female

among the group of college students portrayed in this novel.  Taught by her mother to
assess herself by her looks and her grooming,
aware of her mother's horror at the discovery
that there is black blood in her dead father's
family, Vivian has little sense of her own
worth.  When she falls in love with a boy who
cannot respond to her, she crumbles beneath
a sense of despair and worthlessness and commits
suicide, though the circumstances of the act
leave her specific motivations at the moment
of her death unclear.

170.  Guest, Elissa Haden. *The Handsome Man*.  New
      York: Four Winds Press, 1980.  184pp.

     Fourteen-year-old Alexandra Barnes is attracted
to a handsome young man of about thirty.  She
and her best friend Angie trail the man and in
time actually meet him.  The novel explores
Angie's fantasies about the Handsome Man, the
actual relationship between them, and the tensions within her own family as the relationship
between her father and mother suffers.

171.  Guest, Judith. *Ordinary People*.  New York:
      The Viking Press, 1976.  263pp.

     Two young women figure prominently in the life
of protagonist Conrad Jarret, who is still suf-
fering from guilt over his brother's death.  Karen
Aldrich, a friend from the mental hospital from
which both she and Con have recently been released, stands for the possibility that he will
never fully recover.  In contrast, Jeannine Pratt
represents hope because she helps Con discover
his own worth and learn that he has strength
to share with others.  Con's search for health
and stability is complicated by the fragility
of his parents' marriage.

172.  Gutcheon, Beth. *The New Girls*.  New York:
      G.P. Putnam's Sons, 1979.  347pp.

     Fifteen years after graduation from Miss
Pratt's fashionable New England boarding
school, four former students, Lisa Sutton, Jenny
Rose, Muffin Bundle, and Ann Lacey, have met
for their class reunion.  They are awaiting

the arrival of Sally Titsworth, the fifth
member of their special group, when they
learn of her suicide. Recounting their years
as students in the strict, sheltered environment of the school when they believed the most
important things a girl could be were rich
and beautiful, the book shows the role that
Sally, spirited and rebellious but deeply
troubled and self-destructive, played in their
lives. The story moves back and forth from
the school to the homes and families of the
five girls, exploring their characters and
personalities, and gives us glimpses of their
lives after graduation.

173.   Guy, Rosa. *Edith Jackson*. New York: The
       Viking Press, 1978. 187pp.

       At seventeen, Edith Jackson's chief ambition
       is to keep herself and her three sisters in the
       same foster home until Edith comes of age and
       can get a job to support the family. Because
       she is a minor, Edith must watch helplessly
       as her family is split up. Even her limited
       romantic dreams are shattered when she becomes
       pregnant by a cold-hearted older man. This novel
       depicts the goals of Edith and of fellow blacks
       who seek to influence her life. The novel is
       the third of a trilogy, preceded by *The Friends*
       and *Ruby*.

174.   Guy, Rosa. *The Friends*. New York: Holt, Rine-
       hart and Winston, 1972. 203pp.

       Phyllisia Cathy's difficulties at school and
       in her Harlem neighborhood stem partly from
       the fact that she is West Indian by birth.
       Phyllisia's Americanization and maturation
       are further complicated by the death of her
       mother and by her very strained relationship
       with her father. An awkward friendship with
       Edith Jackson illustrates the differences be-
       tween the girls' families, and their friendship
       eventually becomes the means of Phyllisia's
       growing up. *The Friends* is the first novel
       in a trilogy which includes *Ruby* and *Edith
       Jackson*.

175.  Guy, Rosa. *Ruby*. New York: The Viking Press,
      1976. 217pp.

      *Ruby* is the second of a trilogy which be-
      gins with *The Friends* and concludes with *Edith
      Jackson*. Like *The Friends*, it dramatizes
      racial discrimination and points out the devas-
      tating effect that inept white racist teachers
      can have on their black pupils. Ruby Cathy,
      eighteen-year-old daughter of a strict, violent
      father, feels a desperate need for love. She has
      an affair with Daphne Duprey, a classmate who
      prides herself on her self-control and her
      dedication to her race. The girls' love is
      powerful, but their personalities conflict;
      their goals are divergent, and their families'
      opposition is strong. These forces complicate
      their relationship.

176.  Hahn, Harriet. *The Plantain Season*. New York:
      W.W. Norton & Company, Inc., 1976. 207pp.

      Susannah Ellison, at seventeen, feels over-
      powered by her beautiful mother and is unsure
      in her relationships with men. She is bright
      and values solitude; repeated trips to the
      pier to watch the ocean, think, and feed a pet
      rat are nearly as important to her growing up
      as are her encounters with a variety of boys
      and men. The novel, narrated by Susannah, tells
      of a pivotal year in her life and shows how
      she grows in confidence and gains a sense of
      worth.

177.  Haines, William Wister. *The Winter War*. Boston:
      Little, Brown and Company, 1961. 247pp.

      The character of Lita Littleton, captive of
      the Sioux for eight formative years, presents
      a study in mixed loyalties. Returned to "civil-
      ization," she is sent to a college where she is
      to be trained as a teacher for the Indians,
      but she finds that life unbearable and runs
      away, intending to return to the West. In order
      to reach her destination, she joins a punitive
      military expedition sent West after the Battle
      of Little Big Horn. Falling in love with
      Colonel David Selkirk, the novel's protagonist,
      she finds herself torn between two worlds
      but truly belonging to neither. This his-
      torical novel depicts the prejudices and
      hatreds of its period, which form and

victimize Lita.

178. Hale, Nancy. *Secrets.* New York: Coward, McCann,
     & Geoghegan, Inc., 1971. 126pp.

     Scenes from the lives of five young people
     (the Welches, four children of a painfully
     proper father, and the narrator, who is
     the daughter of artists) comprise this short
     novel. Their childhood games and interests
     (a "lizard farm," secret clubs, and so on)
     and the debutante year of the narrator and
     Jinny, elder of the Welch girls, are most
     fully developed. The novel nostalgically
     evokes youth and youthful friendship.

179. Hall, Lynn. *The Horse Trader.* New York: Charles
     Scribner's Sons, 1981. 121pp.

     Fifteen-year-old Karen Kohler, who lives
     with her mother in a small town in Colorado,
     knows that her mother had to sell her horse to
     pay the expenses of Karen's birth. Karen wants
     to buy back her mother's horse from the horse
     trader, Harley, but instead gets a broken-down
     horse at an excessive price. She learns about
     caring for the horse from Harley, and she also
     learns to love him in a way that is more than
     daughterly. As Karen matures, she and her
     mother develop a close relationship centered
     around a mutual interest in horses, and she
     finally realizes that Harley is a womanizer.
     When her horse foals, Karen knows that her
     money was well-spent, and her joy is complete.

180. Hansen, Joseph. *Skinflick.* New York: Holt,
     Rinehart and Winston, 1979. 194pp.

     Though Charleen Sims appears only briefly,
     her presence is felt throughout this novel.
     Already a teenaged mother who has lost her
     child, Charleen nevertheless still looks like
     a youngster on the brink of adolescence. Her
     willingness to break into the film industry
     (via "kid porn" films) with sexual favors leads
     to murder and to her disappearance. Protagonist-
     detective Dave Brandstetter traces Charleen,
     uncovering facts about her character and her
     past as he searches for a killer.

181. Hardwick, Elizabeth. *Sleepless Nights*. New
     York: Random House, 1979. 151pp.

     The substance of this novel/memoir is a
     series of character sketches of people re-
     markable for their oddity or for their ferocious
     adherence to type. One brief but memorable
     sketch is of an adolescent girl, lovingly
     raised, who turns inexplicably to prostitution
     and self-destruction.

182. Harington, Donald. *Some Other Place. The
     Right Place*. Boston: Little, Brown and
     Company, 1972. 462pp.

     Diana Stoving, a recent graduate of a pre-
     tentious Eastern school, discovers the rein-
     carnation of her grandfather, Daniel Lyam
     Montross, in a high school senior, Day Whit-
     tacker. While attempting to retrace the life
     of Montross, Diana and Day fall in love. Through-
     out this complex novel, which even includes a
     book of poems, we follow the couple's search
     for personal identity.

183. Harnack, Curtis. *Limits of the Land*. Garden
     City, N.Y.: Doubleday & Company, Inc., 1979,
     232pp.

     After a stint in the Army during World War I
     and many years in the city, August, the pro-
     tagonist, returns to his western Iowa hometown
     to farm and to rear a family. Among the
     many problems he must face is the wildly un-
     predictable behavior of his teenaged daughter
     Sheila, who becomes moody when her daily routine
     is disrupted. Harnack ties dissimilar situations
     together by using the land and farm life to
     symbolize a wide range of emotions and experi-
     ences.

184. Harris, Marilyn. *Hatter Fox*. New York: Random
     House, 1973. 241pp.

     The title character, a seventeen-year-old
     Navajo girl, has been repeatedly rejected and
     abused by both Indian and white authority fig-
     ures. Upon first meeting Dr. Teague Summer,
     a young Bureau of Indian Affairs physician, she
     stabs him. First curious and then fascinated,

he sets out to help her. The novel, narrated
by Summer and set primarily in the New Mexico
state reformatory, recounts his attempts to
help her overcome her sporadic violence and
frequent withdrawal. Their relationship
grows deep and ambiguous as she becomes dependent upon him. A sense of doom pervades
this novel, for it seems impossible to imagine
Hatter ever adjusting to society, and indeed,
the reader, and Summer, finally doubt whether
that outcome is truly desirable.

185.  Harrison, G[eorge] B[agshawe]. *The Fires of
        Arcadia*. New York: Harcourt, Brace & World,
        Inc., 1965. 153pp.

A minor but important character is nineteen-
year-old Helen Orr, talented but obnoxious
daughter of the president of Arcadia College.
She follows her theatrical triumph as leader
of the Bacchanals in Euripedes' *Bacchae* by
instigating an actual bacchanalia which leads
to the novel's melodramatic climax. This mystery by an eminent Shakespeare scholar is also
a satiric treatment of the academic scene and
touches on questions of what is permissible
in biological research.

186.  Hassler, Jon. *Staggerford*. New York: Atheneum,
        1977. 341pp.

Essentially the story of the last week in the
life of Miles Pruitt, a high school English
teacher, this novel contains some classroom
portraits of both male and female adolescents.
The most significant of these is Beverly Bingham,
a bright senior with terrible problems: her
father was convicted of murder (only Beverly
and her long-lost sister know the truth of that
episode), and her mother is the town madwoman.
Beverly's adoration of and growing dependence
upon Miles are among the causes of the novel's
surprising climax.

187.  Hauser, Marianne. *The Talking Room*. New York:
        Fiction Collective, 1976. 156pp.

The narrator is B, a thirteen-year-old living
with her hard-drinking and undependable mother,

J, and Aunt V, who is J's possessive lesbian
lover. Perhaps as a result of her unfortunate
situation, B is obese and begins sexual activity
at the age of ten; at thirteen she is pregnant.
Intentionally disconnected in narrative and
sexually explicit, the novel has little plot,
but it does offer some witty scenes.

188.   Hawes, Evelyn. *A Madras-Type Jacket*. New York:
       Harcourt, Brace & World, Inc., 1967. 168pp.

       Margo Brown describes her freshman year at
at an unnamed university. Coming from a close-
knit, small-town family, she is understandably
apprehensive at first, but her thoughtful self-
reliance, her clear values, and her self-aware-
ness and introspection stand her in good stead
as she joins a sorority, makes friends, and comes
to care for the fine young man who wears the "madras-type jacket." The novel, though set in the
late 1960s, presents an almost timeless picture
of college life, both as a time of youthful good
spirits and pranks and as a haven offering
opportunities for learning about oneself and the
world.

189.   Hayes, Joseph Arnold. *Like Any Other Fugitive*.
       New York: The Dial Press, 1971. 446pp.

       Laurel Taggart, a seventeen-year-old slightly
schizoid teenager, runs away from her wealthy
Connecticut home with B.C. Chadwicke III, a
Vietnam veteran. She is fleeing from her
domineering, mentally-ill father, a retired
general, and he is running from a false hit and
run charge. They travel west, dodging police,
bounty hunters, and assassins hired by her
father. During their flight, B.C. discovers
that life has meaning beyond the Vietnam syn-
drome of survival of the most powerful regard-
less of morality, while Laurel develops identity
and self-confidence through him. They fall in
love and plan to marry.

190.   Hazel, Robert. *Early Spring*. New York: W.W.
       Norton & Company, Inc., 1971. 222pp.

       This college novel, set at the University of
Kentucky during the troubled academic year

climaxed by the Kent State killings, centers on
a young professor who narrates. It is a painful year for him, personally as well as politi-
cally, and his affair with Heidi Johnson, a
bright but bigoted student, touches him deeply,
as does his involvement with another couple, a
brilliant black basketball player and a white
girl from a prominent family. The sexually
explicit novel touches on most social problems
of the day.

191.  Hearon, Shelby. *Hannah's House*. Garden City,
      N.Y.: Doubleday & Company, Inc., 1975. 240pp.

      Hannah Landrum, the title character, is second-
      ary to her mother, who is both protagonist
      and narrator. A popular sophomore at the
      University of Texas, Hannah is engaged and
      deeply desirous that the preparations for her
      marriage and the wedding itself be socially
      correct. Her less conventional mother tries
      hard not to embarrass her, even while often
      revealing a rather condescending attitude. But
      by the end of the novel, the mother at least
      has achieved a somewhat better understanding
      of the situation, and Hannah's characterization
      has deepened. The customary generational con-
      flicts are interestingly reversed here.

192.  Heller, Joseph. *Something Happened*. New York:
      Alfred A. Knopf, 1974. 565pp.

      The fifteen-year-old daughter of Bob Slocum
      (a "minor organization executive," as the nar-
      rator-father labels himself) is presented
      as a modern, awkward adolescent who, by her
      own account, has "nothing to do." She bickers
      with her father and mother because she has a
      "poor self-image." She thinks that she is
      untalented and unattractive and so do her
      parents--though they pretend to her to think
      otherwise. She says that she wishes they were
      dead or she were dead, in order to draw their
      attention. Bob Slocum is a self-aware but
      cruel and cowardly man, and his daughter reflects
      these qualities. He concludes that her future
      looks bleak but ordinary and predicts early
      dissipation for her because "she is a strong-
      minded girl who is far too weak to withstand
      a popular trend."

193.  Herlihy, James Leo. *The Season of the Witch*.
      New York: Simon and Schuster, 1971. 371pp.

      In late 1969, the rebellious protagonist, six-
      teen-year-old Gloria Random, runs away from
      her fashionable, upper-class home in Michigan
      to New York with her nineteen-year-old friend
      John, a homosexual who is fleeing the draft.
      In New York, Gloria and John change their
      names to Witch and Roy and move into a Greenwich
      Village commune headed by a maverick ex-psycho-
      analyst from California. In the meantime,
      Gloria searches for her runaway father, a
      Communist whom she finds teaching at a junior
      college. Writing in the first-person form of
      Gloria's diary, Herlihy recreates the hippie
      subculture of the 1960s in this *Bildungsroman*
      about a young girl who sets off on a journey,
      matures, and eventually finds a harmonious niche
      for herself within her family and society.

194.  Higgins, George V. *Kennedy for the Defense*.
      New York: Alfred A. Knopf, 1980. 225pp.

      In this fast-paced humorous novel about
      criminal lawyer Jerry Kennedy, his fifteen-year-
      old daughter plays a small but important role.
      The bright, throughly decent, cheerful Heather
      (nicknamed Saigon because her birth helped
      keep Kennedy out of the Vietnam War) and her
      mother represent the antidote to the sleazy world
      of Jerry's work. Heather also represents an
      optimistic view of the future. Heather's kindness
      endangers her briefly, but Kennedy saves the day.

195.  Hill, Deborah. *This Is the House*. New York:
      Coward, McCann & Geohegan, Inc., 1976. 411pp.

      Details of life on Cape Cod during the Post-
      Revolutionary period demonstrate that the lot
      of many early American women was a hard one
      indeed. The fact that she and her mother
      were nothing more than the possessions of an
      abusive, sexually exploitative drunkard accounts
      in good part for Molly Deems' calculating
      determination to make a good marriage and to
      attain social prominence. Molly devotes her
      adolescence, recounted in a substantial portion
      of the plot, to these ends, exploiting her

looks, her employer, and her suitor, Elijah
Merrick. Accounts of the Merricks' marriage,
the tensions generated by conflicting goals
and by adultery, form the bulk of this historical novel which also touches upon the adolescences of several other young women. Molly's
story implies that submissiveness is women's
key to happiness, a conclusion which conflicts
with the implicit lessons of the early chapters.

196. Hill, Patti. *One Thing I Know*. Boston: Houghton
     Mifflin Company, 1962. 93pp.

     Sixteen-year-old Francesca Hollins narrates
     this tale of her friendships and dates with
     several young men and her brief but intense
     infatuation with Graham von Liddle. Her
     relationship with Graham ends almost casually
     at about the same time as she is observing
     the fragility of her mother's marriage with
     her stepfather. Thus, she concludes that
     "love is just one big fat illusion," and that
     though she is not going to avoid further in-
     volvements she will not fall in love again.

197. Hillerman, Tony. *Dance Hall of the Dead*. New
     York: Harper & Row, Publishers, 1973. 166pp.

     At eighteen, Susanne has rejected her family
     and been rejected by her ambitious boyfriend
     and her hippie commune. A gentle, loving
     person who is not allowed to express her love,
     Susanne is a symbol of the failure of contem-
     porary white American parents. Her brief
     portrait parallels that of an Indian boy who
     is also isolated; each seeks a culture allowing
     genuine growth and development.

198. Hine, Al. *Lord Love a Duck*. New York: Atheneum,
     1961. 367pp.

     Barbara Anne Greene is beautiful, intelligent.
     ambitious, and manipulative. Her only conscious
     morality is sexual, and even that is intensely
     practical, for sexual purity is the only way,
     she knows full well, to maintain her reputation
     and popularity. She lacks malice but is willing
     to be cruel to anyone who stands in her way.
     The plot concerns her relationships with a

brilliant classmate who comes to dominate
her through hypnotism and a handsome college
student whom she eventually marries. Set in
small-town Iowa, this satiric novel is highly
comic.

199. Hoff, Marilyn. *Dink's Blues*. New York: Harcourt, Brace & World, Inc., 1966. 246pp.

Sarah Louise Lodge takes as a college roommate Diane (Dink) Harrison St. Clair, a
drama student, who, as a modern Antigone, as
updated by a black student, steals the heart
of Mr. Jefferson, a married humanities instructor. Sarah begins to date Boots, the black
student; Dink intimates that she is partially
black; and finally, Dink and Mr. Jefferson's
affair becomes campus gossip. Sarah is led
to believe that Dink is pregnant when Dink
deliberately fights with her family and then
drops out of school, and Mr. Jefferson is
suddenly and blissfully reconciled with his
wife. Sarah eventually suspects that Dink
is really not pregnant but is playing "the
biggest, whoppingest, most fantastic practical
joke on the world."

Hoffenberg, Mason--*see* Southern, Terry.

200. Hoffman, Alice. *The Drowning Season*. New
York: E.P. Dutton, 1979. 212pp.

This story of eighteen-year-old Esther and
the grandmother for whom she is named reveals
both their lack of mutual understanding and
their very deep need for such understanding.
Raised by her stern and unloving grandmother,
Esther the White, the younger Esther, called
the Black, marks her years by the passing of
the drowning season, each July and August when
her ineffectual father, Phillip, attempts to
drown himself in the Atlantic near the family's
seaside compound. Three events, however, con-
spire to bring the two Esthers to understanding
and love: the family's loss of much of their
money, Esther the White's discovery that she
has cancer, and Phillip's eventual success in
drowning himself in the Atlantic. As Esther
the White explains her past to her granddaughter,
she is humanized, and the younger Esther gives
up adolescent rebellion for mature understanding

and love.

201.  Hoffman, Alice. *Property Of*. New York: Farrar,
      Straus & Giroux, 1977. 248pp.

      This story of an unnamed narrator, a girl
      of seventeen, begins with her first meeting
      with McKay, leader of a New York City gang
      called "The Orphans," and ends as she leaves
      him a year later. In the meantime she has
      lived with him, helped him commit crimes, taken
      drugs with him, waited for him to serve a brief
      prison term, and watched him destroy his gang
      and gain control of drug traffic in his area.
      She makes few moral judgments except those
      related to her love for him or to her persistent
      sense of self. She always holds herself aloof
      from the gang itself, refusing to become part
      of the "Property of the Orphans," the females
      associated with the gang.

202.  Hogan, William. *The Quartzsite Trip*. New York:
      Atheneum, 1980. 306pp.

      Early 1960s adolescent society is catalogued
      in this account of a pivotal desert trip by
      a large group of high school seniors and their
      English teacher. Leading into a startling
      climax, various segments reveal the preoccupa-
      tions (many sexual) of the young people, for
      whom the trip is primarily a developmental experi
      ence. Four young women are among the main
      characters in this representation of stereotypes
      in American culture.

203.  Holmes, Marjorie. *Follow Your Dream*. Philadel-
      phia: The Westminster Press, 1961. 186pp.

      Tracey Temple, a tomboyish high school junior
      who loves animals and wants to be a vet, lands
      a summer job with a well-known female veterinar-
      ian, only to find that her summer and her am-
      bitions are nearly ruined by men--the handsome
      young men, Whit and Jeff, with whom she becomes
      infatuated and the men who want to keep women
      out of the veterinary profession. Tracey's
      summer is further complicated by her co-worker
      Diane, who is so beautiful that Whit and Jeff
      both fall in love with her, and by Dudley,

Tracey's faithful friend and neighbor, who
falls for Tracey just as Tracey falls for
Whit. Tracey is at an awkward age, not
yet sophisticated enough to be really
grown-up but having to deal with conflicting
grown-up feelings just the same. However,
she finally realizes that neither Jeff nor
Whit is for her, and she remains unswerving
in her adherence to her professional goal.

204. Hood, Margaret Page. *Drown the Wind*. New
      York: Coward-McCann, Publishers, 1961.  220pp.

When the most hated resident of a small
Maine island, Andrew Bruce, is found dead, Gil
Donan, the deputy sheriff, is faced with a
limitless number of suspects. The islanders
are certain that Bill Bickford, a cousin of
Andrew, is the guilty one. Gil must also
suspect twenty-four-year-old blonde, buxom
Sadie Bunker who has been Andrew's housekeeper
since she was seventeen and had hoped to
marry Andrew. Circumstances also make Gil
consider shy, frightened sixteen-year-old Letty
Peaslee who owns land that Andrew wanted to
acquire by marrying Letty. The contrast between
bold Sadie and shy Letty is interesting.

205. Horgan, Paul. *Everything to Live For*. New
      York: Farrar, Straus, Publishers, 1965.  215pp.

Marietta Osborne plays a subordinate but significant role in this novel about Max Chittenden,
twenty-one years old, a Harvard undergraduate
and heir to millions, who lives on his family's
estate outside of Philadelphia in 1921. Max
is portrayed as a Byronic character, attractive,
self-destructive, and remorseful of his relationship with Marietta, his childhood playmate
and fiancée.

206. Horgan, Paul. *Whitewater*. New York: Farrar,
      Straus and Giroux, 1969.  337pp.

Phil Durham, a high school senior, loses
Marilee Underwood to Billy Breedlove before
he is even aware of loving her. Billy is very
engaging, and the young people become a threesome; but Phil eventually becomes the outsider.

Still, Marilee has a special feeling toward
Phil, for they have a close friendship and share
the same books and religious beliefs. As
Billy and Marilee become closer, Marilee's
widowed mother, worried about the possibility
of their "sinning," seeks the counsel of
her priest; but worried as she is, she cannot
foresee the effect the "sin" itself will have
on Marilee when Billy is lost to her. Educated
in a parochial grade school, at the age of
twelve or thirteen expecting to become a nun,
Marilee is depicted sometimes as a sensitive,
intelligent young woman and other times as a
witless worshipper of William (Billy) the People
Conqueror.

207.  Horwitz, Julius. *The Diary of A.N.: The Story
      of the House on West 104th Street*. New York:
      Coward-McCann, Inc., 1970. 220pp.

A.N. is intelligent enough, despite her
youth, to see not only what is wrong with
her black ghetto but also that the inhabitants
contribute to its horrors as well as being
victimized by them. Her story revolves primarily around her mother, sister, and two brothers
and concerns drugs, casual sex, teenaged
pregnancies, crime, and crowded and filthy
housing. The ghetto high school is little more
than a place of daytime detention although
one dedicated white teacher cares about A.N.
and helps her work toward the college education
which will free her. The welfare system is
seen as both humiliating and corrupting to
those who depend on it. The plot line is
thin; however, there is extensive documentation
of slum conditions, and the novel graphically
portrays the lives of ghetto youths.

208.  Houston, James. *Ghost Fox*. New York: Harcourt
      Brace Jovanovich, 1977. 302pp.

The untamed North American wilderness during
the French and Indian Wars serves as the setting
of this adventure-packed book. Sarah Wells
is captured during an Indian raid and is forced
into slavery. Her continuous struggle to
return to white society dissipates as she
begins to accept the Indian way of life. During

the course of the novel, Sarah becomes separated
from her Indian husband, Taliwan, and their
child and thrust back into the white society.
Sarah's empathy for other people and her keen
awareness of the value of life force her to
realize that Indian life is better.

209.  Hunt, Irene. *Claws of a Young Century*.  New
      York: Charles Scribner's Sons, 1980.  292pp.

      In this mildly didactic novel, Ellen Archer
is a beautiful, intense girl of seventeen as
the century "turns over" from 1899 to 1900.
Ellen is determined to fight for women's
rights, as had her aunt who died from pneu-
monia contracted in a British prison.  She
falls in love with Philip Wrenn, becomes pregnant, and reluctantly marries him, but refuses
to give up the cause of women's rights.  Philip
and Ellen separate almost immediately.  The
sacrifices that Ellen makes in terms of marriage,
family, personal comfort, and health reflect
what many feminists of the years 1900-1918 endured.

210.  Hunter, Evan. *Last Summer*.  Garden City, N.Y.:
      Doubleday & Company, Inc., 1968.  256pp.

      A trio becomes a quartet, leading to a
violent denouement.  Peter (the narrator) and
David meet Sandy, a complex and strong-willed
girl.  At first their callousness seems to
contrast with her kindliness, as she rescues
and cares for a wounded seagull.  But then
she commits a surprising act of cruelty in
which the boys become participants after the
fact.  A similar pattern emerges in other episodes, Sandy always being the instigator of their
often cruel fun.  Rhoda, slightly younger and
with a stubborn sense of sexual morality and
a consistent feeling of sympathy for others,
becomes their final victim.  Hunter stresses
the shifting relationships of the four central
characters.

211.  Hunter, Evan. *Love, Dad*.  New York: Crown
      Publishers, 1981.  407pp.

      In Connecticut during the 1960s, when

young people were becoming disenchanted with
the traditional values of home, God, and
country, Leslie Croft, aged sixteen, begins to
assert her independence from her parents. While
still in high school, she begins to rebel, rejects her parents' values, and eventually drops
out of college. She adopts a life-style that
takes her first to the London drug scene, then
to Amsterdam, and finally across Europe to
India. During this time she writes to her
parents only when she needs money. The long
periods of silence cause them anguish and
anger, straining an already weak marriage.
The father's love for his daughter is strong,
but they are alienated when Leslie returns
home to learn of her parents' divorce and of
Dad's remarriage. Leslie is a strong-willed,
selfish, immature individual who wants change
in her own life but does not accept change
for her parents.

212.    Hunter, Kristin. *God Bless the Child.* New
        York: Charles Scribner's Sons, 1964. 307pp.

        The story of Rosalie Fleming's battle with
the American Dream is also the tense story
of her adolescence in this novel which traces
her life from childhood to early adulthood.
As a child, Rosie spends her days skipping
school and killing cockroaches in the tenement
she shares with her mother and grandmother; as
a teenager, she works two jobs, each an eight-
hour shift, and "runs numbers" for the local
crime lord. All these efforts are parallel
attempts to improve the family apartment.
Fascinated by pretty belongings, Rosie literally
cannot rest for wanting something better for
herself, her mother, and her grandmother. Though
her relationships with both older women are
fraught with tension and anger (mostly generated
by their grim economic situation), the bonds
of affection are strong, and her grandmother's
welfare especially is great motivation for her
struggle to move up and out, overshadowing even
a lifelong friendship and sexual initiation.
The novel's ironic conclusion offers little
hope for other Rosies.

213.  Hunter, Kristin. *The Soul Brothers and Sister
      Lou.* New York: Charles Scribner's Sons,
      1968.  248pp.

      The protagonist of this novel, Louretta
      Hawkins, faces numerous problems during adol-
      escence.  She recognizes her mother's strength
      and stability even  while resisting her strict
      rules; she loves her brothers, sisters and
      niece even while resenting her mother's seeming
      preference for them; and she adores her older
      brother, William, though knowing that strong
      William sometimes needs a push from Lou.  Lou's
      life is further complicated by the fact that
      teachers favor white students in her school;
      that she, herself, disapproves of the racist
      attitudes of some of her friends, and that
      there is nowhere for the youngsters to gather
      except the streets.  Lou's efforts to provide
      a clubhouse lead to a direct confrontation
      with a racist police officer but also to her
      new, healthier awareness of her identity as
      a black--and the beginnings of a career.

214.  Hurst, Fannie. *God Must Be Sad.* Garden City,
      N.Y.: Doubleday & Company, Inc., 1961.  284pp.

      Melanie Regan, daughter of a widowed practical
      nurse who eventually marries an employer, is
      beautiful but abnormally shy.  After her mother's
      death, she becomes her stepfather's housekeeper
      and eventually marries him (this is his way of
      protecting her from his hostile brother).  From
      the beginning of the novel we know that she
      will be tried for murder, but we do not learn
      whose until the novel's climax.

215.  Hutchins, Maude. *Honey on the Moon.* New York:
      William Morrow & Company, 1964.  191pp.

      At twenty, Sigourney marries forty-year-old
      Derek Wagstaff, and this sometimes poetic
      novelette is her narrative about their honey-
      moon.  It opens with a detailed description of
      her strange behavior on her wedding night and
      continues through her discoveries of her strange
      resemblance to Peter, a young male friend of
      Derek's, and Derek's unexplained possession of
      Peter's bracelet, a lipstick and a gun.  What is
      fantasy and what is reality is not always clear.

216.    Irving, John. *The Hotel New Hampshire*.  New
         York: E.P. Dutton, 1981.  401pp.

         Franny emerges as the star personality in
         the Berry family circle, the center to which
         the others are drawn or from which they are
         repelled.  Her rape, at about age thirteen,
         is the thread tying together the sexual and
         social themes of the family story, which
         moves from the relative innocence of New
         Hampshire to the decadence of Vienna, on to
         power and success in New York, and finally to
         retreat in Maine.  Along the way, Franny
         settles effortlessly into a lucrative acting
         career, resolves a longstanding love affair
         with her brother John, and marries the black
         athlete who was her avenger many years earlier.

217.    Irving, John. *The World According to Garp*.
         New York: E.P. Dutton, 1978.  437pp.

         Garp is an aspiring writer and son of a
         famous pioneer feminist, Jenny Fields, who
         influences a wide variety of people with her
         forward-looking ideas.  Jenny sets the pattern
         for several strong, assertive, and talented
         adolescent women who play important roles in
         the novel.  In addition, there are several
         young women who are less emancipated and less
         important to the story.  Although the adol-
         escent period as such is not stressed, the
         changes in female role and function may be seen
         through four generations of women.  The validity
         of the novel's feminist viewpoint is the sub-
         ject of disagreement among some readers and
         critics.

218.    Israel, Peter. *Hush Money*.  New York: Thomas
         Y. Crowell Company, 1974.  211pp.

         Robin Fletcher, college student, drug experi-
         menter, and member of the corrupt Society of
         the Fairest Lord, is exploiter, suspect, and
         informer in a "tough" detective's grim report
         of one of his cases.

219.    Jackson, Shirley. *We Have Always Lived in the
         Castle*.  New York: The Viking Press, 1962.
         214pp.

Jackson's modern classic is a combination
horror story and moral fable. It is told in
the first person by Mary Katherine "Merricat"
Blackwood who, with her sister Constance and
their Uncle Julian, is the only survivor of the
mass poisoning of their family six years before. Despite the fact that Constance has
been acquitted of the crime, the local villagers
believe her to have been guilty, and their
relations with the reclusive Blackwoods
steadily build to a climax of destruction. The
reader comes to understand that Merricat, chron-
ologically eighteen, is emotionally much younger,
not so much amoral as pre-moral, and, in fact,
the murderer. Merricat is an odd blend of
perceptiveness, aggression controlled by
magic, and love for her sister. She is an
effective foil for Jackson's portrait of
society's ordinary evil.

220.  Jaffe, Rona. *The Cherry in the Martini*. New
      York: Simon and Schuster, 1966. 190pp.

The title of this novel/memoir comes from
the last line of a story the author tells us
"I wrote when I was thirteen." Five chapters
are a nostalgic reminiscence of what we are
told is an atypical childhood of a girl, never
named, who at nine is in sixth grade in a
private school, who at eleven begins high school,
and who at sixteen enters college. Apparently
autobiographical, the novel demonstrates that
greed is "even worse than a practical joke";
that children are cruel, always needing a
victim; that adolescence is "an island" whose
inhabitants are "half savage and full of the
beginning of tenderness." Schoolgirl crushes,
friendships, fantasies, loyalties--all are
recounted.

221.  Jaffe, Rona. *Class Reunion*. New York: Dela-
      corte Press, 1979. 338pp.

At their twenty-year Radcliffe reunion, four
women are revealed in flashbacks recounting
events which shaped their lives at a time
when college was considered a place for a girl
to have fun and find a husband. Daphne Leeds,
a rich, beautiful debutante, acquired the

reputation of Golden Girl, and in order to
maintain this image of perfection, kept her
epilepsy a secret. Annabel Jones was a fun-
loving individualist whose promiscuous behavior
earned her a reputation that almost destroyed
her. Christine Spark, a shy and witty intellectual, intended to involve herself only with
her studies until she fell in love with Alexander
English, not knowing he was homosexual. Emily
Applebaum saw college as a chance for a new
beginning, but when she discussed her desire
to become a doctor with her advisor, she was
advised to marry a doctor instead. This book
covers twenty years of the lives of a generation
molded by outside appearances and the expectations of women to conform to certain images.

222.  Jaffe, Rona. *Family Secrets*. New York: Simon
      and Schuster, 1974. 511pp.

      This chronicle deals with four generations of
      a Russian Jewish family living in and around
      New York City in the early 1900s. Adam Saffron,
      the patriarch, has traditional values, yet he
      believes in the equality of his sons and daugh-
      ters, all of whom he controls in various ways.
      Leah Vania (later Lavinia), his firstborn,
      challenges tradition by going to college and
      chooses her friends from serious but unliberated
      young women. Through the lives of Lavinia, her
      several sisters, and their daughters, many
      changes in adolescent female roles and functions
      are delineated.

223.  Jaffe, Rona. *Mazes and Monsters*. New York:
      Delacorte Press, 1981. 248pp.

      A sophomore at an eastern college, Kate Finch,
      nineteen, is involved with three male friends
      in the fantasy game of Mazes and Monsters. Her
      freshman year was marked by an unhappy love
      affair and an attempted rape. Kate feels she
      can evade reality and her problems by involving
      herself in this game. She wavers between being
      her own person and doing what other people want
      her to do.

224. Jessup, Richard. *A Quiet Voyage Home.* Boston: Little, Brown, 1970. 274pp.

In this ironically titled novel, a group of American students wreak havoc aboard a luxury liner on a four-day cruise from Europe to America. Manipulated by one young man whose consummate political skill serves no cause at all, the students do some seven million dollars worth of damage, wreck the captain's career, and walk away legally and morally free. None of the students except their Machiavellian leader is examined in any depth, and only one adolescent girl has more than a walk-on role. Cora Ingersoll attaches herself to the leader because she loves "action freaks."

225. Johnson, Charles. *Faith and the Good Thing.* New York: The Viking Press, 1974. 196pp.

Faith Cross fails to observe her eighteenth birthday because her mother dies that day, telling Faith to get herself a "good thing." Faith begins her search by asking Reverend Brown and the werewitch what the "good thing" is. Following the old witch's advice, Faith goes to Chicago and finds that her sheltered life in Hatten County, Georgia, has not prepared her to cope with what she encounters. Robbed shortly after getting off the train and raped by her rescuer, Faith turns to prostitution for her livelihood. The continued search for the elusive "good thing" does not net Faith the happiness she seeks.

226. Johnson, Mendal W. *Let's Go Play at the Adams'.* New York: Thomas Y. Crowell Company, 1974. 282 pp.

Five youngsters, including two girls, imprison Barbara Miller, a twenty-year-old babysitter staying with two of them while their parents are abroad. It all begins as a game, not unlike games the children had previously played among themselves. But with a real victim, they discover within themselves the will to change the game to reality. Cindy Adams, ten, is not really a significant factor, but Dianne McVeigh, at seventeen the oldest of the five, is implacable in her insistence that the game be played out to its ultimate conclusion.

The novel takes us into the minds of all six
participants, demonstrating how all learn of
the dark depths within them. At the end,
Barbara has suffered a cruel and meaningless
death, and we are left with questions: What
did her life signify? How will their participa-
tion in her destruction affect the futures of
the children?

227.  Johnson, Nora. *A Step Beyond Innocence*. Boston:
      Little, Brown and Company, 1961. 274pp.

      Bright, attractive, loved by her well-to-do
      parents, Sally Fraits seems exceptionally
      fortunate. Her Smith College years are filled
      by friendships with other young women and by
      three loves: Victor, a young New York actor
      who she knows is unsuitable; Richard, a Harvard
      business student who is perfect but somehow
      boring; and, finally, Homer, a businessman
      who helps her to be herself. She tries to
      be many different Sallies, and at the end of
      the novel seems to be finding herself through
      a new job which she accepts with Homer's ap-
      proval though it means they will postpone
      marriage. Sally narrates her own story, which
      recreates the mood of college life in the late
      fifties.

228.  Johnson, Sandy. *The CUPPI*. New York: Delacorte
      Press/Eleanor Friede, 1979. 255pp.

      Three twelve-year-old girls are central in
      this novel about child prostitution in New
      York City; Freddie, blonde and knowing beyond
      her years; Winter, partly black and badly
      treated by her foster family; and Donnie, beloved
      daughter of a freelance news photographer. After
      Freddie and Winter run away from home, they are
      soon caught up in the underworld. Freddie's
      mysterious death gives the novel its title:
      CUPPI is police jargon for "Circumstances
      Undetermined Pending Police Investigation."
      Attempts are made to rescue Winter, and Donnie
      is used by the police as a decoy. The novel,
      in form a detective story, includes as subplot
      an adult love affair.

229.  Jones, Craig. *Blood Secrets*. New York: Harper
      and Row, 1978.  199pp.

      Irene, beautiful, charming, and self-assured,
      marries Frank, a tall, plain, introverted man.
      Marriage does not change Frank's secretiveness
      about his family, and he makes Irene promise
      never to contact any of them, especially
      Vivian, his sister.  Frank is very protective of
      their daughter, Regina, not only because she
      had rheumatic fever as a child, but also
      because he is afraid that Vivian will somehow
      win her away.  Spoiled as a child because of
      her illness, Regina is haughty and rude to
      everyone until she starts dating Virgil, who
      is handsome, polite, and seemingly everything
      parents would want for their daughter.  But
      over Irene's objections, Frank becomes obsessed
      with checking into the boy's background and
      finding out where they go on their dates.  His
      suspicions and fears almost break up his
      marriage, and when the truth is finally dis-
      covered, it turns Irene into a murderess.

230.  Jones, Douglas C. *Elkhorn Tavern*. New York:
      Holt, Rinehart and Winston, 1980.  311pp.

      This Civil War novel centers on the tribula-
      tions of the Hasford family from the late-winter
      battle of Pea Ridge through the following
      summer.  Martin Hasford is away fighting with
      the Confederate Army.  His wife Ora, their
      seventeen-year-old daughter Calpurnia, and
      fifteen-year-old son Roman must cope with the
      depredations of the two armies and of civilian
      marauders from both sides.  The indomitable
      Ora is the central figure, but Calpurnia
      provides interest as a strong figure in her
      own right and in her romance with a young
      Union officer.

231.  Jordan, Robert. *Thanksgiving*. New York: E.P.
      Dutton & Co., Inc., 1971.  314pp.

      Linda Jarvis and Elinor Underhill, at twenty-
      one committed to the Vietnam anti-war movement,
      become involved in a plot to blow up a country
      club to which Elinor's parents belong.  At first
      they plan to set the bombs to go off while the

building is empty but then decide (over Elinor's
protests) to set the bombs for a time when the
club is full--during a Thanksgiving party.

232.  Josephs, Rebecca. *Early Disorder*. New York:
      Farrar Straus Giroux, 1980. 186pp.

      This account of fifteen-year-old Willa Rahv's
      life-threatening bout with anorexia nervosa
      is often humorous in tone but clinical in
      detail. Danger signals include Willa's sense
      that her seemingly perfect family is really
      wracked with faults and her perpetual dissatis-
      faction with herself--too fat, too disorganized,
      unable to make friendships she values. Her
      continued resistance to treatment, her family's
      pain and frustration, and; most of all, Willa's
      suffering are clearly and effectively portrayed.

233.  Judson, William. *Cold River*. New York: Mason/
      Charter, 1974. 213pp.

      Lizzie Allison, her father, and stepbrother
      go on a camping trip into the Adirondacks
      in the late autumn. By mischance they make
      a wrong turn, and disasters follow, leading
      to the death of Mr. Allison and the loss of
      much of their gear. Lizzie is older and more
      experienced than her stepbrother, and she
      takes the lead at first as they struggle to
      survive. But both youngsters mature greatly
      as a result of their terrifying adventures.

234.  Kantor, MacKinlay. *Spirit Lake*. Cleveland:
      The World Publishing Company, 1961. 957pp.

      This intricate account follows several pio-
      neer families into the newly opened Iowa
      territory with their varied dreams--from being
      able to buy land cheaply to being a founder of
      a new town. All the settlers, including a
      young doctor and a rich Frenchman, help build
      homes for each family, share their food, and en-
      joy fellowship at community readings. The
      adolescent girls help in the household chores
      and take care of the younger children, but as
      they meet the young men of Spirit Lake, their
      thoughts turn to marriage and their own futures.
      Tragedy strikes during the long, hard winter as

a band of renegade Indians, led by the in-
famous Inkpaduta, attacks the small settle-
ment, killing, pillaging, and abducting four
of the young women. Glimpses of life in the
Indian camp reveal the cruelties endured by
the young women, both Indian and white, during
the rest of the long winter. The memories of
what happened at Spirit Lake will haunt these
former captives for the rest of their lives.

235.  Kaplan, Johanna. *O My America!* New York:
      Harper and Row, Publishers, 1980. 286pp.

At the beginning and the end of the novel
set in 1972, the main character Merry Slavin,
twenty-eight years old, is dealing with the
sudden death of her eccentric and famous father
Ezra "Ez" Slavin. This event is the backdrop
for the story of Merry's childhood, adolescence,
and young adulthood as she tries to cope with
her unusual environment and make some sense
of Ez's life and of her relationship to him.
Ez had considerable charm as an intellectual,
political activist, teacher, and writer; but
he was first to admit that he was not a competent
or dedicated father. Merry wants some family
contact with her brothers and sisters by
Ez and his various spouses and lovers, but
the only other one who also seeks the family tie
is Francesca, a half-sister who is six years
younger and less sophisticated. Merry's personal journey from her Polish grandmother's
Lower East Side home through years close to
Ez and his second wife to her independence and
success contrast to her half-sister's teenage
cult worship, free but fuzzy thinking, and humorous use of trendy, inarticulate language. Both
young women wanted Ez's love; Merry seems
finally to comprehend Ez's struggles and passions.

236.  Kaplow, Robert. *Two in the City.* Boston:
      Houghton Mifflin Company, 1979. 146pp.

David Riddle, from a small East Coast town,
is the main character of this novel. Against
their parents' wishes, he and his high school
girlfriend, Stacey Fahrner, decide to postpone
college to go to New York, get jobs,  and live

together. His uncle helps him get a job in the
Investment Service Unit of a bank, which he
dislikes immensely. Stacey likes her job as a
clerk-typist for the Department of Human Resources. After a very short time, the relationship, which they entered with an idealistic
attitude, degenerates. Stacey wants to consider David a very strong individual but now
she finds him weak. He, in his despair over
his job and the deterioration of their relationship, thinks of returning to his parents' home.
In the end, they decide that they really care
for each other and will try again to make their
relationship a success.

237. Kaufman, Bel. *Up the Down Staircase*. Englewood
    Cliffs, N.J.: Prentice-Hall, 1964. 340pp.

    In a large metropolitan high school during
her first year of teaching, Sylvia Barrett
encounters a multitude of students with
individual problems which no one has the
time to cope with. Alice Blake is a sensitive
teenager with a crush on her English teacher,
Paul Barringer. When Alice writes him a letter
expressing her intense feelings, he casually
grades it and returns it to her as if it were
an assignment. This drives her to attempt
suicide by jumping from the window of his classroom. Alice's story is only one of many in
this complex plot.

238. Kavanagh, Paul. *Not Comin' Home to You*. New
    York: G.P. Putnam's Sons, 1974. 220pp.

    This novel is closely patterned after the
real-life murderous odyssey of Charles Stark-
weather and Caril Fugate. In the novel, friendless fifteen-year-old Betty Marie Dienhardt
lives with harsh parents and a senile grandmother. Coming out of her favorite refuge, the
movies, she is picked up by Jimmie John Hall.
Jimmie John is drifting across the country,
killing people for cars and spending money,
and he takes Betty with him. A relationship
develops between these friendless, loveless
individuals.

239.  Kay, Terry. *The Year the Lights Came On*.
        Boston: Houghton Mifflin Company, 1976.   288pp.

        Megan Priest has a small but important role.
        She is the catalyst for the growing individualism
        and maturation of the protagonist, Colin Wynn.
        Early in the novel, Megan and Colin cement
        their friendship despite the fact that they
        belong to rival "gangs," and later they become
        one another's first loves.

240.  Kazan, Elia. *The Assassins*.  New York: Stein
        and Day, 1972.   377pp.

        A study of society's legal system and its moral
        values, *The Assassins* takes the reader on a
        provocative adventure in which drug-oriented,
        anti-establishment factions force a re-examina-
        tion of what constitutes justice for all.   The
        pivotal character is Juana de Flores, a seven-
        teen-year-old girl of Mexican-German parentage,
        who rejects her home for an uncouth drug pusher.
        Her father, until now a model sergeant in the
        Air Force, kills Vinnie, Juana's lover, and the
        question arises as to whether he will be ex-
        onerated for taking the law into his own hands.
        Juana is less a central character than a repre-
        sentative of the hippies of the early 1970s.
        The book abounds in sexual references and scenes
        of hippie life.

241.  Kellogg, Marjorie. *Like the Lion's Tooth*.
        New York: Farrar, Straus, Giroux, 1972.   147pp.

        Julie Williams and Madeline, the special
        friend of the protagonist, Ben, live in a school
        for abused and abandoned children.   Julie
        fills her days organizing rebellions against
        the school and searching for "the Man," a person
        who may have been her father; she is the only
        character for whom even a small measure of hope
        is allowed.   Madeline, who, like Ben, has been
        repeatedly raped by her father, finds comfort
        in movie magazines and her vaguely maternal
        relationship with Ben.   The girls' histories
        are revealed in a series of flashbacks in this
        episodic novel.

242.   Kennedy, Raymond. *Columbine*. New York:
       Farrar Straus Giroux, 1980. 378pp.

       In a working-class neighborhood of a
       Massachusetts town, the Flynns had lived next
       door to the Kokorisses for as long as Henry
       Flynn could remember. Before he joined the
       Navy during World War II, Henry had dated the
       oldest, then the next oldest of the four
       Kokoriss sisters. After he came home from the
       Navy, he spent some time with Anna, the third
       daughter, but the youngest girl, Columbine, had
       decided that Henry belonged to her. Henry is
       twenty-three years old to Columbine's thirteen
       years, but the determined, provocative child-
       woman amuses him, bewilders him, flatters him,
       and to his chagrin, attracts him. Columbine's
       unsettling pursuit of Henry, followed by out-
       rageous behavior after she feels that Henry
       has betrayed her, make up the major thrust of
       the novel.

       Kenton, Maxwell--*see* Southern, Terry, and Mason
       Hoffenberg.

       Kerr, M.E.--*see* Meaker, Marijane.

243.   Killens, John Oliver. *The Cotillion: or, One
       Good Bull Is Half the Herd*. New York:
       Trident Press, 1971. 256pp.

       Yoruba Evelyn Lovejoy, eighteen, is the
       heroine of a story that the author describes as
       a "Black black comedy." Yoruba is dark, her
       father is a porter, and her light-skinned
       mother is a housewife, but she is one of five
       "culturally deprived" Harlem girls selected
       to take part in the Cotillion, the coming-out
       party for black debutantes. To Daphne, Yoruba's
       mother, the prospect of Yoruba at the Cotillion
       is a dream come true. To Yoruba, her father
       Matt, and her sweetheart Ben Ali Lumumba, the
       Cotillion is a pathetic parody of whiteness,
       to be scorned by those with black pride. How-
       ever, to please Daphne, the three agree to
       participate. The story about the events leading
       up to the Cotillion and the grand event itself
       is told through word play, humorous asides,
       dialogue, slapstick and, at times, savage
       description.

244.  Kingman, Lee. *The Peter Pan Bag*.  Boston:
      Houghton Mifflin Company, 1970.  219pp.

      Seventeen-year-old Wendy Allardyce has come
      home from her junior year at boarding school
      planning to join a girlfriend and spend the
      summer in New York City.  She finds her parents
      opposed to her plans, and Wendy rebels at the
      restrictions she feels her parents have placed
      upon her.  Although her childhood has been
      happy and full of love, she feels a need to
      "find herself" outside the confinement of
      her home.  Taking only her lute and a few
      clothes, Wendy leaves for New York, not knowing
      that circumstances will take her to Boston where
      she will spend the summer with a group of hip-
      pies.  This novel portrays the life of the
      Boston counterculture in the late sixties.

245.  Klein, Norma. *Breaking Up*.  New York: Pantheon,
      1980.  207pp.

      At age fifteen, Ali goes to California from
      New York to spend her usual summer with her
      father and stepmother.  While there she falls
      in love with her best friend's brother, driving
      a wedge between the two girls.  She then becomes
      the object of a custody fight after she and her
      father realize her mother is a lesbian.  Ali
      decides to return to her mother.

246.  Klein, Norma. *Domestic Arrangements*.  New
      York: M. Evans and Co., Inc., 1981.  285pp.

      Complicated and contradictory aspects of love
      and sex in contemporary life are shown from
      the viewpoint of fourteen-year-old Tatiana
      (Rusty), younger daughter of the Engleberg
      family of Manhattan's West Side.  Tatiana has
      just starred in her first movie and the reactions
      of her sixteen-year-old sister, Cordelia, and
      her parents are bewildering and conflicting,
      especially regarding her nudity and sexual
      sophistication in the film.  In spite of the
      glamor, Tatiana resolves never to do another
      movie but to do stage plays and to pursue a
      career in obstetrics.  Tatiana is both typical
      teenager and self-confident, sensitive, and
      serious woman.  Cordelia, who plays a minor role

in the novel, wants to be the first Jewish
woman president of the United States.

247.  Klein, Norma.  *It's O.K. If You Don't Love Me*.
      New York: The Dial Press, 1977.  202pp.

      Jody Epstein is a seventeen-year-old New
      York girl with very modern ideas who lives
      with her mother, younger brother, and her
      mother's current boyfriend.  When she meets
      Lyle, a boy with old-fashioned ideas, who has
      moved to New York from Ohio, they are attracted
      to each other but have very different views on
      love and commitment.  Although the book centers
      on the relationship between Jody and Lyle, it
      also explores Jody's resentment of her father,
      the warm friendship she maintains with her
      former stepfather, and her feelings about her
      liberated mother's lifestyle.

248.  Koch, Stephen.  *Night Watch*.  New York: Harper
      & Row, Publishers, 1969.  212pp.

      Harriet and her brother David Fontana, share
      a sterile, cold, isolated existence broken
      only by sexual experiments with outsiders.
      Finally, however, the two, symbols of modern
      American life, turn to one another for sexual
      release as well as for companionship.

249.  Kotker, Norman.  *Miss Rhode Island*.  New York:
      Farrar Straus Giroux, 1978.  214pp.

      What really goes on in the mind of a Miss
      America contestant?  Yvonne Doucette, a
      twenty-year-old Wellesley student, takes us
      through the ritual from the day she becomes
      Miss Rhode Island until she heads home from
      Atlantic City, shedding tears of defeat.  The
      phone is at last silent; Yvonne has made it to
      the finals but lost the crown to Miss Arizona.
      And she is a very poor loser.  She and her
      friends operate on the premise that casual
      sex is what makes the world go 'round, and she
      unabashedly carries on a pre-contest affair with
      a married forty-four-year-old who admits he
      loves her title and not her.  And Yvonne, who
      has almost made it to the top of the beauty heap,
      weeps in her hotel and bemoans the fact that
      life isn't fair.

250.  Kranidas, Kathleen. *One Year in Autumn*.
      Philadelphia: J.B. Lippincott Company, 1965.
      218pp.

      Joanne O'Reilly, seventeen, is a member of
      a student group drawn together by their
      teacher, protagonist Jessica Courtguard.  Jo's
      growing attraction to Chet Adams and her
      allegiance to Jessica arouse her father's fear,
      envy, and distrust, and he becomes the focus
      of parents' complaints about Jessica's methods.
      Jo and the other students generate the action
      of the plot and motivate  Jessica's movement
      toward fuller understanding of herself.   The
      Jo-Chet romance is a slender subplot.

251.  Krantz, Judith. *Princess Daisy*.  New York:
      Crown Publishers, Inc., 1980.  464pp.

      Daisy Valensky is the daughter of a Russian
      prince and a Hollywood star, and although
      her early life is privileged, she wages many
      battles and carries many scars.  Even as a
      very young child, Daisy carries the responsi-
      bility for her retarded twin sister, and by
      age nineteen, orphaned, penniless, and at the
      mercy of her stepbrother, she must support
      herself and her twin.  Daisy survives and
      thrives.  The novel continues Daisy's story
      until she finds love and freedom from the past
      at age twenty-five.  It also contains a
      great deal of background material on the early
      lives of Daisy's parents and other socialites
      and on the technical aspects of advertising
      and commercial production.

252.  Kubly, Herbert. *The Whistling Zone*.  New York:
      Simon and Schuster, 1963.  348pp.

      In Kubly's gothic, satiric, sometimes didactic
      novel about vicious arch-conservatism (in the
      guise of morality and patriotism) on the
      campus of a midwestern state university, the
      main character is the sincerely humanistic
      associate professor Christian ("Matt") Mawther
      from New England, hired by a national foundation
      to introduce courses on modern cultural concepts.
      Among the females, especially significant in
      young Professor Mawther's year on campus is

Little Crown, the sixteen-year-old albino
midget evangelist with the body of a ten-year-
old, who represents the side-show kind of
conservative religion, and is destroyed by a
group of sexually aggressive male students.

253.  Kumin, Maxine. *Through Dooms of Love*. New
      York: Harper & Row, Publishers, 1964.  278pp.

      Joanna Ferguson's efforts to be independent
      of her father involve her in the labor movement
      of the late thirties, in a complicated love
      affair with a young black leftist, and in open
      scorn for her father's work as a pawnbroker.
      This portrait of father and daughter explores
      their deep affection and the extreme tension
      which arises between them during Joanna's
      eighteenth year.  Kumin provides detailed
      characterizations of both Joanna and Jacob.

      Lambert, Christine--*see* Loewengard, Heida Huberta
         Freybe.

254.  Lambert, Gavin. *Inside Daisy Clover*.  New York:
      The Viking Press, 1963.  245pp.

      The rise and fall and comeback of a child
      star in the Hollywood of the 1950s are chronicled
      in this narrative, which is told by its pro-
      tagonist.  Daisy Clover confides, in a succession
      of theme books, her ambitions, her crushes and
      loves, her attempts at protecting her privacy
      and controlling her fate, and her many defeats.
      At thirteen a beachcomber, at fourteen a star,
      at seventeen a mother and a has-been, and at
      twenty-four a forgotten figure from the past
      trying to rebuild her career, she is through-
      out it all brave, ironically detached and yet
      caring, and fiercely independent.

255.  Lambert, Janet. *Forever and Ever*.  New York:
      E.P. Dutton & Company, Inc., 1961.  182pp.

      This novel is one of several about the globe-
      trotting Campbell family.  Eighteen-year-old
      Sandra, fifteen-year-old Josie, and ten-year-
      old Tenny have been sent home to Wallaceville,
      Indiana, to become "Americanized."  Josie wins
      the lead in the school play, acquires a staunch
      friend, and has her first brush with romance.

For her, life in the small American town
is more exciting and satisfying than in
any of the foreign countries where they have
lived for the past eleven years.

256.   Lamott, Kenneth [Church]. *The Bastille Day
       Parade*. New York: David McKay Company, Inc.,
       1967. 247pp.

       Alec Webb, a successful newspaperman, has
       deserted his wife and daughter Kate by faking
       suicide. After an unexpectedly violent pro-
       test demonstration involving students from
       the Art Institute at which Kate studies, he
       is reunited with his wife and daughter. Kate's
       commitment to her rather nebulous cause is
       first deepened by her experience and then
       shaken by her observation of violence and the
       death of a friend. She remains throughout the
       novel a subordinate though important character.

257.   Langton, Jane. *The Memorial Hall Murder*. New
       York: Harper & Row, Publishers, 1978. 260pp.

       Among the host of characters in this murder
       mystery, Vick Van Horn, college senior and
       musician, stands out. When an explosion in
       Harvard's Memorial Hall is thought to have
       killed Ham Dow, her beloved cello instructor
       and choral director, Vick must undertake some
       of Ham's duties, particularly directing a
       performance of Handel's *Messiah*. The rehearsals
       test Vick's musical skill; the responsibility
       weighs heavily, and she also worries about
       Chem 2, a tough course. Vick's work with the
       chorus is a means of indicating her maturation,
       and the preparations for the concert are counter-
       point to the murder investigation.

258.   Lanham, Edwin. *Speak Not Evil*. New York:
       Farrar, Straus and Company, 1964. 591pp.

       This complex novel with many plot lines covers
       the summer leading up to the tercentenary cele-
       bration of Sagamore, Connecticut. Among major
       interests are the activities of a number of
       eighteen-year-olds. The high school vale-
       dictorian, Faithful Zybioski, comes from a
       prominent old family; out of very mixed motives,

she loses her virginity to a young near-
stranger in town. Pregnant, she is almost persuaded to have an abortion, but ultimately she
and the young man decide to marry. Vera Blane,
the second young female major character, is
not especially attractive, except for her
marvelous breasts. She has been enticed by an
older woman into a group which has sexual
orgies, complete with photographs. When she is
forced to see her behavior through others' eyes,
she reacts with horror and guilt. A dramatic
climax, which even includes a hurricane, brings
the young people to greater maturity and confidence in their futures.

259.   Lauritzen, Jonreed. *The Everlasting Fire*. New
       York: Doubleday & Company, Inc., 1962. 474pp.

       *The Everlasting Fire* pays tribute to the
Mormons, members of the Church of Jesus Christ
of Latter Day Saints. The story begins in
Nauvoo, Illinois, in 1844, where the Saints
are under fire from politicians, greedy land-
grabbers, and moralists who decry the practice
of polygamy. Judge Nathan Eyring, a non-Mormon
who values integrity above all else, champions
the Mormons in many of their battles, never
dreaming that he, his son Rafael, and his
daughter Myra will all fall under the spell of
the church and have their lives completely
changed. Myra, a scoffer at all things religious, becomes, almost against her will, the
seventh wife of Apostle Morton Baird, a truly
fine man, and son Rafael falls madly in love
with young Milly, a Mormon girl for whom he is
willing to commit murder if necessary. Myra's
struggles against the teachings of Mormonism and
Milly's arguments for it play an important role
in this book which chronicles the arduous forced
trek of the Mormons from Nauvoo toward the
Promised Land in Utah where the Saints hope to
live in peace.

260.   Lawrence, Josephine. *The Amiable Meddlers*.
       New York: Harcourt, Brace & World, Inc.,
       1961. 253pp.

       When orphaned Jenny Faler, fifteen, comes to

live with her distant relatives, two maiden
seamstresses, she enters a circle of women,
all of whom are one or two generations older
than she.  The circle is centered in the
dressmaking establishment of her guardians, the
Misses Bruell, who are the hub of neighborhood
gossip and understated female support.  Though
the Bruells fear that Jenny will disrupt their
quiet lives (and their gentle tampering with the
affairs of others), the anticipated problems
of drugs, drinking, and sex never occur.
The girl at first seems politely aloof and totally preoccupied with her studies.  She intends
to win full scholarships to college and law
school and gives every sign of being fully
capable of doing so.  Jenny proves to be better
organized, rather more realistic, and somewhat
more effective in helping others than are her
guardians.  Jenny's story is only one of
several plots.

261.  Lawrence, Josephine.  *I Am in Urgent Need of
      Advice*.  New York: Harcourt, Brace & World,
      Inc., 1962.  216pp.

      Amanda Carpenter, at fourteen, lives with her
lawyer-father, homemaker-mother, and the family
maid in a comfortable city apartment; her maternal grandmother lives in the same building.  All
except the father feel insecure and constantly
refer to outsiders for personal advice and
support: Amanda's mother to a psychologist, her
grandmother to an astrologer, the maid to a
newspaper etiquette columnist, and Amanda herself
to an advice columnist in the same local newspaper.  Amanda's story is of gradually increasing
self-reliance and is developed through three
key episodes: abortive plans for a party, the
death of her closest friend, and a climactic
New Year's Eve date on which she behaves with
a good deal of courage.

262.  Leary, Paris.  *The Innocent Curate*.  Garden City,
      N.Y.: Doubleday & Company, Inc., 1963.  203pp.

      A short but significant passage in this mildly
satirical ecclesiastical novel deals with the
college experience of Rosemary Van Vranken,
whose liberal agnosticism contrasts with the

unquestioning innocence of Sonny Ball, handsome
young curate of respectable St. Clement's
parish. A year or so later, the town of
Schinderhook is shocked and dismayed when the
stigmata of Christ appear on its popular
curate, but the love of the worldly Rosemary
provides the *deus ex machina*.

263.    Leavitt, Caroline. *Meeting Rozzy Halfway*.
        New York: Seaview Books, 1980. 294pp.

At first glance, the Nelsons appear to be
the ideal American family; the parents, Lee
and Len, are attractive and caring; the two
daughters, Rozzy and Bess, are beautiful,
bright, and ambitious. In the course of the
plot (which traces the girls' lives from childhood to young adulthood), however, it becomes
ever more clear that the fabric of family life
cannot withstand the strain of Rozzy's increasingly evident mental illness. More slowly
revealed, but perhaps even more important, is
the toll Rozzy, her needs, and her demands
place upon Bess, her younger sister. Even
Rozzy's apparently impulsive suicide serves to
bind Bess to Rozzy's memory; no real release
seems possible, a concept underscored by the
quiet, ominous concluding sentence. This
study of contemporary family life also examines the bonds and barriers which exist
between sisters.

264.    Lee, Joanna. *I Want to Keep My Baby*. New
        York: New American Library, 1977. 166pp.

When fifteen-year-old Sue Ann Cunningham
becomes pregnant by her high school boyfriend,
she assumes they will marry and have a life
together. The boy refuses, but Sue Ann's
mother convinces her to keep the baby, feeling
it is the only right thing to do. Unable to
live at home because of her mother's inter-
ference, Sue Ann applies for welfare and takes
the baby to live in a rundown neighborhood
until a sympathetic social worker gets her into
a halfway house for teenage mothers. As Sue
Ann struggles to cope with school, a part-time
job and the responsibility of her baby daughter,

she begins to realize how difficult her life
is going to be. With painful new insight
and maturity, she makes the decision to allow
her baby to be adopted.

265. Lee, Marjorie. *The Eye of Summer*. New York:
Simon and Schuster, 1961. 191pp.

Connie, whose father has deserted her and
whose mother doesn't really love her very much,
spends her summers with her cousin Spence, two
years younger than she, on an island retreat.
At ten, she unwittingly almost causes him to
be badly burned; at eighteen, she nearly
causes their relationship to become overtly
sexual, and at twenty-one, she incurs un-
justified guilt feelings over the drowning of
a man with whom Spence was swimming. But it is
Spence who comprehends the dangers of their
relationship and tries to free them both.

266. Lee, Mildred. *The Rock and the Willow*. New
York: Lothrop, Lee and Shepard Company, 1963.
223pp.

Earline "Enie" Singleton is an intelligent
and gifted young girl who sees that the only
way to a life better than that on her family's
farm is through education. During her four
years of high school, she must deal with the
death of a young sister, an older brother's
running away, her father's indifference, her
mother's illness, the proposal of a young man
named Seedy Culpepper, and her family's constant
poverty. After the death of her mother, Enie
must assume the care of her younger brother and
sister and run the house for her father; college
and a career as a writer are more impossible
than ever. Although she is heartbroken when
her father eventually announces his plan to
marry, this event makes it possible for Enie
to attend college.

267. Leffland, Ella. *Rumors of Peace*. New York:
Harper & Row, 1979. 389pp.

Suse Hansen is just about to enter her teen
years in Mendoza, California, when Pearl Harbor
is bombed. Her keen, probing mind is preoccupied
with the war; her best friend Peggy, however,

gradually reverts to typical adolescent behavior. For Suse, the maturation process is
as long and painful as World War II. Leffland
has created a unique young adult figure and
uses people, places, and events of this historical period as a backdrop.

268.  LeGuin, Ursula K. *The Beginning Place.* New
      York: Harper & Row, Publishers, 1980. 183pp.

Two young people, both unwanted misfits with
drab daily lives, discover a magical fantasy
world which seems to offer peace, romance,
even adventure. Irene has escaped there for
several years, ever since she was fourteen,
has learned the language, and has formed close
ties with some of its inhabitants. Thus, when
Hugh discovers Tembreazi, she initially rejects him as an intruder into what she calls
her "ain country." Most of the novel is set
in their fantasy world, but we are given
important glimpses of the appalling families
and narrow lives which are their reality.
Their maturation is shown by their final rejection of the fantasy world as its dream-
like quality turns to nightmare, and they
return, Hugh symbolically wounded, to build
a new reality together.

269.  LeGuin, Ursula K. *Very Far Away from Anywhere
      Else.* New York: Atheneum, 1976. 89pp.

This reflective love story recreates a year
in the lives of seniors Owen Griffiths and
Natalie Fields, adolescents who are loners
with plans and dreams. Owen wins a scholarship to MIT but is reluctant to tell his
parents because they have their own plans
for him. Natalie teaches music, plays the
piano, violin and viola, and composes music
for string ensembles in preparation for studying
musical composition and becoming a full-time
composer. Natalie has committed herself to
music yet is able to accommodate the fact that
she has fallen in love with Owen, as she is
able to see "priorities" and act accordingly.
Owen still conforms to "what is expected" of
him and wants to push their friendship into
a sexual relationship. The story is recounted
by the mature Owen.

270. Leigh, James. *Downstairs at Ramsey's*. New
     York: Harper & Row, Publishers, 1968. 250pp.

     When her mother is killed in an automobile
accident, Delilah Jean Sampson becomes the
ward of her mother's lover, Hardy Brewster.
The Brewster ménage, consisting of Hardy,
Delilah, Jim Long (an old friend of Hardy's)
and, occasionally, Fauna Mayo, who succeeds
Delilah's mother in Hardy's affections, is
observed by Victor Ramsey, Hardy's neighbor
and the novel's narrator. As much a temptress
as her Biblical namesake, Delilah eventually
succeeds in destroying a complex web of
relationships and in seducing Hardy. Though
manipulative and sometimes consciously cruel,
she is nearly as much a victim as Hardy; she
is a mixture of arrogance, vulgarity, and
loving sympathy. Ramsey's first embarrassed
and finally helplessly sympathetic point of
view colors her portrait.

271. Lelchuk, Alan. *American Mischief*. New York:
     Farrar, Straus and Giroux, 1973. 501pp.

     This very graphic novel about extremes of
student rebellion depicts numerous variations
of sex, drug abuse, and the complete rejection
of traditional values. The central characters
are young graduate student leader Lenny Pincus
and his friend and mentor, thirty-five-year-
old dean and literature teacher Bernard Kovell,
at a ficticious Jewish college near Boston.
Women of all ages and social stations serve
the amazingly varied sexual and intellectual
desires of these two men; among the most
prominent are twenty-year-old Lauri Pearlman,
a talented art student from Shaker Heights,
Ohio; and fourteen-year-old Joan "Nugget" Cummings, a runaway from parents preoccupied with
high society in Washington, D.C. With the eagerness of a child discovering new toys, Nugget
quickly enters the world of drug abuse and sexual
perversion, while maintaining for a while her
appearance of angelic innocence.

272. Leven, Jeremy. *Creator*. New York: Coward,
     McCann & Geoghegan, 1980. 489pp.

This story of a mad scientist who is trying
to clone his long-dead wife, write a novel,
and fight against his son's attempts to have
him declared incompetent is populated with
young women who are the objects of his and
his fictional hero's lust. The one mentioned
in greatest detail is a self-described nineteen-
year-old nymphomaniac who is chosen to give
birth to the clone.

273.  Lewin, Michael Z. *Ask the Right Question*.
      New York: G.P. Putnam's Sons, 1971. 190pp.

This rather gentle mystery novel begins when
fifteen-year-old Eloise Crystal asks private
investigator Albert Samson to find her biological father. The bulk of the story is
devoted to Samson's investigative efforts.
However, during Eloise's almost daily visits
to his office, she displays the classic vola-
tility of an adolescent: at times a child,
at times a temptress, occasionally a purposeful
businesswoman.

274.  Lindbergh, Anne Morrow. *Dearly Beloved*. New
      York: Harcourt, Brace & World, Inc., 1962.
      202pp.

During Sally and Mark's wedding ceremony,
the members of the family and of the wedding
party reflect upon the bride and groom, the
meaning of the words of the ritual, and their
own lives. Each person considers this ceremony the symbolic shift for Sally and Mark
from adolescence to adulthood. The thoughts
of the mother of the bride, which open and close
the novel, emphasize the theme that happiness
is hardly ever complete and that the search
for one's self continues throughout one's life.

275.  Linney, Romulus. *Slowly, By Thy Hand Unfurled*.
      New York: Harcourt, Brace & World, 1965.
      214pp.

The two most important female adolescents
of this novel are dead. The book is the self-
examination, analysis, and development through
a personal journal of a widowed, remarried
mother of the two dead daughters and two sons.

She sees her first husband and three of her
children die and endures accusation by her
remaining son and her present husband that
she has somehow been responsible for the
deaths.  The journal is her vehicle for
grasping at reality and sanity, and a succession
of three adolescent female maids is her only
outlet for psychological and physical compas-
sion, confusing as it is to her and to them.
The deceased daughters--Alice who died during
an illegal abortion and Evie who apparently
died from a brain hemorrhage--seem to grow
in the pages of the journal as they begin to
appear as attractive but troubled young women
rather than pitiable children stifled by their
mother's affection.

276.  Lipton, James. *Mirrors*.  New York: St. Martin's
      Press, 1981.  343pp.

Carin Bradley, eighteen, takes the money her
grandfather left her and goes to New York
to fulfill her dream of becoming a dancer.
She will allow neither her diabetes nor her
involvement with Chris, a newspaperman, to
stand in her way.  After six unsuccessful
months, Carin joins the "gypsies," the dancers
who go about auditioning for various shows,
and gets a job in the chorus of a Broadway
show.  Carin becomes a part of the behind-the-
scene world of dancers: the grueling rehearsals,
the competition, the heartaches and disappoint-
ments.  When  Chris visits her in New York,
the show has just closed after one performance,
and one of her roommates has committed suicide.
Carin decides to leave with him.  A call for
an audition with the Joffrey Ballet Company
convinces Carin that she must stay and continue
the pursuit of her lifelong dream.

277.  Lloyd, Norris. *A Dream of Mansions*.  New York:
      Random House, 1962.  274pp.

Set in a small town in Georgia in the 1920s,
this novel explores the theme of loss of innocence.  Hallie Jones and her family have just
moved from South Carolina, which represents to
Hallie all that is beautiful and refined about

the South, to Georgia, which Hallie says everyone knows was settled by jailbirds. Even
though she feels her new hometown is un-
worthy, Hallie tries to impose on it her romantic expectations of Southern "ladies and
gentlemen," subservient Negroes, and beautiful and stately mansions. Hallie's practical
mother and fanatically religious father, although unaware of most of Hallie's fantasies,
recognize the crisis she faces and support her
in dealing with her disillusionments. As
the rest of the community (including Hallie's
siblings) seems blithely to accept outdated
perceptions of the glory of the Old South,
Hallie painfully observes injustice and finds
her own successful ways of dealing with the
world and her changing self.

278.  Loewengard, Heida Huberta Freybe [as Christine
      Lambert, pseud.]. *A Sudden Woman*. New York:
      Atheneum, 1964. 278pp.

      Doro Tenant (a seventeen-year-old free spir-
      it), her mother Lisa, and a brooding, alienated
      man of forty-five form a love triangle. Doro
      meets and loves Mike, seducing him despite
      her knowledge that he does not love her. When
      Lisa, concerned about Doro, meets Mike, they
      fall in love. A trusting mother-daughter
      relationship is broken by their rivalry over
      Mike and by Doro's fury at what she sees as
      her mother's betrayal. All three central
      characters are sympathetically portrayed, as
      the novel examines both love and the need to
      be loved.

279.  Logan, Jane. *The Very Nearest Room*. New York:
      Charles Scribner's Sons, 1973. 249pp.

      When her mother suffers a severe stroke, Lee
      Kramer finds herself, at the age of fifteen,
      faced with the burdens of caring not only
      for her invalid mother but also for her younger
      sister and her sickly younger brother. Her
      father, a busy physician, is rarely at home
      and gives her little help in managing the
      family's daily affairs. Preoccupied by her many
      duties at home, Lee finds little opportunity to
      experience the normal life of a young girl in

her small town in North Carolina. Caught in
a limbo between adulthood and adolescence,
Lee is tempted to retreat from reality into
a world of her own, but by the end of the
novel it is clear that the hardships she has
endured at home have given her the maturity
to survive the painful transition from girlhood to womanhood.

280.  Longstreet, Stephen. *Gettysburg*. New York:
      Farrar, Straus and Cudahy, 1961. 342pp.

      This novel is structured around the three
      days of the Battle of Gettysburg in the Civil
      War. The theme of the book, however, is that
      everyday events go on and hopes, fears, and
      passions are part of life even in the midst
      of battle. A character with a small but im-
      portant role is seventeen-year-old Alice Gross
      who is thought of as a child by her family
      but who is consciously becoming a woman. Alice,
      whose family lives just outside Gettysburg
      and is made up of Union supporters and sol-
      diers, happens to meet and fall in love immedi-
      ately with a young Confederate soldier, Texas
      Chile. They make love on their first encounter
      but must separate the next day to dream youthful
      dreams of the end of bloodshed and the beginning
      of domestic bliss. When the battle is over,
      Alice's life has changed, but she and her re-
      treating lover are the only ones who know it,
      since all the other characters are consumed
      with their own private lives.

281.  Lorimer, L.T. *Secrets*. New York: Holt, Rine-
      hart and Winston, 1981. 192pp.

      The daughter of a minister who has committed
      suicide, Maggie Thompson tells of the events
      which led up to his death. His weakness, his
      inability to face unpleasantness, and his
      adultery are gradually revealed to us, just as
      Maggie had herself slowly realized them. She
      shows much greater maturity and courage than
      he ever possessed, though she takes her own
      sexual initiation lightly. The novel is sus-
      pensefully plotted, and Maggie is an assertive
      narrator.

282.  Lowry, Beverly. *Come Back, Lolly Ray*.
      Garden City, N.Y.: Doubleday & Company,
      Inc., 1977.  230pp.

      This local color novel about Eunola, Miss-
      issippi, a small, class-conscious town in the
      early 1950s, contains a number of portraits
      of townspeople and several rather thin plot
      lines.  Lolly Ray Lasswell and her story serve
      to frame the novel, but she is actually little
      more significant in the novel than are a
      number of others.  She is a high school senior
      a gifted baton twirler, who creates magical
      moments through her performances.  Despite
      her sordid home life (which should make her an
      outcast) and though she is actually quite
      ordinary, she is permitted to attain a special
      prominence in the community because of her
      talent.

283.  Lowry, Beverly. *Emma Blue*.  Garden City, N.Y.:
      Doubleday & Company, Inc., 1978.  231pp.

      This sequel to *Come Back, Lolly Ray* is the
      story of Emma Blue Lasswell, the illegitimate
      daughter of a small Southern town's baton-
      twirling queen who left in disgrace.  Deserted
      by her mother, Emma has been brought up in a
      mobile home by her shy, withdrawn grandmother
      and cantankerous great-grandmother, always in
      the shadow of her charismatic mother.  At
      sixteen, Emma is a plain, stocky girl with
      wild, frizzy hair, a rebellious loner searching
      for her own place in the world.  She enters her
      first romantic relationship with a man twice
      her age, the last survivor of the town's most
      aristocratic family who has a notorious reputa-
      tion left over from his own youth.  However,
      it is her mother's brief visit after an absence
      of more than ten years that finally frees Emma
      from the shadow of the sparkling Lolly Ray
      and allows her to accept herself and her own
      unique style.

      Lucas, Victoria--*see* Plath, Sylvia.

284.  Lurie, Alison. *The War Between the Tates*.
      New York: Random House, Inc., 1974.  372pp.

Matilda Tate, thirteen, is a minor but
significant figure in the story of her
mother's attempt to cope with infidelity (her
husband is having an affair with a graduate
student) and an ensuing separation. Matilda,
always temperamental, is still child enough
to react with open anger. She hates the breach
between her parents, and her feelings complicate
her entry into adolescence. Lurie's treatment
of the girl is humorous, but like Erica, the
protagonist, Matilda offers insights into
families threatened by divorce as well as into
the roles women play both willingly and unwill-
ingly.

285.  Lyle, Katie Letcher. *Fair Day, and Another
       Step Begun*. Philadelphia: J.B. Lippincott
       Company, 1974. 157pp.

After a brief encounter during a canoe trip,
sixteen-year-old Ellen Burd finds herself
pregnant by John Waters. She is a simple
mountain girl who knows all the plants of her
locality and delights in their Latin names;
he is a twenty-two-year-old Yale graduate who,
several months later, scarcely remembers her.
When she informs him of her pregnancy and refuses an abortion, he flees and enters a
small commune. Like Lena Grove (whom she
resembles in other ways) in Faulkner's *Light
in August*, Ellen is sure her former lover truly
does care for her, and she follows him. The
novel is a modern and faithful version of
the old English ballad, "Childe Waters"; the
author had wondered about "Young Waters' strange
behavior to the fair Ellen, [and] her compla-
cent acceptance of it." This poetic novella
explores and tries to explain their motivations.

Macdonald, Ross--*see* Millar, Kenneth.

286.  MacDougall, Ruth Doan. *The Cheerleader*. New
       York: G.P. Putnam's Sons, 1973. 288pp.

Henrietta Snow begins her 1950s high school
career yearning to date Tom Forbes, a junior,
and to become a varsity cheerleader. Snowy
achieves both goals, earns a high grade average,
and becomes a leader in her school. Much

attention is also given to decisions about
"how far to go" in sexual activity, the
responsibilities of friendship, her ambition
to become Queen of the Junior Prom, and the
direction her life should take after graduation.
Dating Tom is both wonderful and painful,
and during Snowy's senior year, they suffer
a prolonged estrangement. Her final, surprising
decision during their passionate reconciliation
marks not only a major step in Snowy's maturation but also the climax of the novel.

287,   MacDougall, Ruth Doan. *The Flowers of the
Forest*. New York: Atheneum, 1981. 275pp.

In tracing the life of Anne Livingston
MacLorne from her seventeenth to her forty-
first year, MacDougall incorporates portraits
of three of Anne's adolescent daughters as
well as a portrayal of the young Anne. As a
teenaged bride, Anne follows Duncan, her husband, away from their desolate factory city
(and its regular paychecks) into the New
England hills to try to win independence as
sheep farmers; she makes this choice partly
because she hates the Huddersfield Shoe Factory
but primarily because she loves Duncan and
chooses to live with him, even if it means a
kind of exile. The woman-killing stress and
bitterness of life on the sheep farm is symbolized by the story of Janet, the eldest
MacLorne daughter, who cannot escape adolescence
until she is twenty-two. A rape victim who
suffers guilt and who makes a terrible marriage
rather than disclose the crime, Janet is an
abused wife and daughter-in-law; only the
death of her husband finally frees her to
act as an adult. The stories of Sarah Mac-
Lorne's escape to the city and to maturity
and of Betsy's transformation from child to
adolescent serve as contrast to their mother's
and sister's harder fates. The lives of all
these characters combine to portray the lots
of many women in nineteenth-century America.

288.   MacDougall, Ruth Doan. *Wife and Mother*. New
York: G.P. Putnam's Sons, 1976. 285pp.

The first quarter of this novel recounts
the circumstances behind the accidental pregnancy which transforms Carolyn Lyman from an
able college student headed for a professional
career into Carolyn Ash, an unwilling wife
and mother. The Ash marriage is desolate;
Carolyn and John share no interests or values;
certainly, they do not share their dreams.
Carolyn is expected to serve as an adjunct
to John's ambition and as a sexual outlet for
him.

289.  Maier, William. *The Temper of the Days*. New
      York: Charles Scribner's Sons, 1961.  381pp.

      Protagonist David Hobgood must choose sides
on a real estate deal that will hurt either
his son or his best friend, Jim Wilkinson.
Some of the flashbacks that constitute the
major portion of this novel deal with the
younger days of the wives of the two friends.
Dottie, a girl of the streets, and Pat, the
daughter of an old Boston family, have little
in common, but both jeopardize their marriages
through other relationships, and both, as
they preserve their marriages, are unswervingly
loyal to their husbands.

290.  Majerus, Janet. *Grandpa and Frank*. Philadel-
      phia: J.B. Lippincott Company, 1976.  192pp.

      At twelve, Sarah MacDermott assumes the
responsibility of protecting her grandfather,
the victim of a stroke. Sarah's Uncle Frank
plans to have old George MacDermott declared
incompetent so that Frank can take control
of the family farm. Enlisting the aid of her
pal, Joey Martin, Sarah takes her grandfather
to Chicago so that a doctor can find him competent. The journey of Sarah, Joey, and George
is the major action of the novel and signifies
Sarah's maturation. The story pictures rural
life in Illinois in the 1940s.

291.  Malamud, Bernard. *A New Life*. New York: Farrar,
      Straus and Cudahy, 1961.  367pp.

      The tragi-comic vicissitudes of S. Levin in
his first year as a college instructor of

English provide entertainment and enlighten-
ment in this early novel by a major American
writer.  One minor character is twenty-year-
old Nadalee Hammerstad, a student in Levin's
freshman composition class with whom he has
a brief but significant affair, complicated
by his inadvertently turning in a lower
grade than Nadalee deserves at the end of
the term.  Recriminations and repercussions
follow.  The episode relates to the principal
theme: the difficulty and variety of moral
decisions one confronts while teaching.

292.   Maloff, Saul. *Heartland.* New York: Charles
       Scribner's Sons, 1973. 279pp.

       Isaiah Greene, a struggling professor, be-
comes an overnight success because he is
interviewed by a reporter as he accidentally
becomes involved in a protest led by militant
Jews.  Consequently, following numerous speaking
engagements, he finds himself at Donner Pass
College for Women, an all-American, all-girl
school high in the Rockies.  To his surprise,
pink-cheeked cheerleaders and class officers
manifest a peculiar interest in the rites of
ancient religions, and on the final day of
the symposium in which he is participating,
these young women become twentieth-century
Amazon priestesses who take their vengeance
on the men who have underestimated them.

293.   Malvern, Gladys. *Wilderness Island.* Phila-
       delphia: Macrae Smith Co., 1961. 190pp.

       Alida Evertsen is one of the first Dutch
immigrants to live in the New Netherlands, to-
day called Long Island.  Her life as a young
girl and as a teenager suggests the restrictions
and privations not only of the colonists, but
of colonial women in particular.  As a child
she observes her brother and a friend accidentally shoot an Indian, an incident which is
indirectly reponsible for the Indian wars
several years later.  When the Indians rebel
against the settlers, she is torn between her
best friend, an Indian, and her loyalties to
her own people.  She reaches maturity in the
closing years of the Indian wars.

294.  Manchester, William. *The Long Gainer*. Boston:
      Little, Brown and Company, 1961. 495pp.

      Daphne Dix, a stunning college cheerleader,
      figures prominently in one subplot of this
      complex novel. The portrait is flat but
      biting, for calculating Daphne uses people
      by flaunting her one asset, her sexuality.
      Daphne and her lover, Red Stacy, a football
      star, base their affair upon mutual exploita-
      tion--she wants his support in her campaign
      for Gridiron Queen, and he wants sexual
      satisfaction without obligation.  Both partners
      are vastly ambitious and need publicity--she
      wants to become a film star; he wants to
      attract the attention of professional team
      scouts.  This need leads  Red to trick Daphne
      into posing for *Sly* magazine.  The exploit not
      only ends their hopes for fame but also
      destroys several careers of university officials.

295.  Marshall, Alexandra. *Gus in Bronze*. New York:
      Alfred A. Knopf, 1977.  242pp.

      Marshall's novel details the struggle of
      Augusta Kaligas, a former dancer, now wife,
      mother, and career woman, to accept death with
      dignity.  The Kaligas family, including Daphni
      and Maya, two teenaged daughters, decides
      that Gus should be allowed to spend her last
      days at home.  Fighting to finish her reading
      of Virginia Woolf, resigning herself to death,
      Gus teaches her family resignation and love.
      The novel dramatizes Kübler-Ross' analysis
      of dying.  As a bronze sculpture of Gus
      breathes life, Gus leaves life, but her anger,
      humor, and acceptance of the strongly distinct
      personalities of her husband, her children,
      and of her siblings affirm life and love.

296.  Marshall, Catherine. *Christy*. New York:
      McGraw-Hill, 1967.  496pp.

      This novel, set in the Appalachian Mountains
      of Tennessee, is based on the life of the
      author's mother.  Christy, a young college
      student, decides to teach in a mission school
      in the mountains.  In spite of her parents'
      opposition, she makes the difficult journey

to the school. Christy encounters poverty,
mountain feuds, murder, rum running, and a
typhoid epidemic, but she learns to love
and understand the mountain people and finds
fulfillment with them.

297. Mather, Melissa. *One Summer in Between*.
     New York: Harper & Row, Publishers, 1967.
     213pp.

     During the summer of her nineteenth year,
     Harriet Brown, a southern black, fulfills a
     college sociology class project: she takes
     a job as mother's helper with a white Vermont
     family and keeps a journal of her experiences
     and her reactions to them. Bright, quick--
     and defensive--Harriet confronts homesickness,
     various forms of racism, including her own,
     and her taxing job. She learns a great deal
     about herself as well as about the North and
     about the human experience.

298. Mathis, Sharon. *Listen for the Fig Tree*.
     New York: The Viking Press, 1974. 175pp.

     Muffin, a sixteen-year-old blind black,
     living in Brooklyn with her widowed mother,
     plans, with great anticipation, the celebration
     of Christmas and the African festival, Kwanza.
     She strives to overcome problems resulting
     from the weaknesses of her mother (including
     alcoholism) and from her own disability. In
     spite of many difficulties and with the
     supportive love of adult friends, she realizes,
     at the celebration of Kwanza, that she has
     reached the time of understanding. She feels
     a sense of belonging to the African past as
     well as to her family and friends, and she
     knows that she has the courage to survive.

299. Matthews, Jack. *Pictures of the Journey Back*.
     New York: Harcourt Brace Jovanovich, 1973.
     176pp.

     After years of strife, Laurel, aged twenty-
     one, and her mother have not seen each other
     for a long time. Now Laurel's mother is
     dying and sends her free-spirited but loving
     boyfriend, J. Dan, to retrieve her daughter

for a final reconciliation. The novel
focuses on the parallels between Laurel and
her mother by highlighting several minor
conflicts between Laurel, her boyfriend, and
J. Dan during the two-day return trip. This
book successfully depicts many trends and
attitudes of the sixties.

300. Maynard, Joyce. *Baby Love*. New York: Alfred
    A. Knopf, 1981. 244pp.

    Set in a small town in New Hampshire, this
book focuses on teenaged girls and their
babies: Sandy, married and trying to create a
perfect life with her husband and son; Tara
and Wanda, unmarried with babies; and Jill,
pregnant by a boy who refuses to marry her.
All of them love and want their babies but
do not realize that this love could be a
substitution for something that is missing
in their lives. Their solutions to problems
they encounter rearing children while they
are still children themselves reflect their
immaturity. Sandy discovers her young husband
with another girl but hopes to ignore this
rather than upset her idealistic dream. Wanda,
overweight and longing for attention, abuses
her baby, then loses her to a deranged grandmother who kidnaps the child and sets fire to
an abortion clinic. Tara, constantly berated
by her mother, and Jill, whose abortion is
interrupted by the fire, set out together
to a commune in Georgia where they believe
babies will be safe.

301. McDonald, Kay L. *Vision of the Eagle*. New
    York: Thomas Y. Crowell Company, 1977.
    312pp.

    Abigail is the well-bred, educated daughter
of an upstate New York banker who, at the age
of nineteen, falls in love with Ross, a handsome pig farmer. When her parents disapprove
of their marriage, Ross and Abigail set out to
make a new life for themselves in the Old West.
In spite of many hardships, they are happy
and very much in love. Abigail has just learned
she is expecting a baby when an Indian named
Snow Cloud kills Ross and takes Abigail back

to his tribe. Thinking the baby is his, Snow
Cloud makes Abigail his wife. It is from her
own background and the love she shared with
Ross that Abigail finds the strength and
courage to survive the rest of her life among
the Indians, secretly teaching her son the
language and ways of white people.

302.  McGraw, Eloise Jarvis. *Greensleeves*. New York:
      Harcourt, Brace & World, Inc., 1968. 311pp.

      Despite the interest and attention of her
      famous, talented, divorced parents and of
      several other adults, Shannon Lightley, eight-
      teen, feels alienated and homeless. To resolve
      her doubts about a career, to come to terms
      with her detested appearance and personality,
      and to become independent from her directive
      mentors, Shannon takes a job as a waitress
      in a small, Portland, Oregon, restaurant and
      lives in a boarding-house nearby. Her adven-
      tures, which include touches of mystery and
      romance, help her to resolve conflicts born
      of a childhood divided among homes and schools
      in Europe and the U.S.

303.  McGuane, Thomas. *The Bushwhacked Piano*. New
      York: Simon and Schuster, 1971. 220pp.

      Ann Fitzgerald is the inspiration for much
      of the offbeat antics of the protagonist Nicholas
      Payne. Ann and Nicholas are both from upper-
      middle-class backgrounds and inclined to rebel
      against these backgrounds by exhibiting anti-
      social behavior. Ann is nearly the only person
      in the world who finds Nicholas amusing. Ann
      eventually, however, opts for a conventional
      marriage to a dull but successful man her
      family approves of. Ann's first photography
      exhibit is half made up of pictures of Nicholas
      in odd activities. Nicholas leaves Ann behind
      as he continues to pursue his fantasies.

304.  McHugh, Arona. *A Banner with a Strange Device*.
      Garden City, N.Y.: Doubleday & Company, Inc.,
      1964. 594pp.

      In Boston in 1948, young veterans try to find

themselves in Harvard graduate school, and
young women try to reconcile their own needs
with society's concept of what their role
should be. Brilliant, pretty Deborah Miller
is nineteen but as innocent as a child, desperately poor, and tyrannized by her father,
a sickly orthodox Jew. Wild, wealthy, beautiful
Sally Brimmer befriends Deborah because her
impotent brother Dudley thinks he might regain
his manhood if he could date an undemanding
innocent. Deborah eagerly siezes the chance
to broaden her horizons, while Sally brings
unhappiness or tragedy to the men who are drawn
to her.

305. McHugh, Arona. *The Seacoast of Bohemia*.
Garden City, N.Y.: Doubleday & Company, Inc.,
1965. 664pp.

This sequel to *A Banner with a Strange Device*
brings the characters to full adulthood. The
beautiful Sally Brimmer blooms as a happy wife
and mother, and Deborah moves into a full,
mature relationship. However, Sally cannot
forgive Deborah for being the innocent catalyst
to Dudley's breakdown.

306. McInerny, Ralph. *Jolly Rogerson*. New York:
Doubleday & Company, Inc., 1967. 261pp.

A pawn in Professor Matthew Rogerson's chess
game of madness is a student named Maureen
Nugent. Because Maureen has been maligned by
one of Matt's incompetent colleagues, she is
easy to manipulate into seeming improprieties.
Matt intends to ruin himself, but he merely
succeeds in ruining everyone else. Although
Maureen is the first victim of Matt's pranks
in that she is asked to leave the school, she
escapes any further damage, setting her apart
from Matt's other victims. Maureen handles
the potentially devastating experience with
maturity and actually foils the professor by
proving to be a most serious student.

McMeekin, Clark--*see* McMeekin, Isabella McLennan.

307.  McMeekin, Isabella McLennan, and Dorothy Pace
      Clark [as Clark McMeekin, pseud.]. *The
      Fairbrothers*. New York: G.P. Putnam's Sons,
      1961. 288pp.

      The efforts of the Fairbrothers, a Kentucky
      family, to regain their emotional and economic
      balance after the Civil War are complicated by
      their reluctant and informal adoption of Zion
      Hobbs, fourteen. Imaginative, impulsive Zion
      is a burden initially but comes to be warmly
      accepted, especially by the elder son, Tolley,
      with whom she falls in love. Zion struggles
      especially to win the approval and affection of
      Mrs. Fairbrother, a spirited, complex woman.
      Zion is the means of reconciling Tolley and his
      mother after a series of ruptures in their
      relationship.

308.  Meaker, Marijane [as M.E. Kerr, pseud.]. *Dinky
      Hocker Shoots Smack*. New York: Harper & Row,
      1972. 198pp.

      Set in Brooklyn, this is a story about the
      intertwined lives and the psychological problems
      of four teenagers, two girls and two boys,
      growing up with parents or guardians preoccupied
      with causes rather than child-rearing. Natalia,
      who has been to a special school for children
      with mental problems, comes to live with her
      relatives, the Hocker family, and develops a
      friendship with one of the boys. As the story
      progresses, the other three make strides forward
      but Susan (Dinky) Hocker regresses. She becomes
      obese, shuns her friends, and even fails to
      give proper care to her cat, a symbol of friend-
      ship and responsibility. She finally strikes
      out to get the attention she so badly needs
      from her parents by writing "Dinky Hocker Shoots
      Smack!" on nearly every surface outside of the
      building where her mother is receiving an award
      for her work with drug addicts. The Hockers
      finally realize how badly Dinky needs their
      attentions and begin to make amends.

309.  Meaker, Marijane [as M.E. Kerr, pseud.]. *If I
      Love You, Am I Trapped Forever?* New York:
      Harper & Row, Publishers, Inc., 1973. 177pp.

Leah Pennington is the "girl" of the narrator-protagonist Alan Bennett. Leah's growing attraction to another boy causes both Leah and Alan very real anguish, and her final decision to leave Alan contributes greatly to his maturation.

310. Meaker, Marijane [as M.E. Kerr, pseud.]. *Little Little*. New York: Harper & Row, 1981. 183pp.

Little Little is the name of a "perfectly formed" high-school-aged dwarf who struggles for independence from her family and tries to evaluate the romantic attentions paid her by two other dwarfs. The chapters alternate between Little Little and Sydney, one of her suitors, and are satirical accounts of both large and small people.

311. Meaker, Marijane [as M.E. Kerr, pseud.]. *The Son of Someone Famous*. New York: Harper & Row, 1974. 226pp.

Adam Blessing, whose mother is dead and whose father is very famous, has trouble staying in private schools. After being again expelled, he decides to go to Vermont to stay with his maternal grandfather and use his grandfather's name so no one will know he is "the son of someone famous." One of his friends at school is Brenda Bell with whom he shares his secret. The school term is a time of growing, and in spite of many misunderstandings and conflicts, Brenda and Adam gain a deeper understanding of themselves, their families, and friends. The story is told as excerpts from Brenda's notes for a novel and Adam's journal.

312. Means, Florence C. *Our Cup Is Broken*. Boston: Houghton Mifflin Company, 1969. 229pp.

Eight-year-old Sarah, an orphaned Hopi, moves east with her adoptive white parents and attends school with white children. Although she is often lonely for the Hopi people and village life, she tries to adjust to the culture but finds she is not really accepted. Following a broken high school love affair, she runs away, back to the Hopi village. Here, life is most difficult, and as Sarah attempts to

gain the acceptance of the Hopis, she finds
they consider her an "outsider" but, neverthe-
less, subject to tribal standards of female
behavior. This story of conflicts between
cultures is told in a realistic way as Sarah
struggles to survive and to find fulfillment
with her own people.

313.  Mercer, Charles. *Beyond Bojador*. New York:
      Holt, Rinehart, and Winston, 1965. 240pp.

      This novel is centered around Judson Lathrop,
      a dutiful New Englander who feels guilt because
      his great-grandfather was a slaver. He has
      become a successful State Department specialist
      on Africa. Judson has fallen in love with a
      beautiful young anthropologist who also loves
      Africa. He comes home to New England from an
      African assignment to tell his wife he wants
      a divorce. The catalyst to the subsequent
      course of events is his twenty-one-year-old
      daughter Ann, who brings home the man she wants
      to marry. Ann's fiancé, George Carveth, is
      black.

314.  Meriwether, Louise. *Daddy Was a Number Runner*.
      Foreword by James Baldwin. Englewood Cliffs,
      N.J.: Prentice-Hall, 1970. 208pp.

      Francie Coffin, eleven when the story opens,
      recounts with lucid and grim detail her life
      in a Harlem tenement from 1934 to 1936, em-
      phasizing her relationships with her parents,
      her two older brothers, and her best friend,
      Sukie. Although Francie's parents are am-
      bitious for themselves and their children, they
      are unable to prevent her brothers from dropping
      out of school, and the constant financial pres-
      sures and inadequate living conditions con-
      tribute to their eventual estrangement. Francie
      maintains an understated, matter-of-fact tone
      even while she describes such sensational events
      as the arrest of her brother, the murder con-
      viction of a next-door neighbor, and a summer
      riot. A climactic moment comes when Francie
      realizes that Sukie has become a prostitute.
      Although Francie records some pleasant, even
      joyous moments, a mood of increasing disillusion-
      ment dominates the novel.

315.  Mertz, Barbara G. [as Barbara Michaels, pseud.].
      *Ammie, Come Home.* New York: Meredith Press,
      1968. 252pp.

      *Ammie, Come Home* is a contemporary ghost story
      set in Georgetown. After Ruth Bennet inherits
      a beautiful old house from an eccentric relative,
      she invites her niece, Sara, to live in George-
      town while she attends college. Sara's presence
      unleashes forces in the house which have lain
      dormant since the Revolutionary War. The
      suspense builds as Sara develops an uncanny
      sympathy for Ammie, the terrified spirit of
      a girl long dead.

316.  Mezvinsky, Shirley. *The Edge.* Garden City,
      N.Y.: Doubleday & Company, Inc., 1965. 210pp.

      Lois Marks has been married for four years
      and has a four-year-old daughter. Although
      she quit college to marry Jerry Marks, a physics
      student who chose to manage his father's furni-
      ture business, she had been a very promising
      drama student. The novel consists of flash-
      backs which trace her adolescence and explain
      her present depression. She believes her
      problems stem from her Jewish background, her
      domineering mother, and her own fears of loss
      of control, coupled with her desires to be
      an actress. In her self-evaluation, she also
      acknowledges conflicting sexual desires that
      she had ignored during her adolescence.

      Michaels, Barbara--*see* Mertz, Barbara.

317.  Millar, Kenneth. [as Ross Macdonald, pseud.].
      *The Underground Man.* New York: Alfred A.
      Knopf, 1971. 272pp.

      Detective Lew Archer is on the trail of a
      runaway teenager, nineteen-year-old Susan
      Crandall, born of the love affair of Martha
      Nickerson Crandall and Leo Broadhurst. At
      first it appears that Susan has kidnapped six-
      year-old Ronny Broadhurst, grandson of Leo.
      Archer discovers that she had witnessed the
      murder of Leo when she was a child, has recently
      been at the scene of the murder of Stanley,
      Leo's son, and has stolen Ronny in order to

protect him. The girl is suicidal as a result
of her drug abuse and tragic circumstances.
After Archer talks her out of jumping off the
San Francisco Bay Bridge, she is reconciled with
her parents.

318.  Millar, Kenneth [as Ross Macdonald, pseud.].
      *The Wycherly Woman.* New York: Alfred A.
      Knopf, 1961. 278pp.

      When Phoebe Wycherly drops out of college
      and disappears, she becomes the object of a
      search by private investigator Lew Archer.
      Various characters give their views of Phoebe's
      personality, and she is suspected of murder.
      Phoebe appears in only a few episodes but is
      the motivational force of the novel, which
      explores the impact of the older generation
      upon their children, a frequent Macdonald theme.

319.  Miller, Heather Ross. *The Edge of the Woods.*
      New York: Atheneum, 1964. 118pp.

      In this brief, poetic novel, Anna Marie Wade,
      a young mother, tries with limited success
      to come to terms with her adolescent memories
      of her grandfather, a violent, stingy, domi-
      neering man.

320.  Mitchell, Don. *Thumb Tripping.*  Boston: Little,
      Brown, & Co., 1969. 182pp.

      Chay and Gary are college students who decide
      to hitchhike and "trip" their way through
      California during the early 70s. Chay is used
      most often as a point of sexual conflict. Will
      Gary, her boyfriend, fight for her honor or sell
      her favors to passing drivers? Chay says "Wow!"
      a great many times and refuses to see anything
      but beautiful souls in the people who pick
      them up. At first proud that they have "turned
      on" an eight-year-old boy to marijuana, Chay
      eventually learns the same boy is now dropping
      acid and decides to fly home to Philadelphia
      rather than continue her adventures with Gary.

321.  Mojtabai, A.G. *The 400 Eels of Sigmund Freud.*
      New York: Simon & Schuster, 1976. 258pp.

A talented group of high school science
students is gathered at Four Winds, former
family home of the owner of Alkavist Research
Labs, for an intensive ten-week workshop under
the tutelage of various research personnel from
the nearby biochemical lab. The author employs
multiple viewpoints, including those of the
emotionally sterile Dr. Eloson, who is in
charge of running the Four Winds program, his
wife Ethel, who is undergoing a mental breakdown, Anna Homay, wife of the ineffectual re-
creation director, and several students. One
of these students is fifteen-year-old Naomi
Heschel. We see her coping with intellectual
demands, the pressure of competition, the first
stirrings of her sexual awakening, and the
death of a brilliant student who was driven to
suicide by the persecution of Ethel Eloson.

322.  Moore, Ruth. *Second Growth.* New York: William
      Morrow & Co., Inc., 1962. 407pp.

In this novel, Constance Wilkerson, aged
twenty, emerges as one of the stronger personalities in a small east-coast village during
the late 1950s. Connie struggles to live a
life acceptable to her fanatical father. Finding
this to be impossible, she believes that escaping with her boyfriend would be more desirable. It is not long before she finds her quasi-
marital relationship unsatisfactory, and her
boyfriend leaves her just before their baby is
born. Connie tries to return home and rebuild
her family relationships, only this time she
honestly tries to deal with her own feelings and
those of others. She struggles with the desire
to reclaim her child who has been abducted by
its father. Eventually, Connie accepts the
fact that this is impossible. Through her
experiences, which are interwoven among stories
of various townsfolk, Connie learns how to
face reality and to continue living even under
difficult circumstances.

323.  Morris, Willie. *The Last of the Southern Girls.*
      New York: Alfred A. Knopf, 1973. 287pp.

The simpering, witless, Southern belle stereotype is replaced in Morris' novel by Carol

Hollywell, a beauty from De Soto Point,
Arkansas, whose urbane humor and liveliness
take Washington, D.C., by storm.  The book
concentrates on Carol's arrival in the nation's
capitol as a young woman, her climb to the
upper echelons of political society, a disastrous marriage, and passionate affair with
a Congressman.  Many passages, however, refer
to childhood and adolescent memories of life
in a river town.

324.  Morris, Wright.  *Plains Song: For Female Voices*.
      New York: Harper & Row, 1980.  229pp.

Morris returns to his native Nebraska in
this psychological novel encompassing three
generations of women.  Cora, the matriarch,
endures and makes do.  As a young girl, Cora,
plain and strong, moves from her parents'
farm to her uncle's restaurant in order to
have a better chance to find a husband and
earn her keep while doing so.  A Nebraska
homesteader thinks she would be a good farm
wife, and after a two-week acquaintance, they
marry.  Morris stresses Cora's stoic bewilderment during her first year of marriage.  Through
the years, Cora raises one daughter and two
nieces.  Madge, her daughter, grows from child
to farm wife and happily continues this rural
tradition.  Sharon, Cora's niece, however,
even as a child is horrified by the bleak
life on the farm.  Sharon's rebellion against
Cora's life provides the major focus for
Morris' paean to pioneer women.

325.  Morrison, James.  *Treehouse*.  New York: The
      Dial Press, 1972.  181pp.

Sam, at twenty-one, returns from the Peace
Corps to learn that he has always been in love
with his younger sister Nell.  Both have been
adopted by a compassionate, forthright couple
who have also had a natural child, Magruder,
who is in many ways the hub of the family.  Sam
and Nell convince their parents and themselves
that the adopted child's search for identity
ends not in the quest for biological parents
but in the deep bonds that have been created
within the family.  Nell, usually the most

insecure child, becomes the force supporting
the family as she draws them together following
a tragedy, and she helps Sam to triumph over
his doubts about their unconventional relationship and his own worth to the family.

326.  Morrison, Toni. *The Bluest Eye.* New York:
      Holt, Rinehart, and Winston, 1970. 164pp.

The arid, desperate life of Pecola Breedlove,
the protagonist, is contrasted with the happier,
more comfortable life of Claudia MacTeer, the
narrator; both youngsters are black. Pecola,
child of loveless, rootless parents, believes
that she would be beautiful and happy if only
she could acquire blue eyes, for she clearly
understands that society values white children
but has no use for her. Her desperate quest
(undertaken through prayer and magic) is complicated by the scorn her fellow blacks display
toward her ineffectual family. Only once is
Pecola granted any real attention--when her
father, violent and self-indulgent, rapes her.
Ultimately, the youngster finds refuge in
madness, the only recourse for this systematical-
ly isolated adolescent.

327.  Morrison, Toni. *Song of Solomon.* New York:
      Alfred A. Knopf, 1977. 337pp.

Brief glimpses into the adolescences of a
number of his female kin--mother, sisters,
aunt, cousin--illuminate the slow maturation
of Macon "Milkman" Dead, protagonist. The short,
intense, poetic flashback into the youth of
Pilate Dead, his aunt, is, however, of central
importance to the saga of the Dead family and
is a parable of the displacement of the non-
conformist within the black community and in
society at large.

328.  Morrison, Toni. *Sula.* New York: Alfred A.
      Knopf, 1973. 174pp.

The adolescences of Sula Peace and Nel Wright
include several episodes which change these
protagonists for life. The girls take comfort
in their friendship, face together the awakening
interest in male eyes, jointly confront overt

racism on the part of white schoolmates, and
share the responsibility for a playmate's
death.  Each incident clearly influences
choices Nel and Sula are to make as women
during lives marked by trouble, separation,
and violence.  The portraits offer insights
into the lot of some contemporary black women.

329.  Mountzoures, H.L.  *The Bridge*.  New York: Charles
      Scribner's Sons, 1972.  373pp.

      This richly detailed novel examines the painful
      acculturation of a Greek immigrant family
      through the eyes of its third son.  Philip Neros'
      mother Thalia, a beautiful but fragile sixteen-
      year-old at her marriage, loses her sanity
      under the strain of motherhood in a foreign
      culture.  Philip's childhood and that of his
      brothers and sisters are marked by alternate
      neglect, forced abandonment, reunion, and
      pain, as his father tries to keep the family
      from final dissolution.  Philip comes to under-
      stand his mother's tragedy and his father's
      courage.  Philip's adolescence and early man-
      hood are enriched by his relationship with
      Joanna Errin, whose maturity and warmth help
      him come to grips with the unexorcised ghosts
      of his past.

330.  Murray, Michele.  *The Crystal Nights*.  New York:
      Seabury Press, 1973.  310pp.

      Elly Josephs, her brother, their Jewish father,
      and their Russian mother and grandmother live
      on a farm in Connecticut.  Elly, a junior in
      high school, despises living on a farm and
      wants to become an actress.  Their life is
      further complicated by the arrival of Aunt Anna
      and cousin Margot from Nazi Germany.  Elly
      finds it difficult to share her best friend, her
      brother, and her room with Margot.  In spite
      of the many conflicts, Elly grows from a jeal-
      ous, irresponsible girl to one who gains self-
      acceptance and the approval of others.

331.  Myrer, Anton.  *The Last Convertible*.  New York:
      G.P. Putnam's Sons, 1978.  526pp.

      The Fusiliers are a group of five Harvard men

of diverse backgrounds who share a large
green Packard convertible nicknamed "the
Empress." The plot traces them and their
girlfriends over a thirty-year period, demonstrating how youthful friendships, romances,
and experiences can influence the rest of
one's life. Though the female roles are
subordinate, they are essential to the themes
of the novel.

332.  Nabokov, Vladimir. *Pale Fire*. New York: G.P.
      Putnam's Sons, 1962. 315pp.

Daughter of a great poet and a significant
character in his long autobiographical poem,
"Pale Fire," Hazel Shade was bright but un-
attractive and never seemed to do anything
right. The presence of a poltergeist in the
family home when she was sixteen seemed connected
with her adolescent vulnerability and emotional
problems. Her suicide, at the age of twenty-
three, deeply affected her father. The novel
as a whole consists of Shade's poem plus a
long and involved commentary, allegedly on
the poem, by Charles Kinbote, a madman who
believes himself the exiled ruler of a mythical
kingdom and who insists that Shade's poem
really is a symbolic telling of his own story.

333.  Nathan, Robert. *The Devil with Love*. New York:
      Alfred A. Knopf, 1967. 200pp.

Father Deener, a small-town Catholic priest
who keeps close watch on his fellow citizens
in Parish, is disturbed at the emanations of
evil that threaten the tranquility of his modest
corner of Christian service. The initial
cause of the impending evil is Gladys Milhouser,
a luscious but far from intellectual seventeen-
year-old, the Homecoming Queen of Parish High
School, who has so titillated a middle-aged
TV repairman, Alfred Sneed, that he offers his
soul to the devil in exchange for her favors.
The devil sends Samael of Hod, a super arch-
demon, to Parish to take advantage of Alfred's
offer, but instead of a soul, he wants a heart,
the noblest thing of all because it can do
something a soul can never do; it can love.
Samael sets up an office in Parish under the

name of Dr. Samuel Hod, and Gladys becomes
his receptionist. Alfred Sneed, his patient,
never succeeds in winning the love of Gladys,
who instead falls for the debonair Dr. Hod,
but he saves his heart because Mary Sebastion,
the lovable Parish postmistress, newly aware
of Alfred as a desirable male, unselfishly
offers her own in order to rescue him. Dr.
Hod, routed by her generosity and completely
undone by the younger generation as represented
by the dauntless Gladys, who has even tried
to teach him to cha-cha, beats a retreat to
Hell shaking his head in defeat and leaving
Parish to a victorious Father Deener.

334.   Nathan, Robert. *Mia*. New York: Alfred A. Knopf,
       1970.   179pp.

       Author Robert Nathan has been called a master
       of satiric fantasy, and in *Mia* he gives us
       an enchanting blend of an autumnal New England
       coast, a philosophical widowed writer, and
       a quiet, middle-aged woman.  The writer,
       Thomas Baggot, winters on the Cape and is happy
       to meet his new neighbor, Emmeline Anderson.
       The two, refugees from life, become warm platonic
       friends, sharing thoughts, excursions, and
       dreams, but Thomas is both charmed and mystified
       by his encounters with a fascinating and bold
       young girl, about fifteen, who darts in and
       out of his life exclaiming, "I want to see
       everything and do everything."  The girl, Mia,
       it later appears, is the eager young Emmeline,
       and the author telescopes yesterday and today
       into a picture of a questing child, vibrant
       with dreams, on a collision course with a
       timorous woman who shrinks from love and ad-
       venture.  Mia is an echo of yesterday intruding
       into today, and in her hunger for life, her im-
       patience at an unfulfilled present, she care-
       lessly destroys a future that at least offers
       possibilities for happines.

335.   Nelson, Shirley. *The Last Year of the War*.
       New York: Harper & Row, Publishers, 1978.
       255pp.

       As the result of a religious conversion

during high school, Jo Fuller rejects her
family's attitudes and plans for her in order to
attend Calvary Bible Institute, her goal being
full-time Christian service. Jo's circle;
the atmosphere of Calvary, demanding but neither
tense nor grim; her work as a student missionary;
and a tentative exploration of love are all
conveyed. Central, however, is the account
of Jo's painful, confusing period of alienation
from God. Nelson uses the final days of World
War II as an analog to Jo's pain.

336.  Neufeld, John. *For All the Wrong Reasons*.
      New York: New American Library, 1973.  220pp.

      Tish Davies and her boyfriend, Peter, are a
very modern high school couple, but when
she becomes pregnant, they make the old-fashioned
decision to get married. As they cope with the
problems of a young married couple, including
the disapproval of their parents, Tish emerges
as a strong and capable young woman. Shortly
after the birth of their daughter, Peter suffers
a mental breakdown, and Tish, newly independent,
faces an uncertain future.

337.  Neufeld, John. *Lisa, Bright and Dark*.  New
      York: S.G. Philips, 1969.  125pp.

      Four high school students find their friend-
ships disturbed by the irrational, sometimes
destructive behavior of one of their group,
Lisa Schilling. The other three try to help her,
reading psychoanalytic studies which are over
their heads and trying unsuccessfully to
persuade her parents to get qualified care for
her. The fears and frustrations of Lisa and of
her friends, especially of the narrator, Betsy
Goodman, are depicted in this study of privileged, middle-class youth.

338.  Nichols, John Treadwell. *The Sterile Cuckoo*.
      New York: David McKay Co., 1965.  210pp.

      John Nichols, barely out of college himself
when he wrote his first novel, set his love
story against a background of fraternity parties,
romantic weekends, and the vocabulary that domi-
nated the campus scene in the first half of

the 1960s. Pookie Adams, the outrageous,
do-or-die heroine, meets Jerry Payne at a
bus stop, and they tumble into an intense love
affair several years later. The hectic pace
and irreverent stunts (drinking Purple Jesuses
on a tombstone) are fated to lose their appeal,
paralleling the demise of Pookie and Jerry's
relationship.

339.  Nixon, Joan Lowery. *The Kidnapping of Christina
      Lattimore.* New York: Harcourt Brace Jovano-
      vich, 1979. 179pp.

Christina Lattimore, a high school junior at
a private school for girls in Houston, is
kidnapped from her front doorstep. When the
police find Christina, the kidnappers embark
upon their backup plan of claiming that Christina plotted the kidnapping to extort money
from her wealthy grandmother, Cristabel
Lattimore. Christina's parents have so completely devoted themselves to following every
whim and wish of Cristabel that they are
willing to do as she says by hushing up the case
and letting Christina appear to be guilty.
Christina is determined to prove her innocence
by solving the mystery of how the crime was
organized. In the process she learns that
she must become independent of the constraints
of her family.

340.  Norman, Gurney. *Divine Right's Trip: A Folk
      Tale.* New York: The Dial Press, 1972. 302pp.

In the early 1970s, Divine Right (David Ray)
Davenport travels from the west coast to St.
Louis, Cincinnati, and finally to the hills of
Kentucky during the course of his road and
drug trips. His companion is Estelle. Nothing
of her past is revealed but we see her join
D.R. in his trips, yet retain enough sense to
mother him, alternately loving and being
intolerant of him and the assorted characters
he attracts. After D.R. parks her at the
Cincinnati bus station for several days while
he visits his sister, she leaves. Alone, D.R.'s
adventures continue until he finally puts out
the word to have Estelle found, and they marry
in Kentucky, attended by hillbillies and hippies.

341.  Oates, Joyce Carol.  *Angel of Light*.  New York:
      E.P. Dutton, 1981.  434pp.

      Kirsten Halleck, nearly eighteen, is a high-
strung and immature prankster continually
testing the limits of her power and freedom.
After her father's death, she plays the self-
important role of a grief-stricken daughter, like
Electra, seeking to avenge her father.  Her
playacting becomes tragic reality, when, re-
fusing to believe that Mr. Halleck's death was
a suicide, Kirsten implicates her own mother
Isabel and Isabel's lover, Nick, as her father's
killers.  It is her brother Owen who becomes
the instrument of Kirsten's retribution.  Owen
first dismisses Kirsten's accusations, then
assumes an equal fury and eventually commits
matricide, losing his own life in the process.
In the end, Kirsten grows weary of the game
and is unable to complete the violent revenge
she'd planned.

342.  Oates, Joyce Carol.  *Bellefleur*.  New York:
      E.P. Dutton, 1980.  558pp.

      The most dominant personality in this Gothic
novel is Leah Bellefleur, whose power exists
by virtue of her independent state of mind:
she retains a virgin strength surpassing other
family women.  As mythic explanation of her
self-assurance, there is her guardian pet
spider, Love, who watches over Leah for five
years, until at the age of eighteen Gideon
kills Love and weds Leah.  Other Bellefleur
women lack protectors; for instance, the lugu-
brious Veronica loses her "second or third"
fiancé while still in her twenties, afterwards
vowing to wear black and avoid sunlight as
an "old maid's" form of self-punishment.  Being
acted upon by men involves both tragedy (rape)
and reward (marriage) for two submissive Bellefleur women: Garnet Hecht (about fourteen) whose
great romantic passion makes her vulnerable to
Gideon's advances; and conversely, Little Goldie
(about nine) whose great innocence makes her an
easy victim, raped by Gideon then by Ewan.
Finally, there are two girls, who by implication,
figure as rebels: Christabel, who is married
off at an early age (about thirteen), appears

to conform, while actually planning to
have an affair; in contradistinction to Yolanda
(fifteen years old) who refuses to conform at
all, leaving the security of the family in
order to choose and form her own destiny.

343.    Oates, Joyce Carol. *Childwold*. New York:
        Vanguard Press, 1976. 295pp.

At the age of fourteen, Laney Bartlett is
rescued from several pushy, mocking teenaged
boys by forty-year-old Kasch, only to be rapa-
ciously seduced by her rescuer. Kasch's interest
in Laney is superseded by his later attraction
to her mother Arlene, who figures as a fecund
Earth Mother. In this experimental novel, with
multiple points of view, the theme is related-
ness with others, and for Laney this entails
submersion of self in a river of life, symbolized by both a childhood incident of near-
drowning and the pubescent experience of life
pulsing within and around her during menstru-
ation.

344.    Oates, Joyce Carol. *Do With Me What You Will*.
        New York: Vanguard Press, 1973. 561pp.

Although Elena Ross is only eight years old
at the beginning of this novel and is thirty
years old at the end of it, she is in a sense a
remarkably passive adolescent throughout most
of the book--that is, until the last thirty
pages. The novel's title appears in the
text only once--as a loose translation of the
legal Latin term *nolle contendere*--but it is
implied throughout, as Elena subjects herself
respectively to her famous and glamorous mother,
to her drunken and vengeful father, to her
wealthy and almost omniscient but unfeeling
husband, and to her idealistic and ingenious
lover. Her awakening comes as a result of
her contact with the intellectual but essentially passive revolutionist Meredith Dawe.
She realizes the futility of the passive life,
and she takes aggressive steps to control her
own destiny.

345.    Oates, Joyce Carol. *A Garden of Earthly
        Delights*. New York: Vanguard Press, 1967,
        440pp.

Oates here presents a stark but understanding
portrayal of how frustrated love and the im-
personal forces of a hostile environment combine
to turn a dreamy adolescent girl into a shallow,
scheming woman with no values to give her son.
At thirteen, Clara Walpole, the daughter of a
poor migrant worker, escapes her bleak life
by running away with an emotionally unstable
man named Lowry. The one love of her life be-
sides her father, Lowry abandons her when she
is pregnant at seventeen, and Clara must find
a protector for herself and her unborn child.
Seducing a wealthy landowner named Revere, Clara
convinces him that the child is his, accepts
a role as his mistress, and eventually marries
him upon the death of his wife. Clara's son
Swan, intended to be her object of revenge on
the world, is too sensitive to share in his
mother's life of hatred, duplicity, and false
emotion. At the age of twenty, Swan becomes
Clara's source of punishment instead, as he
kills himself and his stepfather, leaving
Clara at forty-five to live out the rest of her
life watching the shallow images on a television
screen and never realizing the kind of monster
she has become.

346. Oates, Joyce Carol. *Son of the Morning*. New
York: Vanguard Press, 1978. 382pp.

At fifteen, the innocent, virginal, and
slightly vapid Elsa Vickery is gang-raped,
ironically as she returns one evening from
the country church. Consequently, Elsa becomes
pregnant with Nathan (the name means "gift of
God"), a Christ-figure and the protagonist,
whose sharp awareness of God's presence and
radiating light becomes the central focus of
both his life and the novel. Later, a distraction threatens Nathan's devotion to God in
the form of twenty-year-old Esther Leonie
Beloff, a playful flirt who is, nonetheless, a
virginal temptress. During a picnic, Nathan
becomes nearly mindless in his desire for her
which she encourages and then checks. As a
result, Nathan afterwards blinds his left eye
in church as an act of humiliation, signaling
his reunion with God's purpose and vision and
light.

347. Oates, Joyce Carol. *them*. New York: Vanguard
     Press, 1969. 508pp.

     This thirty-year chronicle (1937-1967) of
     the family relationship of Loretta Wendall
     and her children Jules and Maureen (based upon
     a real family) is Oates' comment on the psycho-
     logical damage that poverty can cause in the
     emotional and moral structure of people's lives.
     Although Loretta is depicted from age seventeen
     to forty-six, it is fifteen-year-old Maureen
     who is the novel's major protagonist. Beaten
     down by the everyday violence and despair that
     punctuates her life in the Detroit slums, Maureen
     is the only family member who seriously fights
     back against the "them" that is represented by
     her family and the impersonal forces of nature.
     Deciding that she needs money to escape, Maureen
     becomes a prostitute and is severely beaten by
     her stepfather when he discovers her plan. Laps-
     ing into a catatonic state for over a year,
     Maureen recovers to move away from home, find
     a job, and enroll in night school where she meets
     and traps the drab married college professor
     who ultimately becomes her husband. Although
     hers is perhaps a hollow victory, Maureen is
     a survivor in a world where even the most pur-
     poseful lives seem to go astray.

348. Oates, Joyce Carol. *Unholy Loves*. New York:
     Vanguard Press, 1979. 335pp.

     Kim, a nineteen-year-old college student, makes
     a brief, but significant appearance midway
     through *Unholy Loves*. The character of Kim
     functions as a foil to that of the protagonist,
     Brigit Stott, who as an eighteen-year-old
     attending Smith, was shocked and offended by
     the sensual poem "Lovesounds," by St. Dennis.
     Conversely, Kim also serves as an ironic parallel
     for the adult Brigit, who at thirty-eight is
     likewise experiencing "apparently insurmountable
     problems" involving family conflicts, a love
     affair full of turmoil, and the alienating
     effects of ambition--all combining with such
     force that Brigit often toys with the notion
     of suicide. (On still another level, Kim is
     a symbolic daughter for Brigit.) Of great

importance, then, to comprehension of the
personality of Brigit is the role played by
Kim, who activates key memories in Brigit.
We conclude that Brigit's unwillingness to
maintain ties with the past stems from her
fear that to do so would be to surrender her soul
or identity, an act equivalent to committing
a form of suicide.

349.  Oates, Joyce Carol. *With Shuddering Fall*.   New
       York: Vanguard Press, 1964.   316pp.

A novelist of adult themes often represented
in the fears and frustrations of adolescent
characters, Oates here presents a detailed
study of alienation and love in family relationships.  At seventeen, Karen Herz wants someone, preferably her god-like father, to give
her the love and security that are so important
to adolescents.  Failing to receive this, she
finds her escape in the company of Shar, a sexually attractive but violent race car driver,
who has tried to rape her shortly after their
first meeting.  Karen's decision to run away
with him is an attempt to be worthy of her
father's love after he has falsely assumed her
complicity in sin with Shar.  The price of her
forgiveness being to kill this man, Karen follows Shar and endures with numbing resignation
rape, brutal lovemaking, and miscarriage.  Eventually she triggers Shar's suicide by denying
her love for him, a cold-hearted act from which
Karen temporarily finds refuge in madness but
which ultimately results in the love and forgiveness from her father that she has so eagerly
sought.

350.  Oates, Joyce Carol. *Wonderland*.   New York:
       Vanguard Press, 1971.   512pp.

Although Oates focuses her story on a pene-
trating exploration of the mind of Jesse Harte
(Vogel), a boy who grows to manhood haunted by
a violent act in his childhood, she offers in
a later part of the novel a particularly important characterization of his adolescent daughter,
Shelley.  As the only survivor of his father's
Christmas-day massacre of his family, Jesse
at fourteen begins a life-long search for an

orderly world, love, and the family unit that
was taken so violently from him.  The disturbing
forces in his own nature unleashed by this
incident surface again years later in his relationship with his teenaged daughter.  Unable
to escape the past, Jesse becomes an absent,
brooding father so that his child must endure
the same "fatherless" adolescence that he has
known.  The third and final chapter of the
novel is a poignant account of Shelley Vogel's
growing alienation from her father, her escape
into the drug culture, and Jesse's last desperate
attempts to save her.

351.  O'Brien, Robert C.  *A Report From Group 17*.
      New York: Atheneum, 1972.  210pp.

      Allison, aged twelve, provides the axis
around which this suspense novel rotates.  Drawn
by her youthful curiosity and her love of
animals, Allison becomes entangled in a web of
international intrigue dealing with chemical
warfare (Group 17 refers to chemical research
reports).  When she is captured and drugged by
enemy agents, Allison triggers the solution of
the mystery.

352.  O'Brien, Robert C.  *Z for Zachariah*.  New York:
      Atheneum, 1975.  249pp.

      Ann Burden, a sixteen-year-old farm girl,
believes she is the only survivor of a nuclear
war.  The story is told in the form of Ann's
diary and reveals many of her thoughts as she
prepares for her future alone.  When John Loomis,
another survivor, appears, Ann has many decisions
to make, and again her strength to survive
overcomes all obstacles.

353.  O'Dell, Scott.  *Sing Down the Moon*.  Boston:
      Houghton Mifflin, 1970.  137pp.

      Based on the years 1863-1865 in the history
of the Navaho Indians, this novel tells the
plight of one tribe routed from their homeland
to Fort Sumner by white men.  Fourteen-year-old
Bright Morning narrates the sad tale in which
she is sold into slavery by Spaniards and escapes to witness the physical and mental deterioration of her family and fellow tribe members.

354. Offit, Sidney. *What Kind of Guy Do You Think
     I Am?* Philadelphia: J.B. Lippincott Company,
     1977. 160pp.

    This novel traces the growing relationship
between Ted, an eighteen-year-old summering
in Southampton, Long Island, and Hilary Mosco-
witz, a twenty-year-old Princeton astro-physics
major who is bitter over her parents' decision
to stop paying her tuition. From their accidental meeting on the beach to their decision to
live together, they feel the pull of opposites.
Hilary is academically ambitious; Ted is content
working as a short-order cook in an all-night
diner. Hilary is sexually aggressive and experienced; Ted feels sexually inadequate and
insecure. Ted's decision to support Hilary so
that she may continue at Princeton concludes
this character study of two young people who,
different as they are, find they are stronger
and more complete together.

355. Ogburn, Charlton. *Winespring Mountain.* New
     York: William Morrow & Co., Inc., 1973. 252pp.

    Ogburn, an author who incorporates environ-
mental themes into his novels, here addresses
the subject of strip-mining. High school
graduate Wick Carter, son of a coal company
president, is sent to Harpersburg, West Virginia, to learn the business. While exploring
the lovely Appalachian countryside, he meets
Letty Sherrod, a beautiful seventeen-year-old
girl whose family lives on a farm at the base
of Winespring Mountain. Although blind, Letty
opens Wick's eyes to the natural wonders that
surround them, and their friendship develops
into a strong love for each other and their
mountain. When the coal company threatens
to strip-mine Winespring, Wick works to preserve
the land that has supported local families and
traditions for generations. The author demonstrates that a balance between using and pre-
serving the land can be achieved.

356. Ogilvie, Elisabeth. *Becky's Island.* New York:
     McGraw-Hill, 1961. 187pp.

    Contrasting with Ogilvie's description of

seventeen-year-old Vicky's privileged summers
in Maine in the early 1900s is the story of
the inhabitants of Becky's Island.  Vicky
is slowly drawn to help the illiterate, outcast
children of the island, hiding her visits from
her relatives and battling the island's self-
proclaimed king.  After she finally reveals
her project in order to secure donations for
a school building, Vicky must struggle to release "her" children to a proper teacher and
her Maine summers to childhood memories.

357. Olsen, Paul.  *Country of Old Men*.  New York:
      Holt, Rinehart and Winston, Inc., 1966.  248pp.

     Lack of communication between young and old
is the major theme of *Country of Old Men*, in
which we discover three young-old men leading
their tangled lives in a small New England
town in 1933.  All three have shameful secrets
in their lives, but two wear an aura of respectability whereas the third is unashamedly a
rebel.  It is not until Matthew, the son of the
rebel, becomes emotionally involved with pretty
Martha Nowell, the seventeen-year-old daughter
of Cass Nowell, one of the respectable members
of the trio, that the underlying violence reaches
its climax.  Martha, the apple of her father's
eye, becomes enamored of the less-than-genteel
Matthew, and repeatedly gives herself to him
without real love or pleasure.  The love-hate
relationships among the characters finally
reach the breaking point, and Matthew, a "born
victim," must pay the price for the follies of
his elders.  Martha, saddened by guilt, is
suddenly older and wiser, and faces her future
with understanding instead of indifference.

358. Osterman, Marjorie K.  *Damned If You Do--Damned
      If You Don't*.  Philadelphia: Chilton Company,
      1962.  397pp.

     In this saga of Meyer Simon, a Jewish immi-
grant, and his descendants, all of the women
must measure themselves against the ideals of
Jewish womanhood and the stereotypes of the
adolescent Jewish princess and the Yiddish mama.
Even the Gentiles find that, where their relationships with Jewish men are concerned, they,

too, must confront the Jewish experience. In
this novel, Osterman follows the lives of six
women from their youth into their womanhood.

359. Pangborn, Edgar. *The Trial of Callista Blake*.
     New York: St. Martin's Press, 1961. 304pp.

At nineteen, Callista Blake encounters both
a criminal trial and an inner trial which is
based on her sensitivity to justice, her ability
to love, and her need to find honesty in her
relationships. The novel recaptures the four
days in which Callista is on trial as a mur-
deress. The hearing itself serves only to
develop her character as it is interpreted by
three people other than Callista: the presiding
judge, her lawyer, and her employer-friend.
These people attempt to unravel Callista's
perplexing personality traits and to demonstrate
the impact she has had on all those involved in
her life. A letter from the judge not only
concludes the novel but also adds the final
touches to the portrait of this profoundly
perceptive yet misunderstood young woman.

360. Parker, Robert B. *The Godwulf Manuscript*.
     Boston: Houghton Mifflin Company, 1973. 186pp.

Terry Orchard, twenty-year-old university
student, is secretary of a radical student
organization and is the first person Boston
Private Investigator Spenser talks to in his
investigation into the theft of the university's
invaluable fourteenth-century Godwulf Manuscript.
Terry is attractive, bright, vulnerable, and
gullible. When Terry's lover is murdered,
Terry calls Spenser and thus involves him
in her defense. Spenser is the only adult Terry
feels she can trust. She becomes enamored of
him but manages eventually to overcome her
feelings and begins to come to terms with her
less than perfect parents.

361. Patterson, Mary. *The Iron Country*. Boston:
     Houghton Mifflin Company, 1966. 403pp.

One year (1943-4) brings torment, excitement,
confusion, and joy to seventeen-year-old
Maxine Johnson. Although the central themes

of the cruelty as well as the beauty of
both death and love are intertwined through
several characters, it is through Maxine and
her best friend John that the story evolves.
Maxine, beginning her senior year of high
school at the opening of the novel, finds
answers to her inquiries concerning mortality
and love after the murder of the local priest,
the burning of the church, the drafting of
fellow students, and most importantly the
death of her father and her own first experiences
with love. A strong character, Maxine combines
youthful inquisitiveness with the sagacity of
a much older person.

362. Peck, Richard. *Are You in the House Alone?*
     New York: The Viking Press, 1976. 156pp.

     Gail Osbourne, pretty and popular, first
feels herself being watched and then is terror-
ized by threatening notes and telephone calls.
While she is babysitting, a classmate, a boy
from a prominent family and the boyfriend, she
thinks, of her best friend, forces his way in
and rapes her. The novel depicts first her
increasing fears and then her recovery from
the rape.

363. Peck, Richard. *Close Enough to Touch.* New
     York: Delacorte Press, 1981. 133pp.

     A middle-class tenth grader, Matt had pledged
his never-dying love for Dory last summer,
and now he is to be pallbearer at her funeral.
Told to put Dory out of his mind, Matt is thus
denied the chance to grieve, so he develops
a plan of escape, a spring "sabbatical" at the
family's summer cabin from which he does not
intend to return. At the cabin, Matt chances
upon and becomes the rescuer of a girl much
different from Dory: Margaret Chosen, who has
an unusual hobby, who has a thriving business
at the Saturday flea market, and who has survived the breakup of her parents' marriage and
the remarriage of her father--in short, a girl
so interesting that Matt is slowly pulled back
into the mainstream of life. A vibrant
teenager, Margaret is presented mainly through
dialogue, but the story itself deals with

several issues relevant to teenagers: step-
parents, half brothers/sisters, social class
(or clique), and the death of a loved one.

364. Peck, Richard. *Don't Look and It Won't Hurt.*
New York: Holt, Rinehart and Winston, 1972.
173pp.

Fifteen-year-old Carol Patterson has grown
up under less than ideal circumstances. She
and her two sisters are raised by a mother who
works nights as a restaurant hostess; their
father is a stranger who is never allowed to
communicate with them; material comforts are
rare. Despite her drab environment, Carol
emerges as a strong character who provides
security for younger sister Liz and aids older
sister Ellen in planning for a better future.
Peck has created a resilient and resourceful
adolescent figure in this first novel.

365. Percy, Walker. *The Last Gentleman.* New York:
Farrar, Straus, Giroux, 1966. 409pp.

Kitty Vaught, who turns twenty-one early
in the novel, is an incidental character in
*The Last Gentleman* as the girlfriend of Will
Barrett, the protagonist. Barrett is a truth-
seeker, one of Percy's "wayfarers." Kitty is
something he stumbles upon in his search. Percy
presents her as a typically modern, upper-middle-
class Southern girl whose ambitions include
becoming a Chi Omega and a college cheerleader
before acquiring a prosperous husband and a GE
all-electric home in the suburbs. Although
Barrett proposes to Kitty soon after they meet
and goes house-hunting with her as a distraction,
at the end of the novel he has not married her.
Percy reprises her as Kitty Vaught Huger for
*The Second Coming.*

366. Percy, Walker. *The Second Coming.* New York:
Farrar, Straus, Giroux, 1980. 360pp.

The story of young and vulnerable Allison
Huger is told in alternate chapters in the
first part of *The Second Coming;* thereafter,
her destiny becomes entwined with that of a
middle-aged man, Will Barrett, and their stories
merge in the narration. Allison is committed

to a private hospital where she is subjected
to electroshock therapy, and as a result, her
memeory is cloudy, her speech sometimes in-
coherent. Percy conveys her communications
in bizarre, original language. She escapes
from the hospital and settles down in a green-
house on property she has inherited. She
then proves, with some help from Barrett, that
she can function and survive.

367. Perrin, Ursula. *Ghosts*. New York: Alfred A.
     Knopf, Inc., 1967. 253pp.

During the 1940s, Eleanor Munson, the protagonist and narrator, experiences the trials
of adolescence in a small mill town. After her
brother's death and her sister's enforced
wedding, Eleanor is left alone with her parents.
Dr. Munson's practice has begun to fail, and
Mrs. Munson's dissatisfaction with marriage
leads her to encourage Eleanor's career aspirations. As Eleanor recognizes the limitations
of small-town life and the roles of those
women who marry and remain in Clifton, she
resolves not to become another of these "ghosts"
and rejects her first lover, choosing instead
to attend a university. She looks back from
adulthood in an attempt to understand her own
decision.

368. Perutz, Kathrin. *The Garden*. New York: Athene-
     um, 1962. 185pp.

Kathy (the narrator), her best friend The
Blossom, and a number of other students at a
prestigious woman's institution in Massachusetts
are depicted in this study of college life.
The relatively plotless novel examines an obsessive (perhaps lesbian) friendship between
Kathy and The Blossom (whom she sometimes
refers to as "my darling" or "my baby") as well
as the heterosexual experiences of both central
characters. Beginning with Kathy's discovery
of the death by suicide of her roommate and
closing with her triumphant yet anti-climactic
loss of her virginity, the novel (written when
its author was only twenty-one) analyzes
college life and students in the 1960s.

369. Perutz, Kathrin. *A House on the Sound*. New
      York: Coward-McCann, Inc., 1965. 213pp.

   A dinner party given by Monika (Nickie) Horn-
   bury and her publisher father gives this novel
   its substance and form. Nickie, a bright
   Barnard college senior, seems largely concerned
   with her own (and others') sexual activities.
   Worth mention also is Delia, the black maid
   who is apparently about Nickie's age and who
   is characterized through dialect and her
   views of her employers and their guests. The
   novel shifts among the points of view of its
   characters, thus revealing their varied backgrounds and feelings. All are shown as shallow
   and lacking in warmth or affection.

370. Pfeffer, Susan Beth. *About David*. New York:
      Delacorte Press, 1980. 167pp.

   *About David* is the journal that seventeen-
   year-old Lynn keeps during the months after
   David, her oldest friend, kills his parents
   and himself. As she progresses through her
   grief and anger with the help of friends,
   family, and a psychologist, Lynn reveals clear
   and positive pictures of herself and her classmates. Beyond the discussion of the tragedy
   and its reasons, the journal focuses on the
   far-reaching effects that one's actions have
   on others.

371. Philips, Judson. *The Twisted People*. New
      York: Dodd, Mead & Co., 1965. 212pp.

   Peter Styles, reporter/detective and hero
   of a series of mystery novels, travels to
   Connecticut in search of the sort of "twisted
   people" who were responsible for a terribly
   destructive accident he was the victim of.
   In Connecticut, he finds a tangle of amorality,
   ruthlessness, and corruption among the family
   of Sam Delafield, an industrial magnate. Sam's
   daughter-in-law Sandra is only twenty, but
   has been prematurely disillusioned by a forced
   marriage to a man who doesn't love her. A
   public sexpot who is secretly chaste, Sandra
   shows, at the end of the novel, a desire to
   "untwist" herself, leave her husband to the
   woman he loves, and straighten out her life.

372. Piercy, Marge. *Dance the Eagle to Sleep*.
     New York: Doubleday & Company, Inc., 1970.
     232pp.

     Named one of *Time's* ten best novels of 1971,
     this book takes a close look at the violent
     lives of adolescent revolutionaries. The
     novel concentrates, in part, on the lives
     of two teenagers, Joanna and Ginny, and how
     they come to realize how little power they
     have been allowed, or have allowed themselves,
     in their counter-culture life. The central
     female characters represent the major alter-
     natives: to join society and become plastic
     or to accept a flawed humanity and continue
     to work for a better future. Joanna is captured,
     given electroshock and insulin therapy, and
     she comes to accept the views of her torturers
     so completely that she tries to get the surviving
     members of her commune to surrender. Ginny,
     pregnant, emotionally hurt, remains with the
     commune, and, surrendering to love, allows the
     two remaining members of the group to co-mother
     her child. Through her own and the child's
     survival, she offers them all a life which
     makes no promises to be wise or just, but
     which does promise, while there are striving
     people, not to surrender.

373. Piercy, Marge. *Vida*. New York: Simon & Schus-
     ter, 1979. 479pp.

     Vida Asch, a woman with once-flaming red hair
     now dyed brown, a charismatic, passionate
     activist, is now forced into hiding, having
     learned to lie, to distrust everyone, to
     move between false identities. The Network
     she has helped to form is depressed and filled
     with infighting, her second marriage cannot
     survive her underground life, and Vida is
     attempting to form a new one for herself.
     Through the use of flashbacks, Vida returns
     to earlier days. Her early relationship to
     her stepsister, Natalie (their political
     bond makes them closer than any blood bond
     could), plays a particularly important role
     in this novel. Glimpses of a younger Vida,
     hard and bright, wanting electricity and some
     faint danger and learning to mistrust what

commands her love (particularly what triggers
her sexuality), blend well with the changes
in the sixties' social movement from peaceful
demonstrations and organization to violence
and bombings.  For Vida, in hiding, the past
is still more real than the present, and her
progress from innocence to experience, from
adolescence to adulthood forms the novel.

374. Pilcer, Sonia.  *Teen Angel*.  New York: Coward,
     McCann & Geoghegan, 1978.  262pp.

     This novel provides a humorous account of
growing up in New York City during the early
sixties.  Using explicit language, Sonny
Palovsky, almost fifteen, deals with an abundance
of adolescent problems--ranging from breast
development to new feelings of sexuality.
Inducted into a celebrated teen gang, Sonny
hopes to make sense out of her confusion about
puberty.  Unlike the other gang members, Sonny
has parents who love her, is in advanced school
classes, and has an innate sense of responsibility.  Although she goes steady and is accepted
as a worthy gang leader, Sonny realizes how
trivial these achievements are and in fact
begins to grow up.

375. Pitkin, Dorothy.  *Sea Change*.  New York: Pantheon
     Book, Inc., 1964.  250pp.

     Vicky Harbison and her family return to
their cottage on the ocean, as they have each
summer.  This summer as she turns sixteen,
Vicky grows from a child to a mature young
woman, loses weight, gains self-confidence,
decides on a career as a marine biologist, and
learns about love.  Vicky follows the basic
romantic pattern of a confused teenager emerging
into the adult world, meeting challenges and
coping with them.  She eventually rises above
difficulties as she becomes a self-assured
person ready for a more sophisticated life.

376. Plath, Sylvia.  *The Bell Jar*.  First pub. (Lon-
     don, England: Heinemann, 1963) under pseud.
     Victoria Lucas.  First Am. ed. pub. anon. in
     New York: Harper & Row, 1971.  First Am. ed.
     pub. under name Sylvia Plath in New York:

Harper & Row, 1973.  275pp.

The experiences of nineteen-year-old Esther
Greenwood--beginning with her month in New York
as one of twelve undergraduate winners of a
fashion-magazine contest and ending with her
gradual recovery from a suicide attempt followed
by a prolonged mental illness--are slightly
fictionalized accounts of Plath's own experiences at the same age.  In a mental hospital, she feels as if she were living under
a bell jar.  In addition, Esther faces the usual
adolescent problems of friction with a parent
(her mother), choice of a profession (writing
and/or editing), plans for continuing her education, experimentation with various life styles,
and introduction to sex.  For a sensitive individual like Esther, even the usual problems
can lead to unusual experiences.

377.  Ponicsan, Darryl. *Andoshen, Pa.*  New York:
      The Dial Press, 1973.  281pp.

Andoshen, Pa., a coal country town, is a
world of both material poverty and great spiritual vigor.  The ethnic Americans of Andoshen live
a life full of excitement, humor, and danger,
which they discuss in a language rich in
pungent idiom, and quite capable of defining
philosophical issues and moral heroism.  Young
Estelle is one of a series of characters
whose lives take crucial turns in the course
of the novel.  Estelle asks herself "What can
I accomplish in this world?"  With no special
resources of talent or competence, Estelle
succeeds in changing her life for the better
through marriage to a man of similar spiritual
ambition.

378.  Portis, Charles. *True Grit.*  New York: Simon
      & Schuster, 1968.  215pp.

Looking back over a long life, Mattie Ross
gives us a first-person account of the time,
some years after the Civil War, when she was
fourteen and tracked down the murderer of
her father.  Dragooned into riding with Mattie
were Rooster Cogburn (a U.S. Marshall) and a
Texas Ranger named LaBeouf.  There is action,

violence, and some sorrow in the novel, but
central are the characterizations of the
decided, forthright Mattie and of Rooster
Cogburn, the man with true grit.

379. Poverman, C.E.  *Solomon's Daughter*.  New York:
      Viking Press, 1981.  268pp.

      Dr. Joseph Solomon has tried to be a good
      and wise parent and yet his daughter, Rose,
      is exceedingly demanding and selfish.  After
      a near-fatal car accident, the adult Rose,
      unable to take care of herself, is again living
      in her parents' home.  In flashbacks we see
      the adolescent Rose in high school--willful,
      strong-minded, selfish, talented, and very
      ashamed of being Jewish.  She cannot get along
      with her mother, and she never tries to re-
      concile their differences.  While Rose has
      matured physically and functioned in the world
      as an adult, she has never really outgrown
      some undesirable adolescent characteristics,
      and her adulthood reflects these attitudes.

380. Price, Nancy.  *An Accomplished Woman*.  New
      York: Coward, McCann & Geoghegan, 1979.  288pp.

      Catherine Buckingham has been raised from
      infancy by Thorn Wade, a young scientist who
      had loved Catherine's mother.  Following her
      mother's wishes with scrupulous care, Thorn
      encourages Catherine to follow her curiosities,
      take care of herself, know and respect her
      own feelings.  Having capped this education with
      a brief love affair, Thorn leaves her to the
      life of an American woman in the 1940s.  Like
      the grid of suburban streets that engulfs the
      isolated house she was raised in, the iron
      pattern of society's expectations slowly
      transmogrifies Catherine.  She becomes "an
      accomplished woman": a person of infinitely
      faceted surface and no core, living in "any
      town of buildings no one like her has built."
      Wade's experiment in non-sexist nurture has
      failed.

381. Price, Nancy.  *A Natural Death*.  Boston: Little,
      Brown, 1973.  376pp.

This poetic evocation of South Carolina
slave society renders the textures of life in
1850.  In examining the moral damage done to
both parties in a slave-holding society, it
focuses on the lives of seventeen-year-old
"Buck" Algrew, who comes as a bride to her
husband's plantation, and fifteen-year-old Joan
King who comes, also a bride, to Abbotsford
as a slave. Both young wives compromise their
best principles.  Buck finds that her power
to do good depends on staying afloat in a
sea of lies, and Joan finds that she must give
at least tacit consent to the Abbotsford system to survive at all.  The portraits of these
two young women, and of Joan's husband Will,
are the heart of this study.

382. Price, Reynolds. *A Generous Man.* New York:
     Atheneum, 1966.  275pp.

Lois Provo is sixteen and traveling with her
aunt's carnival snake show when they become
involved with the Mustian family in rural
North Carolina.  On an intense weekend hunt for
Rato Mustian, his supposedly rabid dog, and the
Provos' Indian python snake, Lois and her
aunt stay with the Mustians and make new dis-
coveries about themselves and each other.  Lois
learns that her aunt is really her mother and
that the stories she has been told all her
life about her parents are lies.  Lois fore-
tells the future of memebers of the Mustian
family and others in the community.

383. Price, Reynolds. *A Long and Happy Life.* New
     York: Atheneum, 1962.  195pp.

During four or five months in the late adolescence of Rosacoke Mustian, in rural North
Carolina, the universal human elements of birth,
death, love, faith, and loyalty take on intense personal meaning.  Unable to win a proposal or even a declaration of love from Wesley
Beavers, whom she has loved for eight years
and dated steadily for three, Rosacoke tries
to hold him by giving the one thing he seems
to want most from her.  Finding herself pregnant and seeing how parenthood can bring
grief to friends and relatives of her own age,

she cannot at first bring herself to tell him
of his new responsibility. When she does tell
him and he promptly proposes an elopement, her
immediate impulse is to reject him. But as
they play their respective roles in the church
Nativity pageant, she suddenly realizes that
she will accept him and will find what happiness
she can in the role ordained by her faith and
her society.

384. Price, Reynolds. *The Surface of Earth*. New
     York: Atheneum, 1975. 491pp.

     Sixteen-year-old Eva Kendal elopes with her
Latin teacher, Forrest Mayfield, who is twice
her age, but she is too immature for the
commitments and responsibilities of a wife.
Cut off from her family in North Carolina,
Eva unhappily awaits the birth of their baby
and begins to doubt that she can be everything
Forrest expects. After her mother commits
suicide, Eva returns home for a visit, hoping
to comfort her family. A letter left by her
mother makes her feel responsible for her
mother's death. As her visit is prolonged by
the illness of her son, Eva is torn between
Forrest and her family. Her father influences
her to remain with them and she never returns
to live with Forrest.

385. Price, William. *The Potlatch Run*. New York:
     E.P. Dutton, 1971. 264pp.

     This darkly picaresque novel focuses on the
lives of three young men, Cleve Timentwa,
a deracinated American Indian, Colin Barnhover,
a psychopath, and Cleve's slow-witted but
gentle friend, Babe. As Colin drives west to
escape the police, he picks up Cleve, who has
gone AWOL from the army, and they have futile,
sometimes brutal, adventures. Several young
girls figure in their lives: Cleve's teenaged sister Fawn, bright and beautiful; twelve-
year-old Echo, whose father Colin murders;
Angela, a waitress who narrowly escapes Colin's
"love"; and Sarah, a WASP college student who
attracts Cleve. The girls are not rendered
as full-length portraits, but rather as they
are perceived by Colin and Cleve--sometimes

as the center of rosy, unrealistic fantasies,
sometimes as objects of indifference or
hostility.

386. Prokosch, Frederic. *The Seven Sisters*. New
    York: Farrar, Straus & Cudahy, 1962.  405pp.

   This moral fable follows the lives of the seven
privileged Nightingale sisters of Bishop's
Neck, Maryland, from their adolescence to their
bizarre fates.  Against vivid backgrounds in
America and Europe, each sister tries to explore her own nature or find her place in the
world.  They variously devote themselves to
passion, art, mysticism, beauty, or love.  Four
of them find that their lives will have meaning
only if they make a moral commitment, and
three must make that commitment to their own
oddly constituted natures.

387. Rabe, Berniece. *The Girl Who Had No Name*.
    New York: E.P. Dutton, 1977.  149pp.

   Girlie Webster is almost thirteen when her
mother dies.  She notices everyone is whispering
around her and giving her furtive looks.  The
youngest of ten sisters, she cannot understand
why her father, who said when she was born that
he could think of no more female names, does
not want her with him anymore.  As Girlie
moves about Missouri, from the home of one
married sister to another, she becomes determined
to solve the mystery of her father's behavior.
In spite of many unhappy situations in the
homes of her sisters, Girlie never loses her
own sense of self-worth.  She remains invincible
each time she returns to her father and is
sent away again, until eventually she opens a
way for him to accept her.

388. Rader, Paul. *Professor Wilmess Must Die*.  New
    York: The Dial Press, 1969.  218pp.

   In this satire of 1960s campus unrest, freshman Susan Rapture, an amoral bubblehead, is
given a key role in the mayhem by her insane
lover.  Prof. Wilmess' daughter Helen is a
portrait of more typical adolescent honesty
and perceptiveness.

389. Randall, Florence Engel. *The Almost Year*.
     New York: Atheneum, 1971. 239pp.

     Can racial tensions added onto the frustrations
     of teen years create a malevolent force strong
     enough to endanger a household? Or can hatred
     alone cause the frightening and eerie happenings
     that occur when an adolescent black female
     spends a school year with an affluent white
     family? Randall's first-person narrative
     offers insight into veiled resentments and
     a struggle for peace and mutual understanding
     among human beings.

390. Raucher, Herman. *A Glimpse of Tiger*. New York:
     G.P. Putnam's Sons, 1971. 222pp.

     This cautionary tale is a deceptively effer-
     vescent character study of two "drop-outs"
     from straight society. Luther, who has con-
     siderable talent for acting, petty graft, and
     mischief, makes their living by a series of
     minor hustles. "Tiger," nineteen-year-old
     Janice McAllister, has dropped out of college
     under the accumulated pressures of a conformity
     she finds meaningless and maddening. Life with
     Luther has imagination, verve, love, satisfying
     sex, and absolutely no future. When Tiger
     leaves him, she unbalances his delicately
     poised sanity and dies for her mistake.

391. Raucher, Herman. *Summer of '42*. New York:
     G.P. Putnam's Sons, 1971. 251pp.

     Herman Raucher nostalgically describes with
     humor, sentiment, and affection the summer of
     1942, when three fifteen-year-old pals from
     Brooklyn--dreamy and poetic Hermie, athletic
     and enterprising Oscy, and clumsy but devoted
     Benjie--long for sexual experience and wonder
     if the war will last until they reach draft
     age. Oscy arranges dates with three girls
     who are slightly older and considerably more
     mature than the boys. Unattractive Gloria
     unselfishly departs after Benjie has abruptly
     made it clear that he cannot face her bracework.
     Big-breasted Miriam, after a brief show of
     self-defense, not only coöperates with Oscy
     but encourages him to the point of exhaustion.
     Half-pretty and more-than-half-willing Aggie

is frustrated by Hermie's ineptness; though
he is eager for sex, he finds himself unable
to experiment with Aggie because he loves
an older woman whose husband is serving in
the war.

392. Read, Piers Paul. *The Professor's Daughter*.
     Philadelphia: J.B. Lippincott Co., 1971.
     276pp.

     The professor is a wealthy teacher of
     political theory at Harvard. His daughter
     has a fairly uneventful adolescence until she
     accompanies her father on a European and
     African trip. They both are made aware of
     her maturity and become increasingly uneasy
     with one another. She leaves for college in
     Berkeley in 1966, and when she returns home
     little more than a year later, she has been
     married, has had an abortion, and is under
     psychiatric care for her sexual preoccupation,
     which leads to a suicide attempt. She joins
     several of her father's students in a plot
     for revolution, a plan which he is ready to
     finance. The budding revolution comes to
     a quick end when the professor is killed by
     one of the conspirators.

393. Rechy, John. *The Fourth Angel*. London, New
     York: W.H. Allen, 1972. 158pp.

     Four Texas teenagers spend several days in
     an orgy of drugs and sex. The spiritual
     and financial leader of the group is Shell, its
     only female. She wants to "get inside people's
     heads" and has been hardened against tears
     since her father raped her at age eleven.

394. Reed, Kit. *At War As Children*. New York:
     Farrar Straus, 1964. 278pp.

     At a major crossroad in her life, Denise
     McLeod, twenty-four, retraces her fondest
     memories and friendships back to their roots
     in her childhood. Throughout the novel, Denise
     explores these important relationships and
     incidents so as to judge their validity and
     their influence on her present values and
     position in life, particularly her lifelong
     dedication to the church.

395. Reed, Kit. *The Better Part*. New York:
     Farrar, Straus and Giroux, 1967. 208pp.

     Teenaged Martha Ewald has lived her entire
     life in a large girls' correctional institution
     run by her father. Isolated from the outside
     world and isolated within by her father's
     preoccupation with dedication to helping the
     girls, Martha is frustrated and desperate;
     she feels that her father's work is useless
     and that the girls will leave the institution
     only to return to their former lives. In an
     attempt to free herself, Martha helps an
     inmate named Marie escape and enters a night-
     marish adventure. Finally, Martha returns to
     the institution with a new understanding of
     her father's work.

396. Reed, Meredith. *Our Year Began in April*.
     New York: Lothrop, Lee and Shepard Company,
     1963. 221pp.

     Waiting anxiously for Papa's return from
     Conference is an annual event for the Suther-
     lands. Yes, they have missed him, but they
     want to know if the bishop has said they are
     to move to another Methodist Church. Short
     of funds, the family has faith and supportive-
     ness to carry them through. Linda, the oldest
     and least aggressive of the three children,
     has a beautiful singing voice which the family
     encourages her to use for others to enjoy
     and to overcome her shyness.

397. Reeve, F.D. *The Brother*. New York: Farrar,
     Straus & Giroux, 1971. 307pp.

     David Spencer, who is nine when the novel
     opens, and his older brother Will, are sons
     of a WASP family whose internal problems are
     seen as a reflection of American society in
     the late 1950s. The Spencers have high
     expectations for their sons and a near-total
     incapacity for warmth or support. In an
     attempt to escape this barren emotional land-
     scape, Will marries Edie, a talented young
     dancer at the beginning of her career, and
     David dates his warm and perceptive high
     school classmate Susan. Neither woman can
     heal the wounds left by an ungiving, hypo-

critical family, and each, unlike her male
counterpart, goes on to take control of her
own public and private lives.

398. Richardson, Anne. *Digging Out*. New York:
     McGraw-Hill, 1966. 181pp.

     Laura Smith, the heroine of this novel, inter-
     rupts her graduate work in history to help
     care for her dying mother. During this time,
     she maturely analyzes Jewish life in America
     and her own place (or lack of place) in it.
     Laura recounts the life stories of the rest
     of her family, giving significantly more
     space to the adolescence and development of her
     male relatives than of her female ones, whose
     only important goal in life is marriage.

399. Richardson, Vokes. *Not All Our Pride*. New
     York: Braziller, 1965. 276pp.

     Although this novel is set in east Tennessee
     in the 1930s, it reflects plantation life
     of the old South. Surrounded by all sorts of
     kin who are still fighting the Yankees, young
     cousins Julie and Hugh grow up together. The
     family assumes they will eventually marry and
     assure the continuity of the line but is
     scandalized when they become lovers at ages
     fourteen and sixteen, respectively. Julie
     is the secondary character, physically mature
     but still a child, a strong-willed tomboy
     who is devoted to her dissipated, aesthetic
     father and the household servants.

400. Richert, William. *Aren't You Even Gonna Kiss
     Me Good-By?* New York: D. McKay Co., 1966.
     247pp.

     Among the characters cavorting through
     Richert's comic and slightly ribald tale of
     twenty-four hours in the life of Jimmy Rearden
     is Suzie Middleburg, who participates in her
     high school friend's wild schemes to raise
     quick money. In fact, Suzie, daughter of
     the Chief Justice of the Illinois State Supreme
     Court, could have been Jimmy's *best* buddy
     had she not made romantic overtures one wintry
     day. This duo complement each other as they

adventure in and around Chicago, for as adroit
as Jimmy is at pulling the wool over family
and friends' eyes, Suzie is just as adept
at whisking away the masks by dispensing gossip and using her father's name to wield power.

401. Richter, Conrad. *A Country of Strangers.* New
     York: Alfred A. Knopf, 1966. 169pp.

   *A Country of Strangers* is a wistful portrait
of a white girl kidnaped by Indians when she
was five, reared as an Indian, and content to
remain one. We first see her at age fifteen,
married to Espan, a young warrior, and already
the mother of Otter Boy, a sturdy son. But
the white man, backed by more soldiers than
there are leaves on the trees, has ordered all
white captives returned to their relatives,
and Mary Stanton, known among the Lenni Lenape
as Stone Girl, goes away with her son to
safety among other tribes until Espan can reclaim her. Her safety, however, is only tempor-
ary, and Mary is finally returned to her own
wealthy and influential family in Pennsylvania,
only to be rejected because an interloper has
been accepted as the real Stanton daughter.
Hired by her own father as a servant, she and
Otter Boy live precariously until Indian raids
endanger the community. In order to save her
younger white sister Nan, who hates her, she
rejoins the Indians, barely escaping with Nan
and the body of Otter Boy, slain by a vengeful
Indian warrior. Instead of gratitude for the
rescue of her sister, she receives vituperation.
Realizing she will never receive justice
or kindness from her own people, she flees
with Wtegowa, like herself a white raised as
an Indian, and the two strike for the freedom
of lands still undefiled by the white man.

402. Richter, Conrad. *The Grandfathers.* New York:
     Alfred A. Knopf, 1964. 180pp.

   When telephones, flush toilets, and automobiles
are still considered "new-fangled," Chariter
(Charity), fifteen, is a member of the Murdoch
clan of western Maryland, a "set-in-its-ways"
family that lives haphazardly and breeds casually

but still places a great deal of importance
on its own brand of respectability. But
Charity is different in looks and in tempera-
ment from the other Murdochs and tries in vain
to discover the identity of her true father
until she obtains a job as a servant in the
home of Squire Goddem. The Goddems are "quality"
folks, and the squire is very probably Charity's
other grandfather, quite a contrast to her
rascally Granpap Murdoch. But although Charity
is never officially claimed as his granddaughter,
there is an unspoken recognition between her
and the lonely squire, and it is in his big
house that Charity, sixteen, marries her suitor,
Gilliam, a prospering young undertaker, who
arrives at the wedding driving a shiny new
hearse. Charity rides off to meet her future,
happier than she has ever been.

403. Rickett, Frances. *A Certain Slant of Light*.
   New York: G.P. Putnam's Sons, 1968. 320pp.

   The narrator of this novel, set in a small
Indiana town during the Depression, is Angel
Crowley, aged ten. She lives with her teenaged sister Kate and their guardian Maggie,
who has achieved the feat of being elected
country auditor. During the two years the
novel spans, Angel faces prejudice and the
violence it breeds, ambition and the cowardice
it breeds, friendship, love, hate, procreation,
and the extraordinary mixture of good and
evil in people. Because she is part of a
strong, intelligent family, she deals with
these difficult lessons courageously. Because
she has been forced to contemplate the worst
in adult behavior, she leave Roseville saddened,
as well as enriched.

404. Rikhoff, Jean. *Dear Ones All*. New York: The
   Viking Press, Inc., 1961. 558pp.

   The Timble women examine their own and each
other's lives. The five sisters, their mother,
a great-aunt and a black housekeeper each, bit-
terly, reviews her youth. Each sees that the
strictures of society and religion placed her,
and caused them to place each other, in roles
from which they found it impossible to emerge

as they sought to realize their dreams.
Life, as they see it, is cruelly disappointing
yet precious.

405. Ritner, Ann. *Seize a Nettle*. New York: J.B.
     Lippincott, 1961. 254pp.

     This lighthearted romance is set in Denver,
     Colorado, and features the five women of the
     Abernathy family. At James Abernathy's death,
     the full responsibility for guiding their
     lives falls upon his wife, mother, and three
     daughters. The fact that the Depression is
     setting in and the family is rapidly running
     out of money merely serves to bring out the
     resourcefulness and character of the three
     daughters. Jessica, the youngest, proves
     capable of turning a profit on her artistic
     talent before she is out of her teens, and
     Margaret is domestic but spunky. The eldest,
     Eugenia, is full of a verve that keeps getting
     her into scrapes and an energy that gets her
     out. All the women in the family believe that
     hard work, solid values, and the development
     of their talents will be their best assurance
     of a satisfying life, and, in the terms of the
     novel, they prove that this is so.

406. Ritter, Margaret. *Simon Says*. Boston: Little,
     Brown, 1966. 248pp.

     Diana Braden, the heroine of this *Bildungsroman*,
     narrowly misses graduating from high school as
     the novel opens. After a childhood of emotional
     neglect by her actor parents, she opts for a
     career in acting and immediately meets the
     enigmatic Simon Furtwangler. Simon becomes
     Diana's emotional and spiritual advisor as
     she deals with the end of adolescence and the
     beginning of maturity: finding her work and
     dealing with guilt and with the early years
     of a troubled marriage. Without losing her
     wit, Diana adds understanding to her underlying
     strength and commits herself to her marriage
     and child.

     Robbins, Harold--*see* Rubin, Harold.

407. Robbins, Tom. *Even Cowgirls Get the Blues*.
     Boston: Houghton Mifflin Company, 1976.  365pp.

   A writer of novels characterized by fantasy
and wit, Robbins here creates a seriocomic
tale of Sissy Hankshaw, a fifteen-year-old girl
from Virginia, whose gigantic thumbs cause
her to become a hitchhiking legend.  Sissy
runs away from home when people try to convince
her that she is a freak, eventually marrying
a Mohawk Indian who also discourages her
individuality and freedom.  She begins to believe
in herself when a visit to a friend's dude
ranch puts her in the company of a group of
militant cowgirls.  These teenagers teach Sissy
to accept people and life and introduce her to
a Japanese guru named "Chink" who reportedly
knows the secrets of time and eternity.  Be-
friended by an anti-establishment psychiatrist
named Dr. Robbins and pregnant by the guru, Sissy
chooses to live with the doctor in a cave in the
desert and have the child who will probably
inherit her thumbs.

408. Robertson, Don. *A Flag Full of Stars*.  New
     York: G.P. Putnam's Sons, 1964.  511pp.

   In this episodic novel set against the backdrop of the 1948 presidential election, Barbara,
aged sixteen, initially plays a minor role as
the daughter of two of the novel's many main
characters.  In love for the first time with
a young man aged twenty-two, Barbara believes
herself to be pregnant, runs away, and marries.

409. Robinson, Jill. *Perdido*.  New York: Alfred
     A. Knopf, 1978.  431pp.

   "Perdido," Spanish for "lost," is the Hollywood mansion built by movie mogul Victor
Levanin, a Jewish immigrant who establishes his
own studio.  He lives in the grand movie
tradition until he dies, leaving behind a
family steeped in dreams of tinsel-town glamor.
*Perdido* is a first-person account of changing
times by Levanin's granddaughter Susanna,
who is fourteen when the novel begins in 1954.
She is drawn to Jackson Lane, a handsome but
unpredictable actor who treats her like a

daughter, which indeed she is, albeit illegitimate, a fact she does not discover until later.
Susanna, a typically willful, headstrong
Hollywood kid, pursues her elusive father, only
to discover he is incapable of real commitment.
In 1960, her marriage of convenience a disaster,
her beloved childhood home sold and condemned,
Susanna struggles toward self-understanding.
She finds peace only in her small son and
in a reunion with her father, who finally
returns willingly and for the first time holds
out his arms to her in parental devotion.

410. Robinson, Marilynne. *Housekeeping*. New York:
     Farrar Straus Giroux, 1980. 219pp.

     After their mother's suicide, Ruth and her
sister are left first with their grandmother,
then with two distant maiden aunts, and then
finally with their mother's sister, a transient.
Although an older Ruth, who has gone on the
road with her aunt, narrates the story with
beautiful language, the teenaged Ruth avoids
people and literature, spending her time
watching and listening. A late bloomer, Ruth
has no desire to break away from her aunt,
unlike her sister who makes friends in school
and leaves home.

411. Robinson, Rose. *Eagle in the Air*. New York:
     Crown, 1969. 159pp.

     The heroine of this picaresque novel finds,
after hitchhiking halfway across the country,
that she has made a spiritual journey as well.
Twenty-one-year-old Jean Pierce is expelled
from college for participating in a civil
rights demonstration and then finds that neither
her family nor her lover can give her a home.
She sets out for San Francisco in a mood of
distrust, which some of her experiences as a
black woman justify. But a one-armed carefree
man named Johnny wins her respect and love
and teaches her not to underestimate human
beings or their capacity for change.

412. Roe, Judy. *The Same Old Grind*. Milbrae, CA:
     Les Femmes Publishing, 1975. 223pp.

Struggling to live in the microcosm Roe
creates at the Majestic Opera House, now a
moribund burlesque theater, are two teenaged
strippers. Roberta Lattimore, who is rebelling
against her black middle-class parents, performs
as Zehyah while dreaming of ascending an African
throne and resisting pressure to undertake a
business career. Elly Mae, an unlettered,
impoverished "cracker" and the loyal pawn of
a pair of carney touts who have exploited her
in peep shows, finds the Majestic a step up
in her career and aspires to become a star.
Both girls sort out their destinies and dreams
as their stories (and a host of others) unfold
while life at the Majestic lumbers toward a
crisis. Moments of grim humor relieve this
story of economic oppression, sexual exploita-
tion--and honor--couched in sexually explicit
language.

413. Rogers, Garet. *The Jumping Off Place.* New
     York: The Dial Press, 1962. 307pp.

At thirteen, Caddy Bartholomew has two main
goals: to become a published poet and to dominate
absolutely her widowed father's attention and
affection. Toward the first end, she smuggles
the poetry of an inmate of the mental hospital
her father administers into the mails, including, as the inmate's, some of her own
verse. This undertaking leads to a dangerous
confrontation with the mad poet. Efforts to
monopolize her father cause Caddy to wage
varyingly effectual battles with her aunt and
with a female member of the staff. Dr. Jane
Carmody, despite personal problems, is gradually
falling in love with Caddy's father, and Al,
the aunt, supports that relationship while
mistrusting Caddy's schemes. The Caddy plot
is only one of several in this broad novel,
but it serves as an important unifying element.

414. Rogers, Thomas, *At The Shores.* New York:
     Simon and Schuster, 1980. 284pp.

Set in Chicago in the late 1940s and early
50s, this novel is a wistful account of a
summer of first romantic love and sexual experimentation between high school seniors

Jerry Engel and Rosemary Ingleside. Rosemary's
characterization is important because she,
as Jerry's willing but unthinking sexual
partner, illustrates the naiveté of adolescents,
physically capable of adult love but emotionally
unprepared for the psychological effects of
the experience. As Jerry's obsession with
lovemaking continues, Rosemary eventually takes
the initiative and tells her mother about their
affair, thus ending this idealistic and immature relationship.

415. Rogers, Thomas. *The Pursuit of Happiness*.
New York: The New American Library, Inc.,
1968. 237pp.

Jane Kauffman, aged twenty-one, and her lover,
William Popper, college students in Chicago,
have lived together for four years, but it is
she who more strongly vetoes the idea of marriage. Her desire to change a lousy world
involves her in various causes, one of which
soon becomes William, whose chronic disregard
of law and respectability lands him in prison
for killing a pedestrian. William, from a
well-to-do family, flouts anything resembling
discipline, and, after several months of his
one-year prison sentence, escapes. Jane joins
him in a family-abetted flight to Mexico where
tranquility and lack of responsibility encourage them to remain permanently. The novel
ends with the two vaguely discussing marriage
but only because of the child Jane is carrying.

416. Rollins, Bryant. *Danger Song*. Garden City,
N.Y.: Doubleday & Company, Inc., 1967. 280pp.

Arla McMahon, whose life between the ages of
fifteen and seventeen is traced in this novel,
is the symbol of the inner corruption of many
white families in the Boston of the early 1960s.
Arla's social-climbing father has trained her
as his tool for attaining the final step on
the social ladder, and he controls her every
move. Part of Peter McMahon's pose is his
guise as a white liberal, and he makes Arla
volunteer at a Roxbury center for black teenagers. There, Arla, still wounded from an
earlier love affair broken off by her father,

falls in love with the novel's young black
protagonist, Martin Williams, who is himself
struggling with problems of identity and
racial discrimination. Once again, Mr. McMahon
interferes, again with tragic results.

417. Rosen, Winifred. *Cruisin for a Bruisin*. New
     York: Alfred A. Knopf, 1976. 150pp.

     Winnie Simon finds her thirteenth year more
     difficult than any she has yet experienced,
     and doesn't like it. Suddenly tension be-
     tween her, her father, her mother, and her older
     sister mounts. Early experiments with sex
     are not very successful, and though eventually
     Winnie develops a relationship with young
     John Miller, severe tests of her maturity still
     await her. Separated from John for most of
     a summer and "bored to death," Winnie drifts
     into a potentially dangerous relationship with
     Timothy, a liar and trickster, which results
     in the loss of her father's boat, a terrific
     family quarrel, and, finally, an accident
     which could cost her dearly. This rash of
     disasters, however, seems to turn the tide,
     and Winnie closes her story considerably more
     mature, more comfortable with herself, than
     she began it.

418. Rosenberg, Jessie. *Sudina*. New York: E.P.
     Dutton and Company, 1967. 236pp.

     Sudina Wraith Howell, a young Southerner,
     becomes convinced that she possesses some
     inherent evil which causes people to die. We
     are shown glimpses of Sudina's relationship
     with family members, especially her grand-
     mother, also named Sudina, and her grandmother's
     beloved servants, Mister and Lulu. Following
     her mother's death, Sudina suffers a nervous
     breakdown. Through help from her doctor and
     those who love her, Sudina is freed from her
     guilt and returns from the brink of madness.

419. Ross, Ivan T. *Requiem for a Schoolgirl*. New
     York: Simon and Schuster, 1961. 243pp.

     Ben Gordon, a high school English teacher,
     becomes obsessed with uncovering the reason

behind the suicide of one of his talented but
off-beat students.  Through his search to
understand why Laurie Mitchell died, Ben
discovers a sensitive girl who was looking for
the meaning of life.  Though she presented a
tough, bohemian demeanor, Laurie was unable
to survive the shattering of her idealized
view of her father.

420. Ross, Sam. *Hang-up*.  New York: Coward-McCann,
     Inc., 1968.  222pp.

In this study of parent-child alienation in
the 1960s, the death of Martha Carson, fifteen,
sets off a murder investigation which also
involves Sherry Loomis, about fifteen; Dave
Grant, seventeen; and Scott Bannister, a
disturbed post-teen youth and Martha's murderer.  Martha's rebellion against her mother's
life style and her vulnerability to peer
pressure brought about her death, and Sherry
learns that even a terrible home (her mother
is an alcoholic and the mother's wino lover
is a potential child molester) is marginally
better than the deadly life on Hollywood's
Sunset strip.

421. Rossner, Judith. *Emmeline*.  New York: Simon
     and Schuster, 1980.  331pp.

In her sixth novel, Rossner makes a strong
statement against the stigma attached to unwed
motherhood by recounting the tragic facts
surrounding a case during the middle of the
nineteenth century.  When not yet fourteen,
Emmeline Mosher is sent from her home in
Maine to support her family by working in a
Massachusetts cotton mill.  There, the naive
and lonely country girl is seduced and im-
pregnated by her womanizing supervisor.  She
returns to her family in silent shame, never
having seen her child or even knowing its
sex.  At thirty-four she marries a young man,
only to discover that he is her son.  When
her family and the community discover her
secret, made more repugnant by the act of
incest, all feel shamed and are able to cleanse
themselves only by ostracizing Emmeline.

422.  Rossner, Judith. *Nine Months in the Life of
      an Old Maid.* New York: The Dial Press, 1969.
      183pp.

      When the world-famous author, Josh Cane,
      and his wife, Lily, both Communist sym-
      pathizers, leave their estate in New York for
      Hollywood in 1929, they leave behind two
      daughters. The elder, Mimi, becomes a surrogate
      mother for the emotionally fragile Beth. Over
      the years, Beth becomes a virtual hermit, leav-
      ing her home only when she must periodically
      be hospitalized for breakdowns. Other than
      Mimi, the only people she will let into her
      world are a half-brother and Mimi's husband.
      Beth is eventually forced into maturity by her
      father's decision to sell a portion of the
      estate and by Mimi's pregnancy. Mimi and Beth
      recognize their reciprocal relationship and
      are able, finally, to achieve independent lives.

423.  Rossner, Judith. *To The Precipice.* New York:
      William Morrow, 1966.  384pp.

      Ruth Kossoff, a poor Jewish girl from New
      York who is a nineteen-year-old freshman at
      Hunter College, accepts a job as tutor and
      live-in companion to the children of a rich,
      Gentile family. This attempt to escape the
      poverty and shame of her childhood is the theme
      of the novel. Ruth is blinded by the trappings
      of the foolish and cruel world of the rich
      in the same way her parents have accepted
      the stagnant environment of poverty. Sexually
      and emotionally she stumbles to the edge of
      a precipice and cannot see the danger because
      of the enticement of a new world of material
      comfort. The price of her blindness is high:
      marriage to and eventually children by the
      father of the young people she has tutored,
      a man she neither knows nor loves; complicity
      in the suicide of her brother; and loss of the
      neighborhood boyfriend she sincerely loves
      because of her inability to give up the luxuries
      of her new life. Although the novel covers
      Ruth's experiences up to age thirty-four, it
      is her adolescence that forces her journey
      into a new world and the hard lessons that
      follow.

424. Roth, Arthur. *The Caretaker*. New York:
     Four Winds Press, 1980. 216pp.

   Pam Sheehy, sixteen, is a complicating factor
in the already complex life of seventeen-year-
old Mark Cooper, the protagonist-narrator.
A runaway who is unhappy with both her home
life and her boarding school, Pam seeks refuge
in her parents' summer home and appeals to
Mark, whose parents are caretakers for the
house, for aid and comfort. Seen only through
Mark's perceptions, Pam, con artist and manipu-
lator, is primarily a plot device rather than
a fully developed character. Still, her
presence allows the author to suggest that
adolescent passion can lead to a sustaining
friendship.

425. Roth, Philip. *When She Was Good*. New York:
     Random House, 1967. 306pp.

   Roth traces the character changes in Lucy
Nelson, a midwestern middle-class WASP, from
her first appearance as a cute and lovable
child, through an adolescence tortured by
frustrations and bitter personal conflicts,
to her final appearance as a shrewish and demanding young wife and mother. Her constant
ally is her maternal grandfather, "Daddy Will"
Carroll, and her chief adversaries are her
undependable father, the daydreaming young
would-be artist whom she eventually marries,
and her husband's aunt and uncle. Presented
through Daddy Will's eyes and affections, Lucy
finds her natural talents for love, music,
and high ideals constantly thwarted by un-
controllable aspects of her environment; she
becomes increasingly reluctant to make allow-
ances for differences of opinion.

426. Rothweiler, Paul R. *The Sensuous Southpaw*.
     New York: G.P. Putnam's Sons, 1976. 253pp.

   Jeri Walker, eighteen, tells of her first
season as a major league baseball player.
The adventure is enacted in richly detailed
accounts of the game as Jeri, trying to win
acceptance from her male teammates and the
powerful men who run baseball, deals with her
celebrity and sexual initiation.

Rowans, Virginia--*see* Tanner, Edward Everett.

427.  Rubin, Harold  [as Harold Robbins, pseud.].
      *Where Love Has Gone*.  New York: Simon and
      Schuster, 1962.  350pp.

      This novel tells of the arrest of Danielle
      (Dani) Carey for the murder of her mother's
      lover and the hearings that follow.  As a
      juvenile, fourteen-year-old Dani can be
      neither tried nor punished in California,
      where the novel is set, so her custody becomes
      the main issue.  Events are presented primarily
      from the viewpoint of Dani's father, long since
      divorced from her mother and now, in a happy
      second marriage, awaiting the birth of another
      child.  Nora Hayden, Dani's mother, is presented
      as a brilliant sculptor but a voracious sexual
      athlete, a totally selfish and possessively
      jealous woman.  Through most of the novel,
      it seems clear that Dani did in fact kill
      her mother's lover in order to protect her
      from his potentially violent rage, but Dani's
      father gradually learns disquieting things
      about the child he deeply loves but does not
      know very well.  This popular novel, which
      depicts a tangle of complex relationships among
      the rich, powerful, and gifted, is loosely based
      upon an actual case.

428.  Rubin, Michael.  *A Trip Into Town*.  New York:
      Harper & Brothers, Publishers, 1961.  216pp.

      Three girls embellish the college years
      of Steven, the protagonist.  Esther, a neigh-
      borhood friend, represents the past he would
      like--at least in part--to abandon.  Caroline
      represents the reluctant balance he will strike
      between wishful rebellion and conformity.  Suki
      represents rebellion, freedom, bohemianism,
      "life."  But though the bond of affection
      between Suki and Steven is powerful, and though
      he sees her through some hard times--a destruct-
      ive affair, its breakup, an abortion-- the
      pair are clearly not a suitable match; Suki
      lacks definition and commitment; Steven lacks
      definition and courage.

429. Rushing, Jane Gilmore. *Mary Dove: A Love Story*.
     Garden City, N.Y.: Doubleday & Company, Inc.,
     1974. 209pp.

     When Mary Dove Pardue's father perishes in
a West Texas snowstorm, the innocent young
woman must fend for herself. Accustomed to
total isolation, she remembers her father's
warnings: when a stranger rides up, she shoots
him. While she nurses Red back to health, they
fall in love. Their strong emotional ties
are tested by Mary Dove's parental background
and the prejudices of pioneers who are gradually
settling into the area after the Civil War.
Jane Rushing, a West Texas native, integrates
her knowledge of the area into all of her
novels.

     Rydell, Forbes--*see* Forbes, [Delores Florine]
Stanton, and Helen Rydell.

     Rydell, Helen--*see* Forbes, [Delores Florine]
Stanton, and Forbes Rydell.
430. Salas, Floyd. *Tattoo the Wicked Cross*. New
     York: Grove Press, 1967. 351pp.

     This tragic novel describes the brutalization
of a young Hispanic in a California reform
school. Aaron D'Aragon, at fifteen, is bright,
brave, capable of idealism, but too small in
stature to command instant respect, and imbued
with the macho ethic of the street gang. A
strong friend protects him from the sexual
predators of the institution but only temporarily: alone again, Aaron demonstrates his bravery
until it makes him a murderer. His family
and his girlfriend Judith are minor but
crucial characters in the drama, as they make
futile efforts to keep Aaron intact inside
an institution they have no control over.
Judith is warm, innocent, decent, and loyal--
she watches the destruction of her friend
with horror.

431. Salinger, J.D. *Franny and Zooey*. Boston:
     Little, Brown, 1961. 201pp.

     In the fall of her senior year, twenty-year-
old Franny Glass, youngest of the seven

brilliant offspring of a Jewish-Irish ex-
vaudeville couple now members of upper-middle-
class New York society, becomes distraught to
the extent of physical illness because of her
doubts regarding her college career, her choice
of a profession, her boyfriend, and her
unsuccessful attempts to find spiritual peace
through prayer. Two extended conversations
with her older brother Zooey lead her first
into a painful soul-searching and later into
a satisfying acceptance of her own relationship
to the world and God.

432. Samuels, Gertrude. *The People vs. Baby*. Garden
     City, N.Y.: Doubleday & Company, 1967. 292pp.

     This documentary novel is the story of Joseph-
ine Delia Gomez, called Baby, a young Puerto
Rican growing up in Spanish Harlem, who falls
victim to her environment. The daughter
of a deeply religious mother and a father she
never knew, Baby, as a child, was pretty and
smart and loved school. In her early teens,
she enters the world of street gangs and crime
and, eventually, prison, drugs, and prostitution.
In spite of her efforts to change and to fight
her way out of this lifestyle, she is too deeply
entrenched to succeed.

433. Samuels, Gertrude. *Run, Shelley, Run!* New
     York: Thomas Y. Crowell Company, 1974. 174pp.

     A reporter covering juvenile justice courts
throughout the country, Samuels was infuriated
by the imprisoning of juveniles "for no other
'crime' than that of running away, truanting,
or victimization by family neglect." Shelley
Clark was guilty of these "crimes." The
oldest illegitimate offspring of an alcoholic
woman who had given away her two younger children, Shelley remained with her mother until
the welfare authorities placed her in a foster
home. At ten years of age she began running
away from foster homes and correctional
institutions. Shelley's desperate need to
rejoin her mother changed to hatred as she
grew more aware of her mother's weak, self-
centered nature. Repeated flights from institutions land this attractive teenager in solitary

where Judge Evelyn Davis finds her during
an inspection visit. This warm and caring
mentor encourages and listens to Shelley and
helps her become a contributing member of
society.

434. Sandburg, Helga. *The Owl's Roost*. New York:
     The Dial Press, 1962. 308pp.

     The lives of the residents of Pine Beach, a sum-
mer resort on the shores of Lake Michigan near
Chicago, are presented from the start of one summer to the end of the next. Characters' reactions
to various affairs, flirtations, marriages,
births, and deaths are investigated. We see
fifteen-year-old Clara Olson, who lives in the
summer house called Owl's Roost, emerging from
her girlhood and exploring the artifices she
sees as embodying mature womanhood. Her
relationship to her mother and her position
as her father's favorite are central to
the novel. We also receive brief insights
into Pearl and Irene Thwaite, seventeen- and
eighteen-year-old daughters of a television
evangelist.

435. Sandburg, Helga. *The Wizard's Child*. New
     York: The Dial Press, 1967. 260pp.

     Marn, daughter of folk-doctor and charm-maker
Wizard Coombs, becomes pregnant on her seventeenth birthday by Henry, the Sheepman's son,
who has promised to marry her. A spell by
Wizard, who does not want his daughter involved
with Henry, turns the young man's thoughts toward her friend Katrin, daughter of a prosperous
farmer. The new Schoolmaster Grim is attracted
to Marn, whom he views as a symbol of innocence
opposing her father's wickedness. The novel,
set in the North Carolina mountains of 1915,
sorts out these relationships and shows how
Marn achieves independence from her father
and selects a man to care for her and her unborn child.

436. Sanguinetti, Elise. *The Last of the Whitfields*.
     New York: McGraw-Hill, 1962. 279pp.

     Two years of familial and regional problems

of the socially prominent Whitfield family,
in a small Georgia town are related by fourteen-
year-old Felicia, the youngest Whitfield: "Father
is a banker, but he's also inclined to a number of spiritual ovulations [sic]." She feels
especially sorry for her chubby and perpetually
fumbling older brother Arthur; she sees herself
as "quite thin and exceedingly atriculated [sic]
for my age." How will Arthur, a misfit even
at home, survive boarding school in Connecticut,
where everybody hates you if you're from the
South? Will Northern Liberals ever allow the
South to face its problems in its own way?
What will the people of Ashton say when they
read the magazine article based on Felicia's
secret interview with the visiting New York
journalist? Will Mother be able to face her
relatives in Charleston, who still think her
move to Georgia was a tragic downfall?

437. Sanguinetti, Elise. *The New Girl*. New York:
      McGraw-Hill, 1964. 272pp.

When Southern-born Felicia Whitfield enters
exclusive Chesney Hall, a boarding school in
Virginia, she desperately misses her ninth-
grade friends at home. An unassuming manner
and eagerness to excel in friendships and
studies aid Felicia in breaking the barriers
at Chesney, and she is even chosen for an
important school position. After befriending
Patsy Dedham who is wealthy, sophisticated,
and pregnant by a married man, Felicia innocently
answers Patsy's plea for help. The consequences
of the naive girl's actions are unfair yet
realistic.

Sara--*see* Blake, Sally.

438. Sarton, May. *As We Are Now*. New York: W.W.
      Norton & Company, Inc., 1973. 134pp.

This novel focuses on the struggles of
Caroline Spencer to protect her integrity of
personality and identity while living in a
horrendous "home" for the aged and infirm.
Some moments of relief and support are offered
Caro by Lisa Thornhill, daughter of a local
minister. Open, friendly, tender, this high

school senior appears only briefly, but she
stands for normality in the extremely abnormal,
destructive world in which Caro lives.  Through
Caro's eventual doubts about her potentially
dangerous influence over Lisa, Sarton fore-
shadows Caro Spencer's terrible fate.  And even
while she represents hope, Lisa, young, strong,
vibrant, also reminds readers that sometime
she (and they) may be as the institution's
residents "are now."

439. Sarton, May.  *Kinds of Love*.  New York: W.W.
     Norton & Company Inc., 1970.  464pp.

     To Joel Smith, a college dropout, and Cathy,
the fifteen-year-old grandchild of the protagonist, Willard, New Hampshire, is a kind
of haven.  Both youngsters are at odds with
their families and both "take time out" from
the antagonisms of their everyday lives during
a rigorous but healing winter in the tiny
village.  Their gently developing love for one
another--and their practical, mature response
to it--form a subplot in a novel which deals
primarily with the problems of the aging,
the lifelong and sometimes prickly friendship
between two elderly women, and the impact of
time upon a once thriving community.

440. Sarton, May.  *The Small Room*.  New York: W.W.
     Norton & Company Inc., 1961.  249pp.

     A major subplot in this novel details the
struggle of a young college professor to
behave properly and humanely when she discovers
that an exceptionally gifted student, Jane Seaman,
has plagiarized a paper.  Professor Lucy Winter,
the protagonist, manages to win Jane's confidence enough to learn that the student has
broken under the pressure of producing better
and better work with each new assignment.  The
lot of gifted academic women, young and old,
is a major theme of several plots, each contributing to Lucy Winter's growth.

441. Savage, Elizabeth.  *The Girls from the Five
     Great Valleys*.  Boston: Little, Brown and
     Company, 1977.  240pp.

Maturation and the changes it imposes upon
adolescent friendships of the 1930s are the
themes in the story of five friends, Hilary,
Amelia, Doll, Janet, and Kathy. Hilary is
ambitious; she wishes to become an influential
woman in Missoula (Montana) society and sees
her friends as partial means to that end until
her mother's serious illness alters her plans.
Motherless, Doll seeks affection, conducts a
courtship, and plans for early marriage. Amelia
is the surrogate head of her household which
includes a feckless mother and a mentally handi-
capped younger sister. Less prominent, Janet
and Kathy serve as points of contrast to their
more dominant companions.

442.  Savage, Elizabeth. *Happy Ending*. Boston:
      Little, Brown and Company, 1972. 308pp.

At nineteen, Maryalyse Tyler is responsible
for the support of her illegitimate baby son.
Although the country is in the grip of the
Depression, she is able to find work. Under
the care of her elderly employers, Thomas and
Carrie Russell, Montana ranchers, Maryalyse
finds security, peace, and substitute parents.
The Russells nurture Maryalyse's growing affection for their hired hand, Bud Romeo, and they
treat her child like a grandson. Though the
book's title is ironic, Savage points out the
value of love and tolerance in the midst of
despair. Maryalyse's story serves as subplot
and counterpoint to the tale of the Russells'
acceptance of the limitations of old age.

443.  Savage, Elizabeth. *The Last Night at the Ritz*.
      Boston: Little, Brown and Company, 1973.
      245pp.

The tensions and tenderness of the long friendship between the unnamed narrator and her college
roommate, Gay, are major themes. Flashbacks
to the women's college years reveal the basis
of their affection for one another. They share
a love of books and a curiosity about life,
and though their adult paths veer sharply in
different directions, the women remain close.
Sharing is, in fact, a major motif. As undergraduates, they have shared a lover, the terror

of unwanted pregnancy, one another's decisions
about sexual activity, and even, to a degree,
Gay's family.

444. Savage, Thomas. *Her Side of It*. Boston: Little,
Brown and Company, 1981. 299pp.

An English professor eulogizes his gifted
and sensitive friend, Liz Phillips, who lets
life wear her down and eventually drinks
herself to death. Her teenaged years, during
the Depression, were ones of oppressive loneliness. Her dearest friend, her father, loses
his mind, and her mother turns to other men
for comfort. Her grandparents impose rigid
rules on the spirited young woman, causing her
to become the willing prey of a high school
athlete who plans to make her his latest trophy.
In her young womanhood she leads a bohemian
life and marries unsuccessfully. Never quite
able to achieve peace in her life, Liz finally
gives in and lets society bury her.

445. Savage, Thomas. *A Strange God*. Boston: Little,
Brown and Company, 1974. 310pp.

Jack Reed grew up with very little in the
way of family life or material comforts, so he
desires success for himself and for his family.
Through he wants the best for Norma and their
children, it is Martha whom he loves above
all. Proud of his beautiful daughter, Jack
makes arrangements for her to attend the
right schools and dreams of her marriage to a
suitable young man. Perhaps it is the protected
life he has arranged for her that severs their
close relationship.

446. Schaeffer, Susan Fromberg. *Falling*. New York:
The Macmillan Company, 1973. 307pp.

Rich in Jewish wit, wisdom, and confusion,
the main character of this novel, Elizabeth
Kamen, unhappily married, vaguely suicidal,
overweight, riddled with feelings of inadequacy,
wends her way through her complicated extended
family and grows into herself with the help
of a psychiatrist, Dr. Greene. Through brief
but important flashbacks, Schaeffer gives the
reader some significant scenes of adolescence,

covering such issues as dating and negative
letters of recommendation for college. Elizabeth finally discovers that all people are
floating free, falling sometimes like a feather,
sometimes like a stone, making their lives
the best they can.

447. Schaeffer, Susan Fromberg. *Time in Its Flight*.
New York: Doubleday & Company, 1978. 782pp.

Ella Steele, over one hundred years old, remi-
nisces about and re-evaluates her family, their
betrayals, and their passions. Ella, the second
daughter in a family of three girls and two
boys, is most like her mother, Edna, the central
figure of the novel; her sister Letitia is
most like her grandmother, Edith; and Anna,
the youngest, is like her grandfather. Edna,
the matriarch, is also shown to us as a curious
child and adolescent, who is the daughter of
a beautiful if simple and chatty mother and a
father who cannot find earthly grounding and
hangs himself when she is sixteen. Edna,
distant from her mother, leaves the city in
search of something natural, which she finds
in the home of her mother's best friend, Ten.
There she meets her husband, Ten's younger
brother, a medical doctor and widower of twenty-
eight, marries him at seventeen, and designs
a complex house and family to match. Female
adolescence is central to this long novel.

448. Schiller, Marvin. *Country of the Young*. New
York: Crown Publishers, Inc., 1966. 281pp.

In 1947, at the age of seventeen, David Wyman,
a clarinetist, wins a scholarship to Tangle-
wood (the summer music school run by the Boston
Symphony) and there meets and falls in love
with Ruth, a talented cello player. David
cannot foresee a life without Ruth; and when
her parents get the young couple to agree to
a two-month separation that Ruth herself ex-
tends, eventually marrying an artist she has
met in Europe, David is unable to stop loving
her passionately and to accept the friendship
that Ruth offers. At thirty, now a stockbroker,
David accepts an invitation to play a walk-on

role in the United States' entry in a Paris drama
festival. There, he is charmed by and sets out
to seduce a fellow performer, Jill, a young American girl whom he comes to love. Although Jill
is an important part of this story, she is developed mainly through David's consciousness, with
very little dialogue used.

449. Schneider, Nina. *The Woman Who Lived in a
      Prologue.* Boston: Houghton Mifflin, 1980.
      479pp.

Ariadne Arkady, a Jewish woman in her seventies who discovers she has cancer, reviews her
life since her family's immigration to America
during her childhood to her becoming an accom-
plice to her grandson's exile in Canada during
the Vietnam era. She sees that as a young
woman she passed from dependency on her family
to dependency on a young husband who was not
strong enough to shoulder life's burdens. In
order to survive, Ariadne became the one to
spar with life. As an old woman who is not
yet ready to surrender, Ariadne is thankful
for the hardships and heartaches of her youth
that gave her the strength to face the coming
battle.

450. Schoen, Barbara. *A Place and a Time.* New York:
      Thomas Y. Crowell Company, 1967. 234pp.

Growing up can be embarrassing, humorous,
and painful at times, and Josie Frost encounters
all these feelings in a short two years. A
tomboy at heart, she prefers sneakers, summers
on the coast of Maine, and Beethoven's Ninth
to the things her cousin Priscilla and Aunt
Anne think are proper for a young lady. Forced
to attend a dance, Josie, who is at first embarrassed with her lack of partners, meets
Henry, and her world is changed. After months
of dreaming and waiting for him to come back
to town, Josie is crushed when Henry doesn't
even recognize her. Rejected, she turns to
Peter, a long time friend with whom she enjoys
going to movies, dog shows, and parties, but
their innocent friendship disturbs both sets
of parents because they are spending too much
time together. The surprise ending reveals

that Josie has indeed left childish relationships
and values behind and is discovering her own
potential as a woman.

451. Schoonover, Shirley. *Mountain of Winter*. New
     York: Coward-McCann, 1965. 256pp.

   This novel portrays a pocket culture of
Finnish-American farmers in the Midwest and
one of their daughters, Ava Knuutinen. The
Finns are hard-working, hard-playing, earthy,
tenacious people with occasional flashes of
prescience. Ava, who is four when the novel
opens and perhaps twenty when it ends, develops the best traits of her people as she emerges,
kicking and screaming, from childhood into
sexual maturity. Emotional maturity comes later
and with difficulty, through a love affair
with a man who betrays her trust and shakes
her self-respect. Helped by the wisdom of her
grandmother and the affection of Paul Yates,
another scarred veteran of the quest for love,
Ava emerges at the end of the novel bereft of
family, with her farm in ruins, but in possession
of herself and her considerable strength.

452. Schwartz, Lynne Sharon. *Balancing Acts*. New
     York: Harper & Row, Publishers, 1981. 216pp.

   A story of the difficulties of old age and
adolescence, this novel juxtaposes the life of
Alison Markman, an intellectually mature thirteen-year-old, with that of Max Fried, a seventy-
four-year-old former circus performer. Although their perspectives are necessarily quite
different, this unlikely pair share similar
wishes to control and order their lives and
ultimately to escape that which is hurtful and
unpleasant. For Alison, the need to escape is
tied to typically adolescent problems: mixed
emotions about stirrings of sexual desire,
feelings of being different from peers, and
frustrations in communicating with her parents.
Falsely assuming that Max does not share her
confusion with life, Alison imitates his past
by attempting to run away and join the circus,
an act whose strain on Max results in his
heart attack and death. The reality of this
event helps Alison turn from the world of make-
believe and make progress toward becoming a
caring and responsible adult.

453. Scoppettone, Sandra. *Happy Endings Are All Alike*. New York: Harper & Row, Publishers, 1978. 202pp.

During their last year in high school, Jaret Tyler and Peggy Danziger become lovers, and for a few months, they are able to conceal their lesbianism from all but a close friend Bianca Chambers, Jaret's mother, and Peggy's college-aged sister Claire. Both Bianca and Kay Tyler are loyal, and both try to understand the relationship, though each unintentionally hurts Jaret or Peggy because of ignorance or thoughtlessness. Claire, however, a young woman with little sense of self-worth, derides Peggy and frequently threatens to "tell" their father. When Mid Summers, an unruly, violent youth, discovers the affair, it inflames his hatred for Jaret. He rapes her, believing that he can ensure her silence by threatening to reveal her secret. Jaret, however, prosecutes Mid, despite the pain this decision gives Peggy and the tension it generates in their small town. The novel's messages are clear: lesbian love is real and natural; rape is a crime of violence, not passion; and even very young women are capable of strength and independence.

454. Scoppettone, Sandra. *Trying Hard to Hear You*. New York: Harper & Row, 1974. 264pp.

Camilla Crawford, aged sixteen, and her best friend, Jeff Grathwohl, are neighbors who share each other's joys and sorrows, and as the summer begins, their greatest concern is what parts they will play in the local summer theater. When Camilla starts receiving attention from Phil Chrystie, a more sophisticated member of the aspiring young actors, she is extremely flattered until it becomes clear his real interest is Jeff. Jeff and Phil establish an "unnatural" relationship, and the group is not only horrified but extremely antagonistic. The dilemma is resolved tragically, affecting all the young people who now disperse into autumn, knowing that a loss of innocence has forever changed their lives.

455. Seelye, John. *The Kid*. New York: The Viking
     Press, 1972. 119pp.

     Appearing in the cattletown after a winter
     that had depleted the herds, the blond youth
     and a big companion are not welcome until their
     gold dust is displayed. The deaf mute African
     is suspect because of his magical powers when
     the men at the saloon engage him in games of
     chance to relieve the two of the gold they
     mined in the hills. The kid gains their atten-
     tion when expounding on the virtues of raising
     sheep. Greed, suspicion, and drinking lead to
     five violent deaths that day. And yet, the
     undertaker shocked the people with his news
     that Blondie wasn't a boy after all.

456. Segal, Erich. *Man, Woman and Child*. New York:
     Harper & Row, 1980. 244pp.

     Jessica Beckwith is almost thirteen and on
     the brink of growing up when she learns that
     Jean-Claude, the nine-year-old French boy visit-
     ing them, is actually her father's child. Her
     reactions are hurt, anger and hatred of her
     father, both at the news and at the fact that
     it was kept from her and her sister. Jean-
     Claude's illness causes Jessica to feel guilty,
     and her approaching maturity is revealed at
     her acceptance of the situation.

457. Selby, Hubert, Jr. *Last Exit to Brooklyn*.
     New York: Grove Press, 1964. 304pp.

     Among the young crowd who hang out in Alex
     the Greek's all-night diner in Selby's frank
     episodic novel of slum life in Brooklyn, the
     one important female adolescent is Tralala.
     From age fifteen to eighteen, Tral rapidly
     develops a tough-guy attitude, using her sexual
     charms (chiefly her enormous breasts) as well
     as her physical strength and her utter ruth-
     lessness to outdo the men in erotic activity,
     financial chicanery, and physical brutality.
     Instead of the admiration she has expected to
     win by these exploits, she earns only jealousy
     and resentment, culminating in a sordid gang
     rape.

458. Seton, Anya. *Smouldering Fires*. Garden City,
     N.Y.: Doubleday & Company, Inc., 1975. 159pp.

     Amy Delatour, a high school senior, obsessed
with Longfellow's *Evangeline* and her own
Acadian ancestors, is plump, dowdy, unpopular,
but a good student. She has an unhappy home
life. A new teacher of Louisiana Creole background brings her out of herself by taking her
glasses off and getting her to let her hair
out of its tight little bun. Under hypnotism,
she relives the eighteenth-century experiences
of a real Evangeline, her ancestor, who was
killed by fire after finding her lover. Now
Amy is released, able to be normal. The novel
is a mixture of popular psychiatry and occultism.

459. Seton, Cynthia Propper. *The Half-Sisters*.
     New York: W.W. Norton & Company Inc., 1974.
     213pp.

     Seton's novel is a study of two women bound
by the sharing of the same father and a deep
love for each other. Through three episodic
encounters, the reader becomes acquainted with
sensible, rather proper Erica Thoroughgood and
her sister Billie, the personification of all
that is beautiful, free, and unconforming.
From their childhood summers together on the
East Coast, they progress through their college years when both love the same man. The
last part of the novel deals with the year
1970 when Erica and Billie are wives and mothers
in their forties.

460. Settle, Mary Lee. *The Scapegoat*. New York:
     Random House, 1980. 278pp.

     *The Scapegoat* is presented in four segments
which, often in flashback, depict events of
two days: Friday, June 7, and Saturday, June 8,
1912. The events are presented mainly through
the eyes of those whose lives are touched by
the efforts of the Imperial Land Company to
defeat the attempt to unionize mine workers
in Lacey Creek, West Virginia. Beverly Lacey,
owner of the Seven Stars Colliery, has three
daughters for whose protection Ann Eldridge

Lacey has insisted her husband install a Gatling
gun on the front porch. Mary Rose Lacey (fifteen), Althea Lacey (sixteen), and Lilly Lacey
(eighteen) are the three adolescent females
who help to tell this story. Privately schooled,
a now liberated Vassar girl, Lilly Lacey's
idealism pushes her stage center to play a
key role in action she only partially comprehends.

461. Shaw, Irwin. *Bread Upon the Waters*. New York:
     Delacorte Press, 1981. 438pp.

     Athletic Carolyn Strand, using her steel
     tennis racquet as a weapon, recsues a stranger
     in New York City's Central Park from muggers
     and sets in motion a series of events that
     nearly leads to her apparently happy family's
     disintegration. Most profoundly affected by
     the well-meant interference in their lives of
     the stranger (a wealthy and powerful attorney)
     is Carolyn's father, the protagonist, but Caro-
     lyn, her older brother and older sister, her
     mother, and several pupils of her father (a
     secondary school history teacher) are also
     depicted in some detail. At the end of the
     novel almost all, including Carolyn, have had
     major flaws revealed and have become alienated
     from the protagonist.

462. Shaw, Irwin. *Rich Man, Poor Man*. New York:
     Delacorte Press, 1969. 629pp.

     Rudolph, Thomas, and Gretchen Jordache are
     rivals for the attention of their domineering,
     immigrant father and self-sacrificing mother.
     Although the story centers around Rudy, the
     favorite child, and Tom, the black sheep, Gret-
     chen is a major character. Her youthful feel-
     ing of rejection drives her to rebel against
     her parents. For consolation and as a means
     of escape, she becomes caught up in a destruc-
     tive affair with an older man. When this re-
     lationship falls apart, a pattern is set for
     her future. Real happiness eludes Gretchen
     as her numerous affairs and marriages finally
     cause the disintegration of her relationship
     with her son.

463. Sherburne, Zoa. *Girl in the Mirror*. New York:
     W. Morrow, 1966. 190pp.

     Ruth Ann Callahan, the sixteen-year-old
main character, struggles with a weight problem.
Tragedy also molds Ruth Ann's personality--
her mother's early death followed by her
father's death in a car accident while on a
wedding trip with new wife Tracy. Ruth Ann
is forced to re-evaluate negative feelings
towards her stepmother when both are left without the man who brought them together.

464. Sherburne, Zoa. *Too Bad About the Haines Girl*.
     New York: W. Morrow, 1967. 191pp.

     Attractive and popular Melinda Haines, a
senior in high school, is faced with the dilemma
of pregnancy. She experiences the problems
of most young women in her predicament--the
reactions of trusting parents and school friends,
the decision to have an abortion or keep the
baby, and the handicap of entering marriage
under such trying circumstances.

465. Sherman, Susan. *Give Me Myself*. Cleveland:
     World Publishing Co., 1961. 232pp.

     Nona Green is only nineteen when she sits
in on a Masefield College class conducted by
Mrs. Evelyn Gordon McKenna, who charms and
electrifies her students in her Principles of
Literary Symbolism course. Nona is an un-
committed person, attending college only for
lack of something more interesting to do. But
Mrs. McKenna, a brilliant Irish scholar, practi-
cally mesmerizes her, and she becomes an eager
servant to the teacher's every whim. As time
passes, Nona discovers that her idol is an
alcoholic and that her lifestyle is bohemian.
Despite this knowledge, she continues to love
Evelyn with a devotion bordering on fanaticism,
vowing to save her from her weaknesses and
even following her to Italy when Evelyn, in a
drunken stupor, sends for her. But in Florence,
where the teacher wallows in dissipation, the
tie binding the two snaps, and a wiser, more
mature Nona returns to her home and school,
realizing that the only real mastery in life
is that of self.

466. Shulman, Alix Kates. *Burning Questions*. New
     York: Alfred A. Knopf, 1978. 361pp.

     Zane IndiAnna spends her teen years in
     Indiana and is encouraged to think for herself
     by her parents and aunt. She migrates to
     New York, marries, has children, is unfaithful,
     and is eventually exposed to radical feminism
     which changes her views forever. Although
     the questions are not so burning as they might
     have been, the influence of learning to think
     for herself as a teenager is highly valuable.

467. Shulman, Alix Kates. *Memoirs of an Ex-Prom
     Queen*. New York: Alfred A. Knopf, 1969.
     274pp.

     In this first-person narrative, flashbacks
     reval Sasha's adolescence and the sources of
     her life-long suppressed anger at men who keep
     women in their place by insinuation, threats,
     and physical force. She is chosen prom queen
     and decides to lose her virginity to her
     steady boyfriend in the back seat of a car.
     Subsequently, her life follows a familiar femi-
     nine pattern--college, marriage, repeated in-
     fidelities, divorce, re-marriage, children--
     with her awareness of what it means to be a
     person first and a woman second only dimly
     manifesting itself. At the end of the novel,
     Sasha cuts her hair quite short in a rebellious,
     symbolic act of defiance and leaves us guessing
     as to the consequences.

468. Siddons, Anne Rivers. *Heartbreak Hotel*. New
     York: Simon and Schuster, 1976. 252pp.

     Maggie DeLoach is a modern Southern belle,
     carefully reared in the traditions that are
     supposed to help her make all the right and
     safe choices in life. At twenty-one, Maggie,
     a senior in college, is pretty, popular, a
     member of the best sorority and pinned to the
     richest boy in school; she is also sensitive,
     caring and intelligent. In 1956, with the
     unrest leading to the civil rights movement
     just beginning, Maggie visits the Mississippi
     Delta with her boyfriend and, while there,
     looks into the face of a black prisoner who has

been captured in the streets.  This prompts
Maggie to return to school and write a sympathetic article for her school newspaper.
The turmoil this creates among the faculty and
her friends on campus forces her to leave her
sheltered existence.  While surrounded by
her frivolous sorority sisters, Maggie becomes
friends with a newspaper reporter and a free-
thinking girl from the East who influence her
new independence.

469. Siebel, Julia.  *For the Time Being*.  New York:
     Harcourt, Brace & World, 1961.  219pp.

   The Kansas plains of the 1920s and 30s, de-
void of any lush landmarks, make an appropriate
background for the Bembroy family.  While
father Paul prefers star-gazing to earthly
matters and his wife Christine exists in her
blind world, the children deal with their
stark surroundings in different ways as they
mature.  Mitchell, slightly ne'er-do-well, is
the most contented; daughters Ann and Nora
are perpetually at odds with their environment.
Nora escapes to pursue an acting career while
her sister bears the brunt of her mother's
handicap.  Only at the end of the novel does
the reader glimpse a vague hope of happiness
for Ann.

470. Slavitt, David R.  *Anagrams*.  Garden City, N.Y.:
     Doubleday & Company, 1971.  335pp.

   This satire on American faculty life spans
one weekend in the life of Jerome Carpenter,
poet and forger of dissertations.  Jerome,
his friend John Royle, and other literati read
from their work, attend parties, engage in
desultory sexual encounters with undergraduates,
and maintain their dignity as best they can.
Marty, John's student and lover, he values
for her gifts of "care, order, admiration,
beauty, lust, and typing--possibly in that
order."  John and Jerome's verbal wit and
moral uncertainties are treated in depth,
while the women in their lives are seen glancing-
ly and from the outside.

471. Smith, Betty. *Joy in the Morning*. New York:
     Harper & Row, Publishers, 1963.  308pp.

     Promptly after her eighteenth birthday, Annie
     leaves her native Brooklyn and moves to the
     Midwest to marry Carl Brown, her childhood
     sweetheart, despite the opposition of both
     mothers.  The year is 1927, and Carl is a
     law student at a state university.  Annie is
     a mixture of warmth, enthusiasm, curiosity, and
     naiveté.  Starved for learning, she longs to
     be a part of the university; listening regular-
     ly outside a classroom leads to an opportunity
     she would not have dreamed of.  Pregnancy,
     however, tests her courage and Carl's stamina,
     as he must work at several menial jobs.  The
     author describes the novel as "the anatomy of
     a marriage; the story of a victory over odds,"
     and characterization, especially of the child-
     like and yet oddly mature (and maturing) Annie,
     is central.

472. Smith, Lee. *Fancy Strut*. New York: Harper &
     Row, 1973.  329pp.

     A small town's preparation for a centennial
     celebration sets the stage for tragedy in
     this seriocomic novel.  All of the characters,
     including the young women, are stereotypical.
     There are a town "bad girl," an All-American
     girl majorette, and a tease who sees herself
     destined for Hollywood.  All are vving for the
     dubious honor of being selected queen of the
     festivities and none matures as a result of
     her experiences.

473. Smith, Mason. *Everybody Knows and Nobody Cares*.
     New York: Alfred A. Knopf, Inc., 1971.  213pp.

     After being seen on a California campus
     while lobbing a tear gas canister back at police,
     Ogden "O.J." Jones leaves wife, children, and
     graduate studies until he can safely return.
     The year is 1969, and with thumb out, O.J. hits
     the open road.  He encounters numerous strangers,
     all with tales to tell, and among his contacts
     is beautiful Erin, who becomes his traveling
     companion.  Her free spirit and youthful ideas
     match O.J.'s temporary needs and exuberance
     for life.

474. Snyder, Zilpha Keatley. *The Changeling*. New
     York: Atheneum, 1970. 220pp.

   Done in flashbacks, the story covers Martha
and Ivy's relationship from ages six to fifteen.
Family and friends' pressure makes it difficult
for Martha to be friends with Ivy, a strange
little girl who lives with her alcoholic
mother and her large, disreputable family.  Ivy,
with her vivid imagination, almost convinces
Martha that she is actually a changeling,
the daughter of a wood nymph or a water sprite.

475. Snyder, Zilpha Keatley. *The Headless Cupid*.
     New York: Atheneum, 1971. 203pp.

   Amanda, the twelve-year-old daughter of their
new stepmother, substantiates David's premoni-
tion that life is going to be very different.
Amanda arrives with her Familiar, boxes of
books on the occult, and an attitude of haughty
coolness.  Soon David and his three younger
siblings become Amanda's neophytes.  They learn
that in 1896 their house had been the scene of
poltergeist activity which ended in the be-
heading of a carved cupid's head on the stair-
way.  In a final plot twist, the cupid's head
is recovered through a genuine ESP experience.

476. Snyder, Zilpha Keatley. *The Velvet Room*. New
     York: Atheneum, 1965. 216pp.

   Growing up in California during the Depression,
twelve-year-old Robin McCurdy, daughter of a
migrant worker, finds refuge from the real
world in a deserted mansion with a book-lined
room and a mysterious past.  Robin, selfish
and insecure, becomes so obsessed by the Velvet
Room that she almost makes the mistake of plac-
ing it above her family in importance.  There
is an air of enchantment about the story.

477. Sonzski, William. *Punch Goes the Judy*. New
     York: Delacorte Press, 1971. 209pp.

   Keyes Bolton, the middle child of a "good
family" (of Indianapolis, Indiana), is called
upon by his desperate parents to help them
reclaim their errant nineteen-year-old daughter Judy ("Punch").  Keyes is sympathetic to

Punch's quarrel with their parents' unforgiving
attitude toward any behavior not meeting their
approval.  Keyes is repeatedly shaken by the
possibility that Punch is indeed mentally ill
and apt to harm herself.  Resolved to do what
is best for Punch, Keyes fails to realize that
he acts as a surrogate parent and is, there-
fore, doomed to failure.  Punch's sensitivity
and insight allow her to see through "the
system," to realize she cannot work to reform
it as Keyes intends to.  Her final act is the
"punch" that destroys any semblance of the
Boltons as a family.

478.  Southerland, Ellease.  *Let the Lion Eat Straw*.
      New York: Charles Scribner's Sons, 1979.
      181pp.

The author treats racial tension, incest,
and family relationships in this episodic story
of a black female who progresses from the age
of six to forty-five.  Some forty pages concern Abeba's adolescent years during which she
and her mother live alone in Brooklyn and are
very poor.  She is an intelligent and musically
talented adolescent who has a partial scholarship to a prestigious music school but falls
in love and chooses to get married over the
objections of her mother, who wants her to be
a concert pianist.  When she is fifteen, she
is raped by an uncle after she walks home
from school with a white male classmate.  This
relationship with her uncle continues for some
time until she retaliates violently.  These
incidents have a detrimental effect on her and,
after she marries, a nearly devastating effect
on her husband.

479.  Southern, Terry, and Mason Hoffenberg [as Max-
      well Kenton, pseud.].  *Candy*.  New York:
      G.P. Putnam's Sons, 1964.  224pp.

This is a commentary on modern life and sex
as revealed through the misadventures of a
young girl, and it employs elements of humor,
satire, and the picaresque.

480.  Speare, Elizabeth George. *The Prospering*.
      Boston: Houghton Mifflin, 1967.  372pp.

      Stockbridge, a mission established to teach
      the English way of life, was begun in 1734 on
      land granted by the General Court of Massachu-
      setts to the Indians. *The Prospering* tells
      the story of the community's development from
      the viewpoint of Elizabeth Williams who came
      to the settlement with her family in 1737 when
      she was seven years old. Elizabeth was curious
      about the Indians from the first and probab-
      ly would have developed a closer association
      if her family had permitted the contacts. She
      was independent in her early years since the
      other family members had different interests,
      but Elizabeth was the one who learned the
      art of caring for the sick and preparing medi-
      cines from herbs as a teenager working with
      her mother. These skills made her welcome
      and respected in the community as did her even-
      tual marriage to one of the ministers serving
      the mission.

481.  Spencer, Scott. *Endless Love*.  New York: Alfred
      A. Knopf, 1979.  418pp.

      This contemporary story of obsessive love is
      told from the perspective of David Axelrod,
      a seventeen-year-old Jewish boy whose object
      of desire is sixteen-year-old Jade Butterfield.
      After a brief love affair becomes too intense
      for even Jade's liberated parents to endure,
      David is barred from seeing Jade or the family
      for thirty days and responds by setting fire
      to their Chicago home. This adolescent act
      (intended merely to gain their attention) has
      shattering consequences, as David is sent to
      a psychiatric hospital for three years, and
      the Butterfield family breaks apart. After
      David's release on probation, his decision to
      regain Jade's and her family's love indirectly
      causes the death of Jade's father, making
      Jade end this self-consuming relationship.
      Although David is the novel's most fully drawn
      character, Jade also participates in his ro-
      mantic idealism. Thus she too serves to il-
      lustrate the theme of the novel: society forces
      young people to trade their dreams for a

stoic belief that the most satisfying part
of their lives may be a brief moment of intense
emotion that will never be repeated.

482. Sprague, Gretchen. *A Question of Harmony.*
     New York: Dodd, Mead & Company, 1965.  271pp.

     Her sixteenth/seventeenth year, her senior
     year in high school, is a complex one for
     Jeanne Blake, an accomplished young cellist.
     Her good luck in meeting and playing with a
     talented young pianist, Dave Carpenter, and
     a violinist, Mel Johnson, deepens her pleasure
     in serious music, polishes her skill, and may
     demand that she make the cello her profession.
     Her perplexing social relationship with Dave,
     who is determined to remain free of serious
     emotional bonds until he has completed medical
     training, is both a joy and a burden.  Female
     friends, especially giddy, opportunistic Dixie
     Thorne and gifted, jealous Marjorie Terry,
     also both nourish and irritate Jeanne.  A
     confrontation with open racism directed against
     Mel, who is black, and preparation for a music
     scholarship contest lend tension and contribute
     to Jeanne's maturation.

483. Sprague, Gretchen. *Signpost to Terror.*  New
     York: Dodd, Mead & Company, 1967.  217pp.

     Fifteen-year-old Gail Schaeffer from Brooklyn,
     along with her parents and sister Karen, goes
     on a camping vacation in the Adirondacks.  The
     story starts out slowly with the two sisters
     constantly arguing and their mother acting as
     peacemaker; then Gail goes walking alone on a
     trail, mainly to get away from Karen.  Soon
     the story becomes suspenseful as Gail inad-
     vertently becomes involved with three bank
     robbers and their hostage.  She falls in love
     with Lew, the mastermind of the robbery, but
     eventually decides that he could be very danger-
     ous and realizes she must try to escape from
     him.

484. Spykman, E.C. *Edie on the Warpath.*  New York:
     Harcourt, Brace & World, Inc., 1966.  191pp.

This book is set mainly in Massachusetts
in 1913. Eleven-year-old Edie's upper-class
family becomes frustrated with her mischievous
retaliations after she marches in a suffragette
parade and is taken to the police station,
declares war on men, isn't taught arithmetic
because she is a girl, isn't wanted at a party
and hunt her brothers give, and hears one of
her brothers say that she has sex appeal. Because of her antics, no one will believe her
and a friend when they report a hotel fire.
Edie is an intelligent, strong, and capable
young female who substitutes prankishness for
growth.

485. Stallworth, Anne Nall. *This Time Next Year*.
    New York: Vanguard Press, 1972. 288pp.

Set in rural Alabama during the Depression,
this book centers around fifteen-year-old
Florrie Birdsong, growing up with her unhappy,
mismatched parents. Torn between her father
with whom she shares a love of the land and
her discontented mother who dreams and plots
constantly of moving to town and away from
farm life forever, Florrie clings desperately
to the hope that some miracle will someday
make them all love each other and be happy
together. As Florrie watches her mother dogged-
ly work at winning newspaper contests and her
father struggle to coax a living out of share-
cropping on his rich sister-in-law's land,
Florrie retreats into a world of books and
dreams, unconsciously fighting growing up.
The sudden death of Florrie's mother causes
her to take the first step toward accepting
responsibility for herself and making her own
choices.

486. Stallworth, Anne Nall. *Where the Bright Lights
    Shine*. New York: Vanguard Press, 1977. 314pp.

This book, set in Alabama, begins in 1939
when Callie and Snow Berryhill and their three
adolescent daughters move to town (after twenty
years on a farm) into a house Callie has
bought with insurance money. Unhappy and unable to find work, Snow deserts his family

and this, along with Callie's obsessive
determination to keep the house at any
cost, deeply affects the girls as the story
covers the next seven years.  Each girl suffers
from the father's indifference, the mother's
possessiveness, and the couple's loveless
marriage, and tries to make her life different.
Maribeth, the oldest, marries a young soldier
she has known a week and moves to California
where she tries for two years to make her
disastrous marriage work while living with
his strange family.  Jo Anna, the youngest,
longing for stability and permanence, marries
the only boy she has ever dated.  Lee Rose,
who had to leave school to help support the
family, harbors the deepest resntment, and,
when she finally visits her father but gets
no admission of love or regret for his having
left them, commits suicide.

487. Stein, Sol.  *Living Room*.  New York: Arbor
     House, 1974.  309pp.

Stein's "successful woman" novel narrates
Shirley Hartman's rise to the top of the
advertising world.  As the Jewish Princess of
Madison Avenue, she has fame and wealth before
she is thirty but experiences growing depression and entrapment.  Of particular interest
to the main character's development are her
childhood and adolescence.  She quickly learned
to assert herself through intelligence, wit,
and beauty in order to reach a precarious
pinnacle of success.

488. Stern, Richard.  *Other Men's Daughters*.  New
     York: E.P. Dutton & Co., Inc., 1973.  244pp.

A middle-aged Harvard professor falls in love
with a young college woman.  After wandering
through several affairs with boys her own age,
Cynthia Ryder finds what she hopes will be a
lasting relationship with Robert Merriwether,
a married physiology professor and the father
of two teenaged daughters.  Told from Merriwether's point of view, the novel portrays
Cynthia as a middle-aged male's fantasy of a
young lover.

489.  Stewart, Edward. *Ballerina*. Garden City,
      N.Y.: Doubleday & Company, 1979. 519pp.

      Stephanie Lang is a talented dancer who
enters the competitive world of ballet in
New York at the age of eighteen. She is bullied,
lied to, and manipulated by her ambitious
mother, by the head of the ballet company, and
by a Russian defector named Sasha, a notorious
womanizer with whom she falls in love. She
shares a deep friendship with her roommate,
Christine Avery, an equally talented dancer,
whose shyness and chronic illness cause Stephanie
deep concern. With the realization of how
people have used her for their own interests
and how valuable friendship and life are,
Stephanie walks out on her most important
ballet role and allows Christine, who has only
a short time to live, to dance in her place.
This decision is a first glimpse of a new and
indendent Stephanie whose caring and sensitivity
have held her back as a dancer but have allowed
her to grow as a person.

490.  Stimpson, Kate. *Class Notes*. New York: Times
      Books, 1979. 225pp.

      Harriet Elizabeth Springer, high school class
of 1955, is the daughter of a conservative
father and a non-conformist mother who binds
Harriet to her in many significant ways. Not
socially successful, Harriet is highly involved
in school, cultural, and intellectual activities. She measures up to the "baffling im-
peratives of femininity" when she is kissed by
a boy on a hayride, but bisexual experiences
at college result in her final recognition
that she is essentially lesbian. Harriet
never realizes her full potential in a career
but finds fulfillment through social action
projects where she can help to eliminate bigotry
and prejudice.

491.  Stolz, Mary. *By the Highway Home*. New York:
      Harper & Row, 1971. 194pp.

      The novel joins Catty shortly after she
turns thirteen and follows her through several
months of upheaval. Her father's job loss

necessitates a move for her family, and as
their lifestyle changes, they gradually begin
to recover from the death of Catty's older
brother in Vietnam.  Catty emerges intact and
touched by first love.

492.  Stolz, Mary.  *Leap Before You Look*.  New York:
       Harper & Row, Publishers, 1972.  259pp.

       The six months leading up to and following
the divorce of fourteen-year-old Janine's
parents are described in this story set between
Christmases.  Adolescent friendships, family
relationships over several generations, and
the growing process are experienced and then
discussed by Janine, her family, and her friends.

493.  Stolz, Mary.  *The Noonday Friends*.  New York:
       Harper & Row, Publishers, 1965.  182pp.

       The Davis family lives in an apartment in New
York City.  Franny and her twin brother have
learned that mother must work away from home,
Franny must baby-sit with Marshall, a younger
brother, and they all must do without many
things their friends enjoy because father
cannot keep a job.  The warmth of family and
friend relationships, the acceptance of a
father's inability to provide for his family,
and the enjoyment found in small pleasures
combine in this story.

494.  Stolz, Mary.  *Wait for Me, Michael*.  New York:
       Harper & Row, Publishers, 1961.  148pp.

       Anny is fifteen and almost ready to admit
she will have to give up her love of fictional
heroes for involvement with real people when
young playwright Michael Vye comes to stay at
her mother's boarding house.  It is love at
first sight for Anny, but she is as young for
him as he is for her mother, to whom he is attracted.  Michael leaves their lives abruptly,
but both Anny and her mother grow and find
their own suitable loves in the next five years.

495.  Stolz, Mary.  *Who Wants Music on Monday*.  New
       York: Harper & Row, Publishers, 1963.  264pp.

       The stories of a mother, her college-aged son,

and her two teenaged daughters are told. The
girls are opposites. Lotta is blond, expert
at feminine wiles, and, according to her sister,
tactful to the point of being mindless. Cassie
is blunt and honest to a fault, and she longs
for a perfect world of art and language. At
odds most of their lives, the girls begin to
round out their personalities and come to face
their futures more realistically.

496.  Stoutenburg, Adrien. *Window on the Sea*.
      Philadelphia: Westminster Press, 1962. 158pp.

    The whole family, even Mom, feels that there
are few things a girl can do--except for home-
making and raising a family--that men can't do
better. Seventeen-year-old Mollie Lucas finds
this infuriating, which creates problems in her
relationships at home and with Glenn Jorgens,
who assumes they will marry when Mollie finishes
high school. It is the newcomer in town, Kingsley Reynal, who opens new doors for Mollie.
Though she thought him the oddest person she
had ever met when he first visited her father's
bait shop, Mollie learns to respect Kingsley's
concern for living creatures and his curiosity
about many things. As her friendship with
Kingsley grows, Mollie is raising her sights
and recognizing the possibility of achieving
higher goals before the summer ends.

497.  Strong, Jonathan. *Ourselves*. Boston: Little,
      Brown and Company, 1971. 228pp.

    Zada Kimberk, seventeen, is the shy, uncertain
daughter of a well-to-do Chicago family, constantly outshone by her charismatic older brother, Jeff. At a time when her classmates are
studying to be doctors and lawyers, Zada, who
wants only to be a housewife, feels compelled
to make a similar commitment in her life. When
she enters college, Jeff's former roommate,
Xavier Fereira, an equally uncertain young man
searching for his own identity, takes a broth-
erly interest in Zada. Because they easily
relate to each other and make each other feel
good about themselves, both Zada and Xavier
grow in self-confidence and assurance. The
platonic relationship slowly turns into a love
for each other that takes them both by surprise.

498. Stuart, Jesse. *Mr. Gallion's School*. New York:
     McGraw-Hill Book Company, 1967. 337pp.

     Although he's been away from teaching for
     some years, Mr. Gallion is persuaded to become
     principal of a small Kentucky high school on
     the Ohio border. The school has been becoming
     progressively weaker: it is lacking in discipline
     and academic standards. Mr. Gallion saves it
     by giving great responsibility to the students
     and by demanding much from them. A great many
     adolescent characters are briefly depicted,
     and though none is developed with any real
     depth, it is significant that more attention
     is given to boys than to girls. The novel calls
     for a return to earlier ethical and intellectual
     standards in education.

499. Susann, Jacqueline. *Once Is Not Enough*. New
     York: Wm. Morrow & Co., Inc., 1973. 467pp.

     January Wayne is the pampered, motherless
     child of famous Hollywood producer Mike Wayne,
     and as she grows up, she accepts the ordeal of
     Miss Haddon's elite boarding school in Connecti-
     cut only to please him. But with graduation
     comes the shocking awakening that Mike has a
     life apart from her, a fact she never completely
     accepts, comparing every man she meets with her
     father and having only one meaningful relation-
     ship, this with a man even older than Mike.
     Jacqueline Susann weaves a tangled web of
     personal relationships not only in the life of
     January but also in the lives of assorted other
     characters, with hardly a normal person in the
     lot. At age twenty-one, January, depressed
     at the death of her father and still halluci-
     nating from drugs, disappears from a lonely
     beach, united at last with her dream man, a
     mirage who looks like her father; this event
     concludes another Electra tale.

500. Susann, Jacqueline. *Valley of the Dolls*. New
     York: Random House, 1966. 442pp.

     Ethel Agnes O'Neill, seventeen, is part of
     a dance group called the Gaucheros, but her
     dream is to have a home and security. She

spent her first seven years in foster homes
until her older sister married and made a
home for her. Using the name Neely O'Hara,
she gets her first break as an understudy in a
Broadway show. When she later takes over the
part, she is discovered to have a natural
talent in singing, dancing, and acting and rises
to stardom in a very short time. To cope with
the pressures, she develops a dependency on
drugs and alcohol to lose weight, to sleep,
and to keep up the energy needed for her career.
This eventually leads to an addiction which
wrecks her personal and professional life.
Neely is one of several women whose lives are
traced in this novel.

501. Swarthout, Glendon. *Welcome to Thebes.* New
     York: Random House, 1962. 372pp.

     Sewell Smith, the protagonist, is a down-on-
his-luck hack writer who once struck it rich
with a novel about his battlefield experiences
during World War II. Drained of inspiration,
he returns to his hometown, Thebes, Michigan,
and finds the clique of town leaders (whom he
blames for ruining his father's career) embroiled in a sex scandal involving a fourteen-
year-old girl. Sewell uses the opportunity to
hatch an extortion plot. Although Carlie, the
girl, does not appear until the end of this
disjointed novel, her off-stage presence throughout defines the principal characters' motives.

502. Tanner, Edward Everett [as Virginia Rowans,
     pseud.]. *Love and Mrs. Sargent.* New York:
     Farrar, Straus and Cudahy, 1961. 277pp.

     Allison Sargent, at eighteen, is a reluctant
prospective debutante and an aspiring artist.
Her widowed mother, a successful advice-to-the-
lovelorn columnist, takes pride in the perfection of her life, including her children,
and unconsciously tries to mold Allison into a
decorative social being like herself when
young and to model her son after his father,
a Pulitzer-Prize-winning writer. Mrs. Sargent's
recognition of how manipulative and blind to
the feelings of others she has become is brought

about through a stormy new love affair and by the rebellions of her two children. Allison is only briefly characterized, but her certainty about her goals and her willingness to take risks for them are stressed.

503. Tanner, Louise [Stickney]. *Miss Bannister's Girls*. New York: Farrar, Straus & Co., 1963. 239pp.

Accurately self-labeled "An Acidulous Novel," this satire on the social pretensions of an upper-class private girls' school traces the lives of sixteen graduates of the class of 1940. And there is much to satirize in the lives of these insular, ignorant, prejudiced girls. But as the narrator tells her classmates' stories, she sees that privilege and polish can mask emotional desperation, that talent and panache don't guarantee success, and that some of the rich are driven to distraction and beyond by the iron-clad habits of their social class. In general, Miss Bannister's girls get what they have deserved: those with life, wit, humor, intelligence, and idealism get to exercise those talents. The meanest snob in the class goes totally to seed. And the narrator finally gains the confidence to withdraw all support, and her daughter, from her futile alma mater.

504. Taylor, Robert Lewis. *A Journey to Matecumbe*. New York: McGraw-Hill, 1961. 424pp.

Flight from the Ku Klux Klan is uppermost in the minds of Davey Burnie (who is modeled after Huck Finn) and his Uncle Jim when they leave Grassy Plantation in Kentucky just after the Civil War. Heading toward Key West with Zeb, a former slave, they encounter many interesting places and people--some posing danger for the trio. At Vicksburg they stop to visit a friend of Uncle Jim's and meet his unusual family including Lauriette Farrow, his youngest sister, a sharp-tongued twenty-year-old beauty. These qualities combine with her intelligence to help Lauriette rescue Davey after he is kidnapped by the Klan and get the two of them to Key West to meet Uncle Jim and Zeb. Lauriette, mellowing as she settles into life in her

new surroundings, relishes her newly acquired
independence and the growing attraction between
herself and Jim Burnie.

505. Taylor, Robert Lewis. *Two Roads to Guadalupé*.
     New York: Doubleday & Company, Inc., 1964.
     428pp.

     Alternating entries from journals kept by
     the Shelby brothers describe the war with
     Mexico during 1846-47. Joining the soldiers
     from Clay County, Missouri, the rambunctious
     fourteen-year-old Sam is attached to the
     Drum-and-Fife Corps while the more scholarly
     Blaine is assigned duties as historian for
     the troops led by Alexander Doniphan. During
     their march, Sam learns that Angeline Hughes,
     a neighbor of the Shelbys, who is attracted
     to Blaine, has disguised herself as a man and
     is in their company. Angeline maintains her
     secret until she is being treated for a shoulder
     wound after one of the battles. That wound
     is minor compared to the injuries inflicted by
     the man who holds her prisoner after she and
     Sam are captured.

506. Thayer, Nancy. *Stepping*. New York: Doubleday
     & Company, 1980. 346pp.

     Zelda is a twenty-one-year-old college student
     when she marries Charlie Campbell, a history
     professor, who is fifteen years older. They
     have nine months of perfect happiness until
     Charlie's two young daughters come to visit,
     and Zelda's ability to cope with a wide range
     of emotions is tested. She must contend with
     the hate and anger of Charlie's ex-wife, the
     children's jealousy and insecurity, and Charlie's
     deep love for his daughters and his determina-
     tion to have them with him in spite of the
     conflicts. Uncertain of her role and having no
     experience with children, Zelda is unprepared
     to find herself so much on the outside of
     Charlie's life. We see Zelda as a bright but
     certainly inexperienced young woman who feels
     resentment, anger, and jealousy at the intrusion
     in her life with Charlie but who also wants to
     prove herself capable of coping with the situa-
     tion.

507. Theroux, Alexander. *Darconville's Cat*. Garden
     City, N.Y.: Doubleday & Co., Inc., 1981.
     704pp.

     Isabel Rawsthorne at eighteen becomes the
     grand passion of Alaric Darconville, the major
     character of this novel. At least in Darcon-
     ville's eyes, Isabel is the epitome of grace
     and beauty. Ultimately, Isabel betrays Dar-
     conville's obsessive love and trust to marry
     the son of a wealthy, neighboring farm family,
     and her motivation is a mystery to Darconville.

508. Thomas, Audrey. *Songs My Mother Taught Me*.
     Indianapolis: The Bobbs-Merrill Company, Inc.,
     1973. 200pp.

     Isobel Cleary recognizes quite early in her
     life that she is a member of a neurotic family
     of social misfits. She spends a painfully lone-
     ly adolescence, never receiving even token ac-
     ceptance from her peers. Fearing she will
     become as neurotic as her mother, each summer
     Isobel flees to the sanctuary of a drifting
     rowboat in the middle of the lake at her
     grandfather's cottage where her family vacations
     each year. When her grandparents sell the
     summer haven, Isobel and her family are forced
     to face each other for every hour of every
     day for what seems to be, to the anxious teen-
     ager, a never-ending succession of summers. To
     escape, Isobel finally accepts a job at a mental-
     institution. There she finds an honest accep-
     tance of neuroses and begins to put her life in
     perspective.

509. Tolan, Stephanie S. *The Last of Eden*. New
     York: Frederick Warne, 1980. 154pp.

     Michelle ("Mike") Caine narrates this story
     of fifteen-year-old students in an exclusive
     and demanding boarding school. To Mike, who
     feels alienated from her mother and a stranger
     in her real home, the school is the Eden where
     she has true friends and a mentor who under-
     stands her deep commitment to writing poetry.
     But during her sophomore and junior years,
     she learns that corruption is present even
     here: in the crush of one classmate on a

male teacher, which leads ultimately to ac-
cuations of lesbianism against the teacher's
wife and another pupil; in the fragility of a
friendship which is first weakened by her own
jealousies and then destroyed by the malice of
another pupil; and finally in her observations
of an actual lesbian relationship between two
pupils. Mike, however, is strong, and, although
deeply hurt by her recognition of evil in her
Eden and in herself, she finds the courage to
recommit herself to her friends and to her
poetry.

510. Topkins, Katherine. *Kotch*. New York: McGraw-
    Hill Book Co., 1965. 190pp.

    Erica Bernheizle is fifteen and pregnant.
    After her boyfriend refuses to marry her, she
    leaves home and eventually sets up housekeeping
    with the central character of the novel, Kotch,
    an old man creeping into senility and dispos-
    sessed by his son and daughter-in-law. Kotch
    fantasizes that Erica and the baby-to-be will
    remain with him forever while Erica fantasizes
    that her boyfriend will take one look at his
    newborn child and marry her. Neither fantasy
    comes true. Erica, a normal fifteen-year-old
    concerned with hairstyles, clothes, and dates
    gives up her baby and returns to her family.

    Traver, Robert--*see* Voelker, John Donaldson.

511. Tucker, Helen. *The Sound of Summer Voices*.
    New York: Stein and Day, 1969. 256pp.

    When Patrick Quincannon Tolson is twelve,
    he begins to search for information about his
    mother, Celinda, who died at his birth and
    whose name is never mentioned in the house where
    he lives with his great-uncle, Darius, and his
    two aunts. From one of his aunts, he finally
    learns about the teenaged Celinda, a beautiful,
    spirited, and rebellious girl who, with her
    two older sisters, was left in the care of
    a bachelor uncle when their parents were killed.
    Celinda felt suffocated by the attention of
    the rest of the family and sensed they were all
    living their lives through her. Feeling that

she could never live up to their expectations,
at eighteen she eloped with Jason Tolson,
choosing him mainly for his indifference toward
her. The marriage failed, and she returned to
her family shortly before Patrick's birth.

512. Turner, Steven. *A Measure of Dust*. New York:
     Simon and Schuster, 1970. 190pp.

This book's central character, Mark Torrance,
thirteen, is a student in a boarding school,
who meets Geraldine Wester in rural Mississippi
during a trip home to visit his parents. Geraldine is a promiscuous fourteen-year-old and
far more worldly than the innocent and religious
Mark, who is just learning about life. In
spite of her seductiveness, Geraldine is a
kind and understanding girl with an underlying
sadness about her family situation.

513. Turngren, Ellen. *Hearts Are the Fields*. New
     York: Longmans, Green and Company, 1961.
     182pp.

Susan's will, like Papa's, had to be law.
Both of them set plans that did not take into
consideration the desires of others and almost
cost them the close relationships which they
want so badly. Complete severance of relationships with these loved ones is averted as Papa
and Susan recognize what they are doing and
determine to change their ways.

514. Tyler, Anne. *The Clock Winder*. New York:
     Alfred A. Knopf, 1972. 303pp.

Independent and unconventional, Elizabeth
Abbott leaves college in her senior year and
takes a job as a gardener and "handyman" in the
Baltimore home of Pamela Emerson, a rich,
eccentric widow with an equally eccentric family of seven grown children. Thinking that her
job will be relatively easy, Elizabeth hopes
to have a great deal of freedom to explore her
own interests and to enjoy life on her own
terms, but her carefree existence comes to a
halt when Matthew and Timothy, two of Mrs.
Emerson's sons, fall madly in love with her
and draw her into their turbulent sibling

rivalry.  Reluctantly, Elizabeth gives up
more and more of her freedom as she becomes
increasingly involved in the strange and complex lives of the Emerson family.  The novel
illustrates the difficulties facing modern
young women who attempt to live on their own
without family or romantic attachments.

515. Tyler, Anne. *Morgan's Passing*. New York:
     Alfred A. Knopf, 1980.  311pp.

     Emily Cathcart always considered her family
pale and ordinary and her childhood quite
unexceptional.  When she meets Leon Meredith,
the son of a Richmond banker with aspirations
to be an actor, she considers his life wonderful
and exciting.  To escape family pressures and
objections, Leon and Emily leave college and
go to New York where they are married, and
Leon pursues his acting career.  When his
improvisational acting group disbands in Boston,
Leon seems ready to give up acting and allows
Emily to draw him into giving puppet shows
for children's parties.  With a quiet serenity,
Emily's inner strength as a survivor shines
through in her relationships with her family,
her friends, her in-laws, and Morgan Gower,
the eccentric main character of the book.

516. Tyler, Anne. *A Slipping Down Life*. New York:
     Alfred A. Knopf, 1970.  214pp.

     Evie Decker is a quiet, dumpy seventeen-year-
old with few friends and no real dreams and
ambitions of her own, living with her bookish,
disinterested father, a mathematics teacher,
in a small town in North Carolina.  After hearing
him interviewed on a radio show, Evie becomes
fascinated with a rock guitarist named Bertram
"Drumstrings" Casey and seeks him out at a
rock concert and, later, at his performances
in a local nightclub where one night she is
found with his name carved in her forehead.
The book follows Evie's involvement with the
ambitious musician into their marriage which
is not so much for love as an attempt to better
their lives.  Although they are strangely
compatible, their lifestyle does not improve
as they are faced with unemployment, poverty, and

Casey's waning career as a rock star. When
her father dies suddenly, Evie, now pregnant,
asks Casey to come and live in her father's
house, and when he refuses, she leaves him,
showing a new strength and determination to
make a better life for herself without him.

517. Updike, John. *Rabbit Is Rich*. New York:
     Alfred A. Knopf, 1981. 467pp.

     In this third novel featuring Harry ("Rabbit")
Angstrom, Teresa ("Pru") Lubell follows Nelson
Angstrom from Kent State to Colorado, then to
his parents' home in Pennsylvania, visibly
pregnant when she arrives. A hasty wedding is
arranged for her and the immature Nelson,
and they move in with his family. Cool and
aloof, Pru sticks by Nelson even when he runs
away and later writes that he is enrolling
again at Kent State. She stays on with his
family who are left to wonder if she actually
loves Nelson or just considers him a good catch.

518. Updike, John. *Rabbit Redux*. New York: Alfred
     A. Knopf, 1971. 407pp.

     Eighteen-year-old flower-child Jill Pendleton,
a runaway from her wealthy home in Connecticut,
is one of the leading characters in this sequel
to *Rabbit, Run*. Before meeting middle-aged
Harry ("Rabbit") Angstrom, Jill has been in-
doctrinated with the 1960s anti-Establishment
ideals of pacifism, uninhibited sex, and drugs.
While Rabbit's wife Janice is living with a
lover, Jill and her black, intellectual, drug-
pushing friend Skeeter move into Rabbit's home,
where they "educate" Rabbit and his thirteen-
year-old son. Though Jill is adored by the
three males of the household, her life seems
doomed because of her drug addiction and her
inability to cope with her problems. As she
sleeps alone in the house, both Jill and the
house are destroyed in a blaze presumably set
by one of Rabbit's conservative neighbors.
Jill's story contributes to the theme: the
futility of both the conservative Establishment
and the youthful revolution of the 1960s.

519. Valin, Joseph. *The Lime Pit.* New York: Dodd,
     Mead, 1980. 245pp.

This crime novel centers around the murder
of Cindy Ann Evans, sixteen, who has escaped
from the safety and boredom of life with an
aged male "protector" into the excitement and
hazards of life among the members of a child
prostitution-pornography ring. Detective Harry
Stoner's search for the missing girl, who never
herself appears in the novel, slowly reveals
her personality and the grim realities of her
life. Even more important, perhaps, is Valin's
use of Cindy Ann's life as a symbol of the
corruption, wastefulness, and brutality of
contemporary American culture; Valin shares
his methodology and concern with such other
detective fiction writers as Ross Macdonald,
Robert B. Parker, and Margaret Millar. This
child-as-victim pattern is an important motif
in current crime fiction.

520. Vasquez, Richard. *Chicano.* Garden City, N.Y.:
     Doubleday & Company, Inc., 1970. 376pp.

The author's Mexican-American heritage illumi-
nates the Sandoval family saga. Several generations are traced from their southern origin
to the East Los Angeles barrio where they re-
locate. The story culminates with Mariana Sandoval, a young, beautiful girl who represents
all that is good and tragic to this segment
of the American peoples.

521. Vliet, R.G. *Rockspring.* New York: The Viking
     Press, 1973. 120pp.

At fourteen, Jensie is the somewhat petulant
daughter of a frontier family in west Texas
in 1830. Kidnapped and cruelly treated by
three Mexican bandits, she first tries to kill
herself but fails, and from then on her fierce
hunger for life prevails. The closest she
subsequently comes to defeat occurs when she
is forced to recognize that attempts to escape
are fruitless, for she is incapable of surviving
alone or of finding her way back to her family.
Her stubborn independence and courage never-
theless stand her in good stead, as she learns

to speak Spanish with her captors, comes to
understand and ultimately to love one of them,
and finally returns home, only to see one of
her fellow countrymen perform an act of violence
as senseless and brutal as her own kidnapping
had been.

522.   Voelker, John Donaldson [as Robert Traver,
          pseud.]. *Laughing Whitefish*. New York:
          McGraw-Hill Book Company, 1965.  312pp.

   *Laughing Whitefish* is a tale of a twenty-one-
year-old Chippewa Indian who fights the
greedy white man to a victorious finish in the
Michigan courts, claiming her inherited but
strongly challenged shares to the Jackson Ore
Company, which her grandfather, Marji, helped
to found by leading the initial surveyors to
the rich iron deposits.  William Poe, a young
and inexperienced lawyer, has her case literally
dumped on his lap by Civil War veteran
Cassius Wendell, a shrewd but often besotted
attorney.  Laughing Whitefish is beautiful,
intriguing, and well-educated, dedicated to
spending her life in the service of the rem-
nants of her people, desiring money from the
powerful Jackson Ore Company only to help her
tribe.  The novel is based on a true story and
is to a great degree a condemnation of whites'
wanton dispossession of the Indian from his
rightful lands.  Traver, himself a lawyer,
takes us through the tangles of litigation.
Laughing Whitefish wins more than money in her
battle--becoming a heroine to her people and
the bride-to-be of William Poe, who has fallen
madly in love with the spunky Indian beauty.

523.   Voigt, Cynthia. *Homecoming*. New York: Atheneum,
          1981.  312pp.

   Dicey Tillerman finds herself in charge of
her young sister and brothers when their mother,
no longer able to cope with life and its responsibilities, abandons them.  Alone, with little
money but fearing foster homes and possible
separation should they go to the police, the
children travel cross-country to explore their
limited options.  As head of her nomadic household, Dicey provides a strong and positive

female role model. Only thirteen, she handles
the grave responsibility thrust upon her in a
shopping mall parking lot and achieves her
goal--finding exactly the right home for her
special sister, brothers, and herself.

524. Von Hoffmann, Nicholas. *Two, Three, Many More*.
Chicago: Quadrangle Books, 1969. 251pp.

Although she is not a major character, Ellie
Rector's political coming-of-age is important
in this novel of radical campus politics in the
late sixties. Fuzzily apolitical, Ellie finds
herself irresistibly drawn to the commitment
and zeal of the campus radicals and surprises
herself by giving her name to a dean who is
seeking organizers of a demonstration. On
the periphery of political activities, she is
the innocent through whose eyes the reader
sees the escalating conflict between students
and administration, and at the end of the
novel, Ellie is becoming concerned with politics
and the events and people that shape and change
her life.

525. Wagoner, David. *The Road to Many a Wonder*.
New York: Farrar, Straus & Giroux, 1974.
275pp.

Set in 1859, this story dramatizes Ike's
escape from his worthless father to the gold
fields of Slab Crick off the South Platte River.
Ike Bender sets out to join his brother Kit
in the search for gold. His father gives him
a near-broken head to speed him on his journey, but sometime employer Tom Slaughter and
his fifteen-year-old daughter Millicent wish
him well. Acquiring a pistol as well as a
man-shy burro from an unsuccessful "bushwhacker,"
Ike meets a number of odd fellows before arriv-
ing in Dogtown where, to his surprise and
bewilderment, is waiting young Milly Slaughter.
Having decided that "Mr. Bender" is the only
man for her, Milly has run away from home to
join him and to become his wife rather than
sit home to wait for him while he helps all
the "damsels in distress" he comes across and
gets won over by one of them. The rest of the

adventure belongs to Ike and Milly; but however many wonders they discover along the
road they follow, the "greatest wonder" lay
under the wheelbarrow.

526. Waldron, Ann. *The Integration of Mary-Larkin
     Thornhill.* New York: E.P. Dutton & Co., Inc.,
     1975.  137pp.

     Written from personal experiences, Ann Wald-
     ron's story has a familiar theme with a twist of
     circumstances.  Desegregation of schools in
     the southern city of Stonewall prompts many
     parents of Mary-Larkin's friends to move away
     from their white neighborhood or enroll their
     children in private institutions.  But the
     Reverend and Mrs. Thornhill, staunch supporters
     of equal rights and Christian doctrines, refuse
     to alter their beliefs.  The author conveys
     the emotional impact of Mary-Larkin's initi-
     ation into a predominately black junior high
     school and her ostracism from the white com-
     munity  in a story in which mutual trust and
     understanding are gradually achieved.

527. Walker, Alice. *Meridian.*  New York: Harcourt
     Brace Jovanovich, Inc., 1976.  228pp.

     Substantial chapters recount Meridian Hill's
     girlhood and treat her guilt toward her mother,
     her perplexity about sex, her growing awareness
     of herself as a black, and her participation
     in the Civil Rights movement.

528. Walker, Alice. *The Third Life of Grange Cope-
     land.*  New York: Harcourt Brace Jovanovich,
     1970.  244pp.

     This Georgia novel, which examines the vio-
     lence, ignorance, and desperation of three
     generations of blacks, at first focuses on a
     "plump" and pretty teenager, Mem, who lives
     with Josie, a black prostitute, as an "adopted"
     daughter.  Mem is educated, a schoolteacher,
     but makes an unfortunate alliance with Brown-
     field Copeland, a wild and bitter black man
     who has made Josie's brothel his home after his
     father's desertion and his mother's suicide.
     Their marriage produces three daughters.  After

Brownfield murders her mother, Daphne, the
oldest daughter, goes north where she ends up
in a mental institution; Ornette turns to
prostitution to live; Ruth, the youngest, lives
happily with her grandfather, Grange, who has
returned to Georgia, regretful about deserting
his family. Brownfield and Grange fight for
custody, or "possession" of Ruth. Grange
shoots his son and is later killed by police.
The novel closes just as Civil Rights activism
and the end of family conflict provide some
peace and opportunity for Ruth.

529. Walker, Margaret. *Jubilee*. Boston: Houghton
     Mifflin, 1966. 497pp.

*Jubilee* describes, with some historical detail,
the daily living and hardships of slaves and
freed men and women in Georgia and Alabama.
The novel focuses on the life of Vyry, a mulatto
slave born to a plantation owner, John Dutton,
and Hetta, one of his slaves. Vyry begins her
working life as a teenager and at sixteen takes
a lover, Randall Ware, who is a free black man.
She has two children by him, but they are never
allowed to marry. After enduring the depriva-
tions, separations, and horrors of the Civil
War and the vigilantism and injustices of
Reconstruction, she is reunited with Ware, but
by then she has found a peaceful and hopeful
life in a legal marriage to Innis Brown.

530. Waller, Leslie. *The Brave and the Free*. New
     York: Delacorte Press, 1979. 602pp.

This novel examines the intertwined lives
of several members of the high school class of
1964 from their graduation night in a small
Midwestern town to their ten-year reunion.
Sarah Scudder, class valedictorian and potential
liberal, loves Hurd Banister, rich young ROTC
student headed for West Point and the Vietnam
war. We follow their stormy relationship, with
Hurd's year-older half-sister as the connecting
link. These two girls, as well as Peaches,
Jane's roommate, investigate the political,
social, sexual, and economic avenues open to
them.

531. Walter, Eugene. *Love You Good, See You Later*.
     New York: Charles Scribner's Sons, 1964.
     183pp.

     Margaret Bergeron is the main adolescent char-
     acter in this tale of a bizarre, free-thinking
     Southern family. She and her eccentric grand-
     mother Amelie vie for the attention and affec-
     tion of Amelie's visiting lover. The battle
     of wits is set against a backdrop of faded
     gentility and Bergeron persistence in embracing
     traditions and land holdings.

532. Ware, Clyde. *The Innocents*. New York: W.W.
     Norton and Company, Inc., 1969. 240pp.

     Living among the Indians who killed her
     parents, she was known as the Dog Girl because
     she was left to survive alone among the half-
     wild dogs of the tribe until a prospector
     traded for her and renamed her Doe. When she
     is about nineteen, the prospector's old age
     and illness make him realize he must prepare
     her for a life in civilization after his death;
     he must also, however, lead a band of outlaws,
     convinced the old man can take them to gold, on a
     treacherous and fruitless search, followed by
     Doe. The old man's only intention is to protect
     Doe and see that she is free from the outlaws,
     but Doe's devotion is equal to his; she stays
     with the band to take care of him, refusing
     any attempt to escape. In his final ploy,
     the old man drinks from a poisoned stream so
     the outlaws will do the same, and after their
     deaths, Doe escapes with Glade Mowrey, a Civil
     War veteran, who has come to understand their
     values.

533. Watson, Sally. *Jade*. New York: Holt, Rinehart
     and Winston, 1969. 270pp.

     Blending fact and fiction, this story of
     high adventure and romance in the early 1700s
     introduces sixteen-year-old Melanie Lennox,
     called Jade by those who love and respect her
     for the strong-willed individual she is. Her
     sense of right and wrong often places her in
     a position to clash with those in authority and
     consequently to receive frequent punishments.

Especially strong are her feelings about freedom, which earn her a flogging from the captain of a slave ship when she releases most
of his human cargo. Rescued by pirates, Jade
chooses to stay with them and to try to free
other slaves from their captors, but she refuses
to join in attacks on other ships or to take
a share of the loot.

534. Waugh, Hillary. *The Young Prey.* Garden City,
     N.Y.: Doubleday & Co., Inc., 1969. 206pp.

Virginia Hall, a fifteen-year-old from a
small Pennsylvania town, becomes a statistic
within five "chapters" of prologue (forty-one
pages), and Frank Sessions is the New York
detective assigned to the case. Virginia,
an overly protected and naive adolescent, and
her best friend are by chance included in a
joy ride to New York City to see a hippie festival in Washington Square. But once in New York,
the group learns there had been no plans for a
festival and, moreover, finds itself stranded.
Waugh's main thesis seems not to be directed
as a warning to young females but as a plea
for the restructuring of the American system
of justice.

535. Webb, Charles. *Love, Roger.* Boston: Houghton
     Mifflin Co., 1969. 188pp.

The author of *The Graduate* ventures into
fantasy. Travel agent Roger Hart, contemplating
a marriage proposal from nursing student Beth,
is locked in a Boston department store overnight with mysterious and melancholy Melinda.
His intention to design his life around both
young women leads to a compatible *menage à trois*
with all three characters merrily house-hunting
in the suburbs.

536. Weidman, Jerome. *The Sound of Bow Bells.* New
     York: Random House, 1962. 531pp.

Jennie Broom exploits protagonist Sam Silver's
trust and affection to transform their high
school's pre-commencement exercises into an
attack on their anti-Semitic principal. This
episode, one of many flashbacks into the adult

Sam's adolescence, not only changes Sam's life
(he is barred from graduation and also loses a
vital scholarship) but also characterizes Jennie
as a person of indomitable will and intense
passions who uses anyone conveniently placed
to feed her boundless ambition. The novel
traces Sam's adult life as a writer who turns
his back on his true ability partly because of
Jennie's disastrous influence; it recounts their
brief, destructive, youthful marriage and his
eventual adult efforts to free himself of her
impact and memory.

537. Weingarten, Violet. *A Loving Wife*. New York:
     Alfred A. Knopf, 1969. 241pp.

     This novel focuses on the middle-aged crises
and love affairs of Molly Gilbert, but two
adolescents, for a time, draw the heroine's
attention. Susan, the college girlfriend of
Molly's son, is a trendy and liberated young
woman who shocks Molly, but only briefly, by
sharing the son's bed in Molly's house. Barbara
Jean is a gifted, fifteen-year-old black whom
Molly, as a social worker, tries to rescue from
a New York slum and a life of poverty and despair.

538. Weingarten, Violet. *Mrs. Beneker*. New York:
     Simon and Schuster, 1968. 224pp.

     Carla, a college student, is living with Tommy
Beneker when she goes to his mother and asks
for money to have a safe abortion. Carla is
a girl of little conscience or concern for anyone except herself and is in direct contrast
to the kind and gentle Mrs. Beneker, a woman
who admits she never learned to get angry.
Relying on Mrs. Beneker's compassionate nature,
Carla admits she has not told Tommy and does
not know for sure if he is the father of her
baby. Mrs. Beneker refuses until Carla hints
that without the money, she might take sleeping
pills, and Mrs. Beneker relents and sees her
through the abortion.

539. Welles, Patricia. *Babyhip*. New York: E.P.
     Dutton & Co., Inc., 1967. 256pp.

Sarah, at sixteen, is aggressively verbal
and irreverently funny as she grows up in her
1960s Detroit Jewish home. Her parents are
pathetic, her two friends (one a black male
named Moses and one a female Catholic named
Jenny) are predictable, and her lovers are
shallow. She schemes and carefully plans her
escape from hopelessly square Detroit to Cam-
bridge to live with her fiancé, whom she has
no intention of marrying. There, her encounter
with Bobbie (a sensitive, rich boy who wears
opera pumps) has a strong impact, and Sarah
finally becomes painfully aware of the consequences of thoughtless actions.

540. Wells, Rosemary. *Leave Well Enough Alone.*
     New York: The Dial Press, 1977. 218pp.

The main character of this book, which eventually turns out to be a mystery, is fourteen-
year-old Dorothy Coughlin, who lives in Newburgh,
New York, in 1956. She has been reared in a
lower-middle-class Catholic home and goes to
a very strict parochial school. She gets a
summer job babysitting for a wealthy family
in Llewellyn, Pennsylvania, taking care of
nine- and twelve-year-old girls who are spoiled
and neglected. Dorothy lies several times and
steals a pair of boots, but due to her religious
background, she repents. She also tries to be
modest instead of proud and passive instead of
inquisitive but fails and is constantly bothered
by her conscience. Her curiosity leads her to
the truth about a death and a hidden will, the
contents of which she is ill-prepared to handle.
The summer proves to be very taxing on her
resourcefulness, maturity, and religious faith.

541. Wells, Tobias. *A Matter of Love and Death.*
     Garden City, N.Y.: Doubleday & Company, Inc.,
     1966. 191pp.

When her unoffical guardians are brutally
murdered, nineteen-year-old Judy Carter is the
obvious suspect. Detective Severson, the protagonist and narrator of this mystery, soon
realizes that she is lying; she tells him two
different versions of how she came to be taken
in by her guardians and of her discovery of the

murders, and he then hears yet a third version
from an apparently more trustworthy source.
After he has solved the case, the reasons for
Judy's lies are revealed, in a secret about her
background which has nothing to do with the
murders.

542. Welty, Eudora. *Losing Battles*. New York: Random House, 1970. 436pp.

In *Losing Battles*, a novel laden with Mississippi hill country dialogue, a picture of Ella
Fay Renfro, the sixteen-year-old sister of
Jack Renfro (the hero), emerges from the stories
told about her. A misadventure of hers opens
the novel: she loses Granny's gold ring to a
disreputable storekeeper, and Jack steals the
store's safe to regain the ring--an action
that lands Jack in state prison. Ella Fay is
characterized as a lively, mischievous teenager in a large, impoverished, sometimes foolish
family.

543. West, Jessamyn. *Leafy Rivers*. New York: Harcourt, Brace & World, Inc., 1967. 310pp.

Set early in the nineteenth century, this
novel depicts the maturation of Mary Pratt
Converse Rivers, who, before she has emerged
from adolescence, has survived the frustration
of her dreams for as much real education as
her frontier community can offer and substituted
a sometimes difficult marriage, a liberating
affair, and a dangerous but economically necessary journey. Her final emergence into womanhood is signaled by the birth of her daughter
and her assumption of her baptismal name, Mary
Pratt, instead of the nickname, Leafy. Ulti-
mately.capable, strong, independent, and nur-
turing, Leafy learns how best to love her handsome but weak-willed husband by loving another
and by driving their herd of hogs from their
Indiana home to the Cincinnati market. The
arduousness of life in the wilderness is depicted in this *Bildungsroman*.

544. West, Jessamyn. *The Life I Really Lived*. New
York: Harcourt Brace Jovanovich, 1979. 404pp.

By the time she is twenty-three, Orpha Chase
has become the widow of a murderer-suicide,
having lived in innocent blindness for two
years with a stunningly handsome man who is
certainly bisexual, possibly homosexual. Orpha's account of this courtship and marriage
and the violent events which ended it, along
with glimpses of life with her parents and
other incidents of her adolescence, form an
important portion of this long, leisurely
novel which is the mature woman's account of
life as she really finds it rather than as
she has depicted it in the many novels she
has written. Implicit in the statement is
Orpha's awareness that the events of her adolescence established patterns of thought and
feeling which influenced every later decision
she has made.

545.   West, Jessamyn. *The Massacre at Fall Creek*.
New York: Harcourt Brace Jovanovich, 1975.
373pp.

Set in 1824, this novel evokes the Indiana
frontier just at the period when it was turning
from wilderness to "civilization"; the symbolism of this change is twofold. West depicts the first trial of whites for the crime
of murdering Indians (heretofore condoned)
and uses the maturation of seventeen-year-old
Hannah Cape to parallel the development of
the area. The courtship between Hannah and
a  young attorney, Charlie Fort, is sweet,
intense, and difficult, for Hannah, guilty
and confused, retreats from the initial inti-
macy of the relationship. As Hannah learns
to govern her emotions and to forgive Charlie
for his affair with another woman, the community learns to govern its racism and bent
toward violence.

546.   West, Jessamyn. *A Matter of Time*. New York:
Harcourt Brace & Jovanovich, 1966. 310pp.

The flashbacks devoted to the adolescence
of Tassie and Blix Murphy are few but important. Tassie, the elder of two mature sisters,
is nuring Blix, a terminal cancer patient.

When the time comes, Tassie also helps Blix to
die easily and painlessly by her own hand.
Before Blix's death, the sisters confront the
void which has separated them for a number of
years and discover that their mother's use
of Tassie to dominate Blix was the chief cause
of their partial estrangement.  Only now, late
in her life, for instance, does Tassie learn
that when she pleaded, at Mrs. Murphy's insti-
gation, that Blix break off an adolescent affair, she permanently altered and probably
diminished her sister's life.

547.  Westheimer, David. *My Sweet Charlie*.  Garden
      City, N.Y.: Doubleday & Company, Inc., 1965.
      255pp.

      Ousted by an unsympathetic father, seventeen-
      year-old Marlene Chambers, pregnant and alone,
      seeks refuge for the winter months in an empty
      summer home on the Gulf Coast.  Charlie Ro-
      berts, too, needs shelter and a hiding place
      and breaks into the same house.  Thus begins
      a relationship that develops into a strong
      bond between two frightened people.  What
      makes the gradual friendship and mutual af-
      fection so unusual is that Marlene is a poorly
      educated, white Southern girl, and Charlie
      is a black Northern lawyer who, while taking
      part in a civil rights demonstration, acci-
      dentally murders a man.  Westheimer's novel
      poses the question: can racial prejudice be
      eradicated if both sides use time, patience,
      and listening ability to bridge the gap?

548.  Wetzel, Donald. *A Bird in the Hand*.  New
      York: Harcourt Brace Jovanovich, Inc., 1973.
      149pp.

      A triangle of forty-eight-year-old Claude
      Drover, his wife Ruth, and nineteen-year-old
      Naomi Fisher (a friend of Claude's son) leads
      to the break-up of Claude's marriage and the
      ecstatic union of Claude and Naomi.  Though
      the point of view of each of the central
      characters is used from time to time, Claude
      is the protagonist and the only one we get
      to know really well.  Naomi seems alluring,

vital, and loving to Claude: to Ruth she seems
merely immature. Her own character and feelings (except for her reiterated statements of
love for Claude) are less clear.

549.   White, M.E. *In The Balance*. New York: Harper
       & Row, Publishers, 1968. 218pp.

       Baylor Irish, a sometime college student
       and aspiring actress, seems always to be
       fleeing something without any sense of what
       she is running to. Her chaotic, meaningless
       drifting through life is reflected in the
       formlessness of this novel. It is through
       Baylor's eyes we see the action and in Baylor's
       stream of consciousness we seem to be as we
       shift from present to past and from reality
       to fantasy.

550.   Whitney, Phyllis. *Columbella*. Garden City,
       N.Y.: Doubleday & Company, Inc., 1966.
       306pp.

       Jessica Abbott, while recovering from the
       death of her mother, is summoned to St. Thomas
       in the American Virgin Islands by her aunt
       Janet. Upon arrival she learns that she is
       to be offered a position as tutor to a neigh-
       bor's fourteen-year-old granddaughter, Leila
       Drew. The problems between Leila and her
       mother seem similar to those Jessica had with
       her mother, and the two older women feel she
       will be a strong influence upon Leila. As
       the story involving Leila, her mother, and
       Jessica unfolds, the strong character of
       each individual is demonstrated, and the
       reader is reminded how critical one's devel-
       opment is at age fourteen. Leila is forced
       to face reality in a mature way and learn
       to accept her mother as she is. She learns
       to be an individual in her own right, not
       one made in the image of her mother.

551.   Wilkinson, Sylvia. *A Killing Frost*. Boston:
       Houghton Mifflin Co., 1967. 216pp.

       Ramona ("Ramie") Hopkins is thirteen. Dur-
       ing school sessions, she lives in town with

her Aunt Cecie, although she visits extensive-
ly with her grandmother, Miss Liz, whom she
calls "Mama," since Ramie spent her early
childhood years on her grandmother's farm.
Through this first-person account of Ramie's
hopes, fears, reactions, and dreams, we discover, along with her, various truths about
her deceased parents and the relationships
and personalities of family members, especially
her grandmother and grandfather, "Papa," who
died some five years earlier. Although only
four months or so of actual time pass, Ramie
delves deeply into both her own childhood
memories and those of her aunt and grandmother
converning her parents, grandfather, and dead
baby brother. A central issue is the response
of Ramie and Miss Liz to Dummy, an old, dumb
man who lives off the charity of the southern,
rural neighborhood.

552.  Wilkinson, Sylvia. *Moss on the North Side*.
       Boston: Houghton Mifflin Co., 1966. 235pp.

Cary, the central figure of the novel, is
the fourteen-year-old illegitimate daughter
of a Cherokee tenant farmer and a promiscuous
white woman. When Cary's father dies from
rabbit fever, she burns their cabin down
around his body in a last rite. Afterwards,
she is forced to live with her mother whom
she hates. In her loneliness, she becomes
engrossed in the oddities and cruelties of
nature. When she returns to work at the
Strawbrights' farm, Johnny's love and understanding provide her with the security she has
lacked since the deaths of her grandmother
and her father. Eventually she comes to an
acceptance of herself, her Indian heritage,
and the natural order of her rural world.

553.  Williams, John. *Stoner*. New York: The Viking
       Press, 1965. 278pp.

Although primarily concerned with the long
unhappy history of William Stoner's career
as an English professor at the University of
Missouri, this novel includes a touching portrait of Stoner's only child, Grace, a quiet,
introspective girl whose deep affection for

her father contrasts sharply with her mother's
open hostility toward him. Jealous of the
love that her husband and daughter share,
Edith Stoner tries to monopolize Grace's life
and to alienate her from her father. Frustrated by her mother's domination, Grace grows
distant from both her parents, leaving her
father confused and hurt. In her last year
of high school, she spends as much time as
possible away from home, and shortly after
graduation, she makes the final break from
her parents when she becomes pregnant, marries,
and moves to St. Louis. This disintegration
of the close relationship between Grace and
her father is one of the most tragic episodes
in a very tragic novel.

554. Willingham, Calder. *Rambling Rose*. New York:
     Delacorte Press, 1972. 309pp.

     Rose is a pretty nineteen-year-old in the
summer of 1935 when she comes to the narrator's
home in Alabama to work as domestic help. The
narrator recalls that summer when he was thirteen in an attempt to understand Rose, a girl
with a generous heart and a very active sex
life. For all her sexual escapades, some
explicitly described, Rose is an extremely
naive and trusting girl, terrified of loneliness and illness, desiring a home and family
intensely. Yet, even when she meets and marries Mr. Right, she is incapable of fidelity,
and that nearly costs her her life. She is,
as the song lyric goes, a rambling rose. It
is her nature to love widely.

555. Wilson, S.J. *To Find a Man*. New York: The
     Viking Press, 1969. 185pp.

     Rosalind Berk is a totally self-involved
young woman who asks Andrew Greenstone, her
childhood friend, to help her find a man to
take care of a friend who is "in trouble."
Andrew realizes that her only friend is herself and that it is Rosalind who is pregnant,
so he sets out to arrange an abortion. Although Rosalind is definitely selfish and
self-centered, we see her also as somewhat
naive and vulnerable and not nearly as worldly

as she would have everyone believe. Her dependence upon Andrew and their love-hate relationship is clear and funny. Rosalind emerges
from the experience unscathed and is still
insisting on her wedding day that it all happened to a friend.

556.   Wilson, Sloan. *All the Best People*. New York:
       G.P. Putnam's Sons, 1970. 510pp.

In this saga of two generations of two families, Caroline Stauffer develops along conventional lines as the daughter of a socially
prominent family. Caroline becomes the only
hope of her mother when the family loses almost everything during the Depression, a role
she accepts with relish. The years of her
adolescence are molded by a father who cannot
show his love for her except by yelling as
she crews his sailboat, by a mother who pushes
her toward marrying for money, and by a teenaged boy who worships her. Caroline rejects
the young man's true adoration, accepts her
mother's image of herself as worthy because
of her beauty, and substitutes an ever-increas-
ing number of brief encounters with young
men for a real relationship with her father.
These adolescent years form the woman who
finally marries the worshipping boy turned
man and foreshadow the eventual outcome of the
novel.

557.   Wilson, Sloan. *Georgie Winthrop*. New York:
       Harper & Row, Publishers, 1963. 304pp.

Charlotte Harkin, at seventeen, has lived
beyond her years because her mother insisted
that she should combine the experiences of
both their lives. The girl is uninhibited
and sophisticated when, as the catalyst in
George Winthrop's life, she pushes him to
continue with her the affair that he had
begun with her mother. Although it would
appear that this adolescent is merely a precocious sex object, abundant psychological
undercurrents are revealed in Charlotte's being
mother to her father, pushing George to become a man, analyzing and rejecting the predictable life of George's teenaged son, and

struggling to grasp the experiences of adolescence that have passed over her. While the action of the novel covers only a few months, the story covers many years and many experiences which leave a teenaged girl from a very untraditional background struggling to fill a traditional role.

558. Winter, Alice. *The Velvet Bubble*. New York: William Morrow & Co., 1965. 221pp.

This psychological study of an adolescent's abnormal love for her father is told in the first person by Dorrie Lawson, fourteen, whose existence is focused on her desire to be the only woman in her father's life. A delicate mental balance deteriorates as Dorrie tells of her lifelong hatred of her mother and of her past and current struggle to eliminate anyone who threatens her goal. The actual story unfolds during the year between Dorrie's mother's death and Dorrie's attempt to murder the woman her father grows to love, but much of the telling also includes earlier unbalanced episodes in Dorrie's life.

559. Winters, Nancy. *The Girl on the Coca-cola Tray*. New York: The Dial Press, 1976. 181pp.

This humorous novel gives an overview of social forces at work on young women in the 1950s. Led through the story by Jennie Sue Massengill, New York-born and educated within the strict boundaries of Catholic and private schools, the reader sympathizes with her struggle to reflect her mother's image of the all-American girl--a blonde, smiling, wholesome girl who adorns the Coca-cola tray. Jennie's pseudo-expression of independence is her marriage to Hyman ("Feen") Feinstein, a bright but unambitious man who demands slavish devotion and emulation. Only after a family crisis in which mother-daughter roles are reversed does Jennie recognize personal worth and individual rights.

560. Witheridge, Elizabeth. *Never Younger, Jeannie*. New York: Atheneum, 1963. 150pp.

"You'll never learn younger" was the ex-
pression used frequently by Grandmother during
the year Jeannie spent at Seven Pines Farm
with her grandparents. Throughout this time,
the eleven-year-old Californian has an opportunity for many varied experiences of Michigan
farm life in 1914.

561.  Woiwode, Larry.  *Beyond the Bedroom Wall: A*
      *Family Album.*  New York: Farrar, Straus and
      Giroux, 1975.  619pp.

      This lengthy novel is, indeed, a literary
      album which provides more than a glimpse of
      two families--the Joneses and Neumillers.
      The latter family is developed with extreme
      detail, and the female characters are sharply
      defined, particularly Alpha Jones.  This re-
      markable woman's life is traced from her
      childhood and adolescence in North Dakota to
      marriage to Martin Neumiller to her death at
      age thirty-four.  Her calm exterior, religious
      convictions, and determination to encourage
      self-expression in her children are traits
      which dramatically shape her offspring.  Even
      after her death, Alpha remains a strong in-
      fluence on the thoughts and words of the other
      main characters.

562.  Woiwode, Larry.  *What I'm Going to Do, I Think.*
      New York: Farrar, Straus and Giroux, 1969.
      309pp.

      Woiwode's rather bleak first novel is a
      study of two young people tormented by their
      pasts and trying desperately to overcome fear
      through their marriage.  Ellen, twenty-one
      and just barely pregnant when they wed, was
      raised by wealthy grandparents who protected
      her from her parents' mysterious deaths (al-
      ways referred to as "the accident").  Her
      husband Chris Eenanam is a bright graduate
      student with a promising future, but Ellen's
      love and reassurances cannot erase his self-
      doubts and deep depressions.

563.  Wolff, Maritta.  *Buttonwood.*  New York: Random
      House, 1962.  343pp.

Susie, the adolescent female in this novel, is a minor character involved in a subplot in the story of Paul Maitland, war hero, son, brother, lover, protector. In his life, Susie is the questioner for whom he has no honest answer. She is a young woman on a pedestal, admired and cared for: part of the reason that he is still a bachelor in his late thirties, part of the reason he takes care of her mother but never marries her. Paul is not Susie's biological father, but he acts as a surrogate and watches over her rearing. Susie's questioning his actual place in her life reveals her struggle to understand herself outside the boundaries of a traditional family life.

564. Wolff, Ruth. *A Crack in the Sidewalk*. New York: The John Day Company, Inc., 1965. 282pp.

In a small town setting in mid-America, Linsey Templeton, aged thirteen, is growing up in a loving family who live above a hardware store on Main Street. She has a lovely voice and enjoys singing with the family, but still she knows that very soon she and her older sister will be leaving their parents' home. The story centers around Linsey's growing up and learning to accept adult responsibilities at an early age. Her character is strong and determined, yet never does she forget others. As she matures and accepts a job singing with a folk music trio for the summer, she learns that true love may be found close at hand in someone whom she considered only a good friend.

565. Wolff, Ruth. *I, Keturah*. New York: The John Day Company, Inc., 1963. 285pp.

Brought up in an orphanage, Keturah Brown, aged sixteen, did not know what it meant to be part of a family until the summer she went to live with an older couple, the Dennys. During her three years in their home, Keturah learned about love and caring for others and began to yearn to be a lady. Then she accepted a position in the Hawthorne home where she

cared for the small, frail child Adrianne, and
came under the influence of Miss Hawthorne,
a grand, stately, but cold and very private
person. Keturah brings to the Hawthorne house
her warmth and understanding and in return
learns how to be a lady.

566.  Wolitzer, Hilma. *Hearts*. New York: Farrar,
      Straus and Giroux, 1980. 324pp.

      *Hearts* recounts the oftimes troubled journey
      of two strangers toward understanding and
      emotional maturity. In addition, it tells of
      a physical journey across America reminiscent
      of Steinbeck's *Travels with Charlie*. Newly
      widowed dance teacher Linda Reisman, aged
      twenty-six, leaves New Jersey with her bel-
      ligerent thirteen-year-old stepdaughter Robin,
      driving a newly mastered green Maverick and
      heading for that great American magnet for
      the dispossessed, California. Robin carries
      hate in her heart and a murderous fork in her
      pocket, both intended for her real mother who
      deserted her as a small child. But many things
      happen on the trip across the country, includ-
      ing Linda's botched abortion, her passionate
      fling with an engaging hitchhiker, and Robin's
      discovery that her real mother is not, after
      all, a monster. The two resolve their dif-
      ferences with love and mutual respect, Linda
      deciding to keep her baby, and Robin, finally
      able to release her resentments through the
      luxury of tears, choosing to accompany her
      in a new life. As they cross the state line,
      the book ends on that upbeat note: "California,
      here we come."

567.  Wood, Phyllis Anderson. *I Think This Is Where
      We Came In*. Philadelphia: Westminster Press,
      1976. 155pp.

      When Paul and Mike, both eighteen, and Paul's
      seventeen-year-old sister Maggie head for a
      camping trip in the high Sierras, their in-
      tention is to "take it easy and have fun" be-
      fore fall and a return to school. During
      their holiday, they first become nursemaids
      to a very sick dog, then owners of a mis-

chievous pup, and finally heartbroken kids
abandoned by their dog.  Maggie is a mature,
responsible young woman who makes this trip
as one partner of a threesome, taking on no
more cooking and cleaning chores than either
of the boys: "one of the new breed of females."
Because of Maggie's empathy with others and
the comradery of the youngsters, they develop
a closeness over this vacation that generates
a gentle shift from a "brother-sister" relationship between Mike and Maggie to that of
boyfriend-girlfriend.

568.  Woodfin, Henry.  *Virginia's Thing*.  New York:
      Harper & Row, Publishers, 1968.  185pp.

This private detective novel reveals an
adolescent female image through the eyes of
those who knew her before her body was found
on the shore of a lake.  Virginia, a twenty-
year-old college junior, was a civil rights
activist who worked in Mississippi, pledged
herself to the social democratic values of
her union organizer father, studied political
science, and secretly married a black activist
whom she loved.  She had been deserted by her
mother when she was very young but had been
reared by a stepmother and had accepted her
middle-class values.  Her accidental death
was the culmination of a cruel hoax which
falsely persuaded her that her father had
committed her real mother to a mental institution so that he could marry again.  That destruction of her faith in the rightness of
her father's ideals led to her death.

569.  Yafa, Stephen H.  *Paxton Quigley's Had the
      Course*.  New York: J.B. Lippincott Co., 1967.
      195pp.

Pax, fraternity boy and womanizer, meets his
match in Tobey Clinton, a Bennington College
student whose heart and mind cry for revenge
when "Tobe" learns Pax "the Quig" has been
screwing Jan and Eulice while secretly pinned
to her.  Eventually Pax decides Tobey is the
only woman for him--but it's too late.  Tobey
plots with Jan and Eulice to lock Quig in the
attic of her dorm.  The reader first meets

Quig after he has spent two weeks in the attic,
surviving on yogurt and wheat germ and sex
every four hours. The bantering tone, the
militant action of its female characters, and
the sentimental unhappy ending mark this book
as angry satire.

570.  Yates, Richard. *The Easter Parade*. New York:
      Delacorte Press, 1976. 229pp.

Included in this forty-year chronicle of the
lives of two sisters, Sarah and Emily Grimes,
are vivid accounts of their romantic encounters
in adolescence. When she is nineteen, Sarah,
the oldest, meets an English-bred young man who
looks like Laurence Olivier, and it is not long
before the two marry and settle into what Sarah
hopes will be a story-book marriage, a dream
symbolized for her by a romantic photograph of
her and the dashing young man at the Easter
Parade on Fifth Avenue. Less attractive but
more intellectual than her sister, Emily longs
to find a man as attractive as her sister's
husband but instead gives up her virginity to
a strange soldier in Central Park whom she will
never see again. Uncompromisingly bleak, the
novel examines the ways that both sisters fail
to find satisfying relationships with men and
suggests that women are too often doomed to
suffer either the agonizing bondage of a
"dream marriage" turned sour or the agonizing
freedom of casual affairs that lead nowhere.

571.  Yglesias, Helen. *Sweetsir*. New York: Simon
      and Schuster, 1981. 332pp.

Morgan Beauchamp Sweetsir is a sadistic bum
who engages in wild sexual frolics and thumps
his women now and then to keep them in line,
but he has a charm which mesmerizes his friends
and victims into rationalizing his dangerous
eccentricities. Sally, wife number five, finally slips a knife into him, but before she is
acquitted for his murder, we see her in flashbacks as a fifteen-year-old marrying the mild
little Italian who has made her pregnant (later
educating herself to become a secretary) and
her efforts to "have things nice" for herself
and her daughter Laura. Bored with her marriage

to middle-aged Vin, she divorces him and falls
prey to the love-hate relationship between her
and the irresponsible Sweetsir. The sixteen-
year-old daughter Laura, a prominent figure
in the book, is her mother's joy, but ultimately
disappoints her badly by leaving school to
live with a youth of questionable origin,
possibly one of Sweetsir's progeny. Her ration-
ale, "But we're in love," is as old as time,
and just as fatal, as Sally has learned in the
battle of the sexes. She is freed by the jury,
but it remains uncertain whether she will ever
be free of the masochistic leanings some women have toward brutal mental and physical exploitation.

572. York, Carol Beach. *Sparrow Lake*. New York:
    Coward-McCann, 1962. 155pp.

    Shy and book-bound Liddie Howard, raised
by artistic Aunt Alice and groomed by status-
conscious Aunt Ila, is momentarily displaced
from an ivory tower during her sixteenth year.
Aunt Alice and Liddie occupy their summer home
on Sparrow Lake for a winter, and the young
girl's attendance at the local school brings
her in contact with commonplace adolescent
experiences--going to the drugstore after
school, having a flirty best friend who wears
too much make-up, and being infatuated with
a handsome high school drop-out. Carol York's
story conjures memories of every girl's special
year while stressing the sad dilemma of social
restraints imposed by class distinctions.

573. Zacharias, Lee. *Lessons*. Boston: Houghton
    Mifflin Company, 1981. 342pp.

    In a series of extensive flashbacks, the
adult Janie Hurdle reconsiders her adolescence,
dwelling particularly on several important
junior high and college experiences. These
include the beginnings of her lifelong devotion
to musicianship (she is a fine clarinetist),
some dreary moments of sexual initiation during junior high, a doomed college affair, and
an appallingly unwise marriage. Each event,
however, ultimately contributes to Janie's

growth, and she emerges stronger, wiser than
any individual situation could foreshadow.
Zacharias stresses the drive and dedication
necessary to the true artist.

574.  Zindel, Paul. *The Girl Who Wanted a Boy*.
      New York: Harper & Row, Publishers, 1981.
      148pp.

      Sibella Cametta, a fifteen-year-old student
      who is a scientific whiz, feels like a freak
      among her friends.  Her special abilities
      in physics seem to set her apart from the
      social life at high school, and she longs to
      have a boyfriend as the other girls do.  One
      day she sees Dan's picture in the newspaper
      and is instantly in love; she is convinced he
      is the one who will fulfill all her dreams.
      This is a story of a teen's first tender,
      fragile love and how she copes with the unex-
      pected disappointment of love not returned.
      Sibella comes to realize that a one-sided
      love is indeed very painful, but that it is
      not the end of everything and life will go on.
      Her father's law of love reciprocity--"Don't
      give your heart away to anyone unless you know
      he wants it and wants to give you his"--is
      a lesson Sibella finally comes to understand.

575.  Zindel, Paul. *I Never Loved Your Mind*.  New
      York: Harper & Row, Publishers, 1970.  181pp.

      Pulitzer-Prize-winner Zindel, writer of
      numerous works for young adults, frankly and
      humorously presents the turbulent and outspoken
      attitudes of the late 1960s through the char-
      acter of Yvette Goethals, a high school drop-
      out who works as a hospital aide.  Yvette's
      communal life style and disgust with the
      Establishment contrast with the standards of
      Dewey Daniels, a seventeen-year-old who lives at
      home but quit school because "they weren't teach-
      ing anything urgent."  After being hired at the
      same hospital, Dewey schemes his way to
      Yvette's heart, and mutual sexual attraction
      temporarily binds them.  Philosophical dif-
      ferences, however, end the relationship.

576. Zindel, Paul. *My Darling, My Hamburger.* New
     York: Harper & Row, Publishers, 1969. 168pp.

   Although high school seniors Marie and Liz
are best friends, popular Liz is going steady
with confident Sean while mousey Marie is still
being "fixed up" with boys like Dennis. The
parents of both Dennis and Marie appear very
supportive, while both Sean and Liz have real
problems at home. The night Liz feels that she
has been cut loose from trying to please her
parents, she seeks comfort in the persistent
Sean's arms; as a consequence, Liz becomes
pregnant and is eventually dropped by Sean
after he seeks the advice of his father, saying
that "his friend" got this girl in trouble
and doesn't know what to do. Liz requests
Marie's help in arranging a time when she can
have an abortion without her parents' know-
ledge--prom night; and Marie must break her
prom date with Dennis to help her friend.
Somewhat dated, this novel depicts many of the
painful decisions youth encounters on the way
to adulthood--particularly that of the young
female whose boyfriend wants her "to go all
the way."

577. Zindel, Paul. *The Pigman.* New York: Harper
     & Row, Publishers, 1968. 182pp.

   Paul Zindel has been praised for his ability
to create characters who honestly represent
the pleasure and pain of adolescence. Lorraine
Jensen and her best friend John Conlan, both
slightly maladjusted to school and home life,
befriend Mr. Pignati ("The Pigman"). The
lonely widower showers them with all types of
favors and trusts the young people to the
point where his home is always available.
Against Lorraine's better judgment, however,
John uses the house for a party while Mr. Pignati is in the hospital. The old man is shocked
to find his belongings in disarray and does
not recover after being hospitalized again.
The two teenagers must cope with the guilt and
sorrow of The Pigman's death.

578. Zindel, Paul. *The Pigman's Legacy*. New
     York: Harper & Row, Publishers, 1980. 183pp.

     The sequel to *The Pigman* begins with Lorraine
     Jensen and John Conlan experiencing depression
     and guilt over the death of Mr. Pignati. To
     ease the pain, they return to his house only
     to find another elderly occupant. Colonel
     Parker Glenville made and lost a fortune de-
     signing subway systems, and as with the Pigman,
     Lorraine and John provide support and affection
     for a lonely, dying man. With the death of
     the Colonel, however, comes a rebirth of
     belief in themselves and an acknowledgment of
     their romantic attraction to each other.

579. Zindel, Paul. *The Undertaker's Gone Bananas*.
     New York: Harper & Row, Publishers, 1978.
     239pp.

     A loner who bumbles into trouble if he hasn't
     already jumped smack into it eyes opened, Bobby
     Perkins is first befriended by Lauri Geddes
     when Bobby is unjustly carted off to the sta-
     tionhouse to be "booked." Lauri's action
     cements the bond between them, for Bobby sees
     that Lauri had undertaken what was for her a
     courageous act. In fact, Bobby soon learns
     that Lauri is frightened of everything and
     works at creating "adventures" to help rid
     her of her fears. Their adventures serve not
     only to help Lauri but also to put them in
     conflict with the local police patrols. When
     Mr. and Mrs. Hulka (he is the undertaker of
     the title) move into the apartment next door
     to the Perkins', Lauri's mother prepares a
     meal with which Lauri and Bobby can welcome
     the Hulkas, and the real adventure in Zindel's
     "first murder-mystery" is "off and running."
     Though Lauri's involvement with Bobby is thera-
     peutic (both she and her mother realize she
     has "a thing" for Bobby), in this last adven-
     ture, she is never far from fainting, but
     she is not about to desert her best and only
     friend.

# CHRONOLOGY

434. Sandburg, Helga, *The Owl's Roost*
436. Sanguinetti, Elise, *The Last of the Whitfields*
496. Stoutenburg, Adrien, *Window on the Sea*
501. Swarthout, Glendon, *Welcome to Thebes*
536. Weidman, Jerome, *The Sound of Bow Bells*
563. Wolff, Maritta, *Buttonwood*
572. York, Carol Beach, *Sparrow Lake*


*1963:*

 22. Barker, Shirley, *Strange Wives*
 59. Calisher, Hortense, *Textures of Life*
 64. Carter, Mary, *A Fortune in Dimes*
123. Faasen, Neal, *The Toyfair*
252. Kubly, Herbert, *The Whistling Zone*
254. Lambert, Gavin, *Inside Daisy Clover*
262. Leary, Paris, *The Innocent Curate*
266. Lee, Mildred, *The Rock and the Willow*
376. Plath, Sylvia, *The Bell Jar*
396. Reed, Meredith, *Our Year Began in April*
471. Smith, Betty, *Joy in the Morning*
495. Stolz, Mary, *Who Wants Music on Monday*
503. Tanner, Louise, *Miss Bannister's Girls*
557. Wilson, Sloan, *Georgie Winthrop*
560. Witheridge, Elizabeth, *Never Younger, Jeannie*
565. Wolff, Ruth, *I, Keturah*


*1964:*

 33. Betts, Doris, *The Scarlet Thread*
 86. Cores, Lucy, *The Misty Curtain*
 91. Crawford, Joanna, *Birch Interval*
 97. Cuomo, George, *Bright Day, Dark Runner*
 98. Curtiss, Ursula, *Out of the Dark*
106. Disney, Doris Miles, *The Hospitality of the House*
113. Downey, Harris, *The Key to My Prison*
120. Ehle, John, *The Land Breakers*
125. Farrell, James T., *What Time Collects*
136. Friedman, Bruce Jay, *A Mother's Kisses*
156. Gover, Robert, *Here Goes Kitten*
160. Grau, Shirley Ann, *The Keepers of the House*
164. Greenberg, Joanne, *I Never Promised You a Rose Garden*
169. Grumbach, Doris, *The Short Throat, the Tender Mouth*

212.  Hunter, Kristin, *God Bless the Child*
215.  Hutchins, Maude, *Honey on the Moon*
237.  Kaufman, Bel, *Up the Down Staircase*
253.  Kumin, Maxine, *Through Dooms of Love*
258.  Lanham, Edwin, *Speak Not Evil*
278.  Loewengard, Heida, *A Sudden Woman*
304.  McHugh, Arona, *A Banner with a Strange Device*
319.  Miller, Heather Ross, *The Edge of the Woods*
349.  Oates, Joyce Carol, *With Shuddering Fall*
375.  Pitkin, Dorothy, *Sea Change*
394.  Reed, Kit, *At War As Children*
402.  Richter, Conrad, *The Grandfathers*
408.  Robertson, Don, *A Flag Full of Stars*
437.  Sanguinetti, Elise, *The New Girl*
457.  Selby, Hubert, Jr., *Last Exit to Brooklyn*
479.  Southern, Terry, and Mason Hoffenberg, *Candy*
505.  Taylor, Robert Lewis, *Two Roads to Guadalupe*
531.  Walter, Eugene, *Love You Good, See You Later*


*1965:*

  6.  Allen, Elizabeth, *The Loser*
 12.  Armstrong, Charlotte, *The Turret Room*
 35.  Blake, Katherine, *My Sister, My Friend*
 36.  Blake, Sally, *Where Mist Clothes Dream and Song Runs Naked*
 68.  Chappell, Fred, *The Inkling*
 89.  Cormier, Robert, *Take Me Where the Good Times Are*
114.  Drexler, Rosalyn, *I Am the Beautiful Stranger*
118.  Echard, Margaret, *I Met Murder on the Way*
128.  Fikso, Eunice, *The Impermanence of Heroes*
166.  Grossman, Alfred, *Marie Beginning*
185.  Harrison, G.B., *The Fires of Arcadia*
205.  Horgan, Paul, *Everything to Live For*
250.  Kranidas, Kathleen, *One Year in Autumn*
275.  Linney, Romulus, *Slowly, By Thy Hand Unfurled*
305.  McHugh, Arona, *The Seacoast of Bohemia*
313.  Mercer, Charles, *Beyond Bojador*
316.  Mezvinsky, Shirley, *The Edge*
338.  Nichols, John Treadwell, *The Sterile Cuckoo*
369.  Perutz, Kathrin, *A House on the Sound*
371.  Philips, Judson, *The Twisted People*
399.  Richardson, Vokes, *Not All Our Pride*
451.  Schoonover, Shirley, *Mountain of Winter*
476.  Snyder, Zilpha Keatley, *The Velvet Room*

188.  Hawes, Evelyn, *A Madras-Type Jacket*
256.  Lamott, Kenneth, *The Bastille Day Parade*
296.  Marshall, Catherine, *Christy*
297.  Mather, Melissa, *One Summer in Between*
306.  McInerny, Ralph, *Jolly Rogerson*
333.  Nathan, Robert, *The Devil with Love*
345.  Oates, Joyce Carol, *A Garden of Earthly Delights*
367.  Perrin, Ursula, *Ghosts*
395.  Reed, Kit, *The Better Part*
416.  Rollins, Bryant, *Danger Song*
418.  Rosenberg, Jessie, *Sudina*
425.  Roth, Philip, *When She Was Good*
430.  Salas, Floyd, *Tattoo the Wicked Cross*
432.  Samuels, Gertrude, *The People vs. Baby*
435.  Sandburg, Helga, *The Wizard's Child*
450.  Schoen, Barbara, *A Place and a Time*
464.  Sherburne, Zoa, *Too Bad About the Haines Girl*
480.  Speare, Elizabeth George, *The Prospering*
483.  Sprague, Gretchen, *Signpost to Terror*
498.  Stuart, Jessie, *Mr. Gallion's School*
539.  Welles, Patricia, *Babyhip*
543.  West, Jessamyn, *Leafy Rivers*
551.  Wilkinson, Sylvia, *A Killing Frost*
569.  Yafa, Stephen H., *Paxton Quigley's Had the
      Course*


*1968:*

27.   Baumbach, Jonathan, *What Comes Next*
29.   Benchley, Nathanie, *Welcome to Xanadu*
46.   Bradford, Richard, *Red Sky at Morning*
61.   Carpenter, Don, *Blade of Light*
66.   Chappell, Fred, *Dagon*
78.   Cleaver, Vera, and Bill Cleaver, *Lady Ellen
      Grae*
95.   Culp, John H., *A Whistle in the Wind*
144.  Gasner, Beverly, *Girls' Rules*
157.  Gover, Robert, *J C Saves*
210.  Hunter, Evan, *Last Summer*
213.  Hunter, Kristin, *The Soul Brothers and Sister
      Lou*
270.  Leigh, James, *Downstairs at Ramsey's*
302.  McGraw, Eloise Jarvis, *Greensleeves*
315.  Mertz, Barbara, *Ammie, Come Home*
378.  Portis, Charles, *True Grit*
403.  Rickett, Frances, *A Certain Slant of Light*

415. Rogers, Thomas, *The Pursuit of Happiness*
420. Ross, Sam, *Hang-up*
538. Weingarten, Violet, *Mrs. Beneker*
549. White, M.E., *In the Balance*
568. Woodfin, Henry, *Virginia's Thing*
577. Zindel, Paul, *The Pigman*


*1969:*

 23. Barrett, B.L., *Love in Atlantis*
 49. Breslin, Jimmy, *The Gang That Couldn't Shoot Straight*
 77. Cleaver, Bill, and Vera Cleaver, *Where the Lilies Bloom*
 83. Connell, Evan, *Mr. Bridge*
132. Forman, James, *The Cow Neck Rebels*
161. Graves, Wallace, *Trixie*
206. Horgan, Paul, *Whitewater*
248. Koch, Stephen, *Night Watch*
312. Means, Florence C., *Our Cup Is Broken*
320. Mitchell, Don, *Thumb Tripping*
337. Neufeld, John, *Lisa, Bright and Dark*
347. Oates, Joyce Carol, *them*
388. Rader, Paul, *Professor Wilmess Must Die*
411. Robinson, Rose, *Eagle in the Air*
422. Rossner, Judith, *Nine Months in the Life of an Old Maid*
462. Shaw, Irwin, *Rich Man, Poor Man*
467. Shulman, Alix Kates, *Memoirs of an Ex-Prom Queen*
511. Tucker, Helen, *The Sound of Summer Voices*
524. Von Hoffman, Nicholas, *Two, Three, Many More*
532. Ware, Clyde, *The Innocents*
533. Watson, Sally, *Jade*
534. Waugh, Hillary, *The Young Prey*
535. Webb, Charles, *Love, Roger*
537. Weingarten, Violet, *A Loving Wife*
555. Wilson, S.J., *To Find a Man*
562. Woiwode, Larry, *What I'm Going To Do, I Think*
576. Zindel, Paul, *My Darling, My Hamburger*


*1970:*

  4. Adleman, Robert H., *The Bloody Benders*
 13. Arnow, Harriett Simpson, *The Weedkiller's Daughter*

   51.  Bristow, Gwen, *Calico Palace*
   52.  Brown, Kenneth, *The Narrows*
  108.  Dizenzo, Patricia, *Phoebe*
  124.  Fall, Thomas, *The Ordeal of Running Standing*
  135.  Friedman, Bruce Jay, *The Dick*
  138.  Gagarin, Nicholas, *Windsong*
  207.  Horwitz, Julius, *The Diary of A.N.*
  224.  Jessup, Richard, *A Quiet Voyage Home*
  244.  Kingman, Lee, *The Peter Pan Bag*
  314.  Meriwether, Louise, *Daddy Was a Number Runner*
  326.  Morrison, Toni, *The Bluest Eye*
  334.  Nathan, Robert, *Mia*
  353.  O'Dell, Scott, *Sing Down the Moon*
  372.  Piercy, Marge, *Dance the Eagle to Sleep*
  439.  Sarton, May, *Kinds of Love*
  474.  Snyder, Zilpha Keatley, *The Changeling*
  512.  Turner, Steven, *A Measure of Dust*
  516.  Tyler, Anne, *A Slipping Down Life*
  520.  Vasquez, Richard, *Chicano*
  528.  Walker, Alice, *The Third Life of Grange Copeland*
  542.  Welty, Eudora, *Losing Battles*
  556.  Wilson, Sloan, *All the Best People*
  575.  Zindel, Paul, *I Never Loved Your Mind*


*1971:*

    1.  Abbey, Edward, *Black Sun*
   16.  Athos, Daphne, *Entering Ephesus*
   30.  Berkley, Sandra, *Coming Attractions*
   38.  Blatty, William Peter, *The Exorcist*
   45.  Bradbury, Bianca, *A New Penny*
   48.  Brautigan, Richard, *The Abortion*
   58.  Calisher, Hortense, *Queenie*
   74.  Chute, B.J., *The Story of a Small Life*
   84.  Connolly, Edward, *Deer Run*
   90.  Covert, Paul, *Cages*
  101.  Davis, Mildred, *Three Minutes to Midnight*
  107.  Dizenzo, Patricia, *An American Girl*
  109.  Doctorow, E.L., *The Book of Daniel*
  117.  Dunn, Katherine, *Truck*
  141.  Gallagher, Patricia, *Summer of Sighs*
  178.  Hale, Nancy, *Secrets*
  189.  Hayes, Joseph Arnold, *Like Any Other Fugitive*
  190.  Hazel, Robert, *Early Spring*
  193.  Herlihy, James Leo, *The Season of the Witch*
  231.  Jordan, Robert, *Thanksgiving*

243.  Killens, John Oliver, *The Cotillion*
273.  Lewin, Michael Z., *Ask the Right Question*
303.  McGuane, Thomas, *The Bushwhacked Piano*
317.  Millar, Kenneth, *The Underground Man*
350.  Oates, Joyce Carol, *Wonderland*
385.  Price, William, *The Potlatch Run*
389.  Randall, Florence Engel, *The Almost Year*
390.  Raucher, Herman, *A Glimpse of Tiger*
391.  Raucher, Herman, *Summer of '42*
392.  Read, Piers Paul, *The Professor's Daughter*
397.  Reeve, F.D., *The Brother*
470.  Slavitt, David R., *Anagrams*
475.  Snyder, Zilpha Keatley, *The Headless Cupid*
477.  Sonzski, William, *Punch Goes the Judy*
491.  Stolz, Mary, *By the Highway Home*
497.  Strong, Jonathan, *Ourselves*
518.  Updike, John, *Rabbit Redux*


*1972:*

 82.  Colter, Cyrus, *The Rivers of Eros*
122.  Eyerly, Jeannette, *Bonnie Jo, Go Home*
134.  Friedman, Alan, *Hermaphrodeity*
148.  Gilbert, Julie Goldsmith, *Umbrella Steps*
154.  Gould, Lois, *Necessary Objects*
162.  Greenan, Russell H., *The Queen of America*
163.  Greenberg, Joanne, *The Dead of the House*
174.  Guy, Rosa, *The Friends*
182.  Harington, Donald, *Some Other Place. The Right
         Place*
240.  Kazan, Elia, *The Assassins*
241.  Kellogg, Marjorie, *Like the Lion's Tooth*
308.  Meaker, Marijane, *Dinky Hocker Shoots Smack*
325.  Morrison, James, *Treehouse*
329.  Mountzoures, H.L., *The Bridge*
340.  Norman, Gurney, *Divine Right's Trip*
351.  O'Brien, Robert C., *A Report from Group 17*
364.  Peck, Richard, *Don't Look and It Won't Hurt*
393.  Rechy, John, *The Fourth Angel*
442.  Savage, Elizabeth, *Happy Ending*
455.  Seelye, John, *The Kid*
473.  Smith, Mason, *Everybody Knows and Nobody Cares*
485.  Stallworth, Anne Nall, *This Time Next Year*
492.  Stolz, Mary, *Leap Before You Look*
514.  Tyler, Anne, *The Clock Winder*
554.  Willingham, Calder, *Rambling Rose*

*1973:*

  67.  Chappell, Fred, *The Gaudy Place*
  80.  Coffey, Marilyn, *Marcella*
  93.  Crews, Harry, *The Hawk Is Dying*
 116.  Duncan, Lois, *I Know What You Did Last Summer*
 142.  Gallagher, Patricia, *The Thicket*
 143.  Gardner, John, *Nickel Mountain*
 165.  Greene, Bette, *Summer of My German Soldier*
 184.  Harris, Marilyn, *Hatter Fox*
 197.  Hillerman, Tony, *Dance Hall of the Dead*
 271.  Lelchuk, Alan, *American Mischief*
 279.  Logan, Jane, *The Very Nearest Room*
 286.  MacDougall, Ruth Doan, *The Cheerleader*
 292.  Maloff, Saul, *Heartland*
 299.  Matthews, Jack, *Pictures of the Journey Back*
 309.  Meaker, Marijane, *If I Love You, Am I Trapped
         Forever?*
 323.  Morris, Willie, *The Last of the Southern Girls*
 328.  Morrison, Toni, *Sula*
 330.  Murray, Michele, *The Crystal Nights*
 336.  Neufeld, John, *For All the Wrong Reasons*
 344.  Oates, Joyce Carol, *Do with Me What You Will*
 355.  Ogburn, Charlton, *Winespring Mountain*
 360.  Parker, Robert B., *The Godwulf Manuscript*
 377.  Ponicsan, Darryl, *Andoshen, Pa.*
 381.  Price, Nancy, *A Natural Death*
 438.  Sarton, May, *As We Are Now*
 443.  Savage, Elizabeth, *The Last Night at the Ritz*
 446.  Schaeffer, Susan Fromberg, *Falling*
 472.  Smith, Lee, *Fancy Strut*
 488.  Stern, Richard, *Other Men's Daughters*
 499.  Susann, Jacqueline, *Once Is Not Enough*
 508.  Thomas, Audrey, *Songs My Mother Taught Me*
 521.  Vliet, R.G., *Rockspring*
 548.  Wetzel, Donald, *A Bird in the Hand*


*1974:*

  19.  Baldwin, James, *If Beale Street Could Talk*
  63.  Carroll, Gladys Hasty, *Next of Kin*
  65.  Cassill, Ronald Verlin, *The Goss Women*
 103.  Deal, Babs H., *The Reason for Roses*
 147.  Gerber, Merrill Joan, *Now Molly Knows*
 192.  Heller, Joseph, *Something Happened*
 218.  Israel, Peter, *Hush Money*
 222.  Jaffe, Rona, *Family Secrets*

175. Guy, Rosa, *Ruby*
176. Hahn, Harriet, *The Plantain Season*
187. Hauser, Marianne, *The Talking Room*
195. Hill, Deborah, *This Is the House*
239. Kay, Terry, *The Year the Lights Came On*
269. LeGuin, Ursula K., *Very Far Away From Anywhere Else*
288. MacDougall, Ruth Doan, *Wife and Mother*
290. Majerus, Janet, *Grandpa and Frank*
321. Mojtabai, A.G., *The 400 Eels of Sigmund Freud*
343. Oates, Joyce Carol, *Childwold*
362. Peck, Richard, *Are You in the House Alone?*
407. Robbins, Tom, *Even Cowgirls Get the Blues*
417. Rosen, Winifred, *Cruisin for a Bruisin*
426. Rothweiler, Paul R., *The Sensuous Southpaw*
468. Siddons, Anne Rivers, *Heartbreak Hotel*
527. Walker, Alice, *Meridian*
559. Winters, Nancy, *The Girl on the Coca-cola Tray*
567. Wood, Phyllis Anderson, *I Think This Is Where We Came In*
570. Yates, Richard, *The Easter Parade*


*1977:*

26. Bartholomew, Cecelia, *Outrun the Dark*
34. Blackwood, Caroline, *The Stepdaughter*
79. Cleaver, Vera, and Bill Cleaver, *Trial Valley*
88. Cormier, Robert, *I Am the Cheese*
151. Gordon, R.L., *The Lady Who Loved New York*
186. Hassler, Jon, *Staggerford*
201. Hoffman, Alice, *Property Of*
208. Houston, James, *Ghost Fox*
247. Klein, Norma, *It's O.K. If You Don't Love Me*
264. Lee, Joanna, *I Want to Keep My Baby*
282. Lowry, Beverly, *Come Back, Lolly Ray*
295. Marshall, Alexandra, *Gus in Bronze*
301. McDonald, Kay L., *Vision of the Eagle*
327. Morrison, Toni, *Song of Solomon*
354. Offit, Sidney, *What Kind of Guy Do You Think I Am?*
387. Rabe, Berniece, *The Girl Who Had No Name*
441. Savage, Elizabeth, *The Girls from the Five Great Valleys*
486. Stallworth, Anne Nall, *Where the Bright Lights Shine*
540. Wells, Rosemary, *Leave Well Enough Alone*

1978:

47.  Brancato, Robin F., *Blinded by the Light*
126.  Fast, Howard, *Second Generation*
173.  Guy, Rosa, *Edith Jackson*
217.  Irving, John, *The World According to Garp*
229.  Jones, Craig, *Blood Secrets*
249.  Kotker, Norman, *Miss Rhode Island*
257.  Langton, Jane, *The Memorial Hall Murder*
283.  Lowry, Beverly, *Emma Blue*
331.  Myrer, Anton, *The Last Convertible*
335.  Nelson, Shirley, *The Last Year of the War*
346.  Oates, Joyce Carol, *Son of the Morning*
374.  Pilcer, Sonia, *Teen Angel*
409.  Robinson, Jill, *Perdido*
447.  Schaeffer, Susan Fromberg, *Time in Its Flight*
453.  Scoppettone, Sandra, *Happy Endings Are All
        Alike*
466.  Shulman, Alix Kates, *Burning Questions*
579.  Zindel, Paul, *The Undertaker's Gone Bananas*


1979:

2.  Abrams, Linsey, *Charting by the Stars*
9.  Andrews, V.C., *Flowers in the Attic*
11.  Applewhite, Cynthia, *Sundays*
71.  Childress, Alice, *A Short Walk*
87.  Cormier, Robert, *After the First Death*
94.  Culin, Charlotte, *Cages of Glass, Flowers of
        Time*
96.  Cummings, Betty Sue, *Now Ameriky*
115.  Duncan, Lois, *Daughters of Eve*
121.  Epstein, Jacob, *Wild Oats*
133.  Freely, Maureen, *Mother's Helper*
150.  Goldman, William, *Tinsel*
172.  Gutcheon, Beth, *The New Girls*
180.  Hansen, Joseph, *Skinflick*
181.  Hardwick, Elizabeth, *Sleepless Nights*
183.  Harnack, Curtis, *Limits of the Land*
200.  Hoffman, Alice, *The Drowning Season*
221.  Jaffe, Rona, *Class Reunion*
228.  Johnson, Sandy, *The CUPPI*
236.  Kaplow, Robert, *Two in the City*
267.  Leffland, Ella, *Rumors of Peace*
339.  Nixon, Joan Lowery, *The Kidnapping of Christina
        Lattimore*

348.  Oates, Joyce Carol, *Unholy Loves*
373.  Piercy, Marge, *Vida*
380.  Price, Nancy, *An Accomplished Woman*
478.  Southerland, Ellease, *Let the Lion Eat Straw*
481.  Spencer, Scott, *Endless Love*
489.  Stewart, Edward, *Ballerina*
490.  Stimpson, Kate, *Class Notes*
530.  Waller, Leslie, *The Brave and the Free*
544.  West, Jessamyn, *The Life I Really Lived*


*1980:*

  3.  Adams, Alice, *Rich Rewards*
 10.  Andrews, V.C., *Petals on the Wind*
 21.  Bambara, Toni Cade, *The Salt Eaters*
 28.  Beattie, Ann, *Falling in Place*
 69.  Cheatham, K. Follis, *Bring Home the Ghost*
104.  DeVries, Peter, *Consenting Adults*
111.  Doty, Carolyn, *A Day Late*
170.  Guest, Elissa Haden, *The Handsome Man*
194.  Higgins, George V., *Kennedy for the Defense*
202.  Hogan, William, *The Quartzsite Trip*
209.  Hunt, Irene, *Claws of a Young Century*
230.  Jones, Douglas C., *Elkhorn Tavern*
232.  Josephs, Rebecca, *Early Disorder*
235.  Kaplan, Johanna, *O My America!*
242.  Kennedy, Raymond, *Columbine*
245.  Klein, Norma, *Breaking Up*
251.  Krantz, Judith, *Princess Daisy*
263.  Leavitt, Caroline, *Meeting Rozzy Halfway*
268.  LeGuin, Ursula K., *The Beginning Place*
272.  Leven, Jeremy, *Creator*
324.  Morris, Wright, *Plains Song*
342.  Oates, Joyce Carol, *Bellefleur*
366.  Percy, Walker, *The Second Coming*
370.  Pfeffer, Susan Beth, *About David*
410.  Robinson, Marilynne, *Housekeeping*
414.  Rogers, Thomas, *At the Shores*
421.  Rossner, Judith, *Emmeline*
424.  Roth, Arthur, *The Caretaker*
449.  Schneider, Nina, *The Woman Who Lived in a
        Prologue*
456.  Segal, Erich, *Man, Woman and Child*
460.  Settle, Mary Lee, *The Scapegoat*
506.  Thayer, Nancy, *Stepping*
509.  Tolan, Stephanie S., *The Last of Eden*
515.  Tyler, Anne, *Morgan's Passing*

519. Valin, Joseph, *The Lime Pit*
566. Wolitzer, Hilma, *Hearts*
578. Zindel, Paul, *The Pigman's Legacy*


*1981:*

  8. Alther, Lisa, *Original Sins*
 18. Bach, Alice, *Waiting for Johnny Miracle*
 40. Blume, Judy, *Tiger Eyes*
 70. Childress, Alice, *Rainbow Jordan*
105. Dew, Robb Forman, *Dale Loves Sophie to Death*
130. Flagg, Fannie, *Coming Attractions*
139. Gallagher, Patricia, *All for Love*
179. Hall, Lynn, *The Horse Trader*
211. Hunter, Evan, *Love, Dad*
216. Irving, John, *The Hotel New Hampshire*
223. Jaffe, Rona, *Mazes and Monsters*
246. Klein, Norma, *Domestic Arrangements*
276. Lipton, James, *Mirrors*
281. Lorimer, L.T., *Secrets*
287. MacDougall, Ruth Doan, *The Flowers of the Forest*
300. Maynard, Joyce, *Baby Love*
310. Meaker, Marijane, *Little Little*
341. Oates, Joyce Carol, *Angel of Light*
363. Peck, Richard, *Close Enough to Touch*
379. Poverman, C.E., *Solomon's Daughter*
444. Savage, Thomas, *Her Side of It*
452. Schwartz, Lynne Sharon, *Balancing Acts*
461. Shaw, Irwin, *Bread Upon the Waters*
507. Theroux, Alexander, *Darconville's Cat*
517. Updike, John, *Rabbit Is Rich*
523. Voigt, Cynthia, *Homecoming*
571. Yglesias, Helen, *Sweetsir*
573. Zacharias, Lee, *Lessons*
574. Zindel, Paul, *The Girl Who Wanted a Boy*

# TITLE INDEX

Marcella, 80
Marie Beginning, 166
Mary Dove, 429
Masquerade, 55
Massacre at Fall Creek, The, 545
Matter of Love and Death, A, 541
Matter of Time, A, 546
Mazes and Monsters, 223
McCaffrey, 153
Measure of Dust, A, 512
Meeting Rozzy Halfway, 263
Memoirs of an Ex-Prom Queen, 467
Memorial Hall Murder, The, 257
Meridian, 527
Mia, 334
Mirrors, 276
Miss Bannister's Girls, 503
Miss Rhode Island, 249
Misty Curtain, The, 86
Moon and the Thorn, The, 73
Moonflower Vine, The, 60
Morgan's Passing, 515
Moss on the North Side, 552
Mother's Helper, A, 133
Mother's Kisses, A, 136
Mountain and the Feather, The, 14
Mountain of Winter, 451
Moveable Feast, 44
Mr. Bridge, 83
Mr. Gallion's School, 498
Mrs. Beneker, 538
My Darling, My Hamburger, 576
My Father's House, 119
My Sister, My Friend, 35
My Sweet Charlie, 547

Narrows, The, 52
Natural Death, A, 381
Necessary Objects, 154
Never Younger, Jeannie, 560
New Girl, The, 437
New Girls, The, 172
New Life, A, 291
New Penny, A, 45
Next of Kin, 63
Nice Italian Girl, A, 72
Nickel Mountain, 143

SUBJECT INDEX

Please note: Index listings indicate only the most
important themes which directly affect the adolescent
female characters. Only those subjects most promi-
nently identified in the annotations are cited here.
No more than three subject listings are assigned to
any one entry.

Racism, 19, 25, 55, 62, 69, 71, 75, 95, 100, 124,
    142, 157, 160, 161, 167, 169, 174, 175, 177,
    184, 190, 207, 208, 213, 243, 293, 297, 301, 312,
    313, 326, 327, 328, 353, 381, 389, 401, 416,
    468, 478, 482, 504, 522, 526, 527, 529, 533,
    537, 547, 552
Rape, 9, 57, 81, 216, 223, 225, 343, 346, 349, 362,
    453, 457, 478
Religion, 11, 38, 47, 56, 80, 137, 206, 252, 259,
    262, 333, 335, 346, 394, 396, 431, 540
School, 2, 20, 27, 28, 53, 55, 56, 115, 172, 177,
    186, 188, 207, 220, 221, 227, 237, 241, 250,
    252, 262, 266, 271, 286, 291, 292, 294, 296,
    306, 321, 335, 338, 368, 388, 437, 440, 465,
    467, 468, 470, 488, 490, 498, 503, 509, 524,
    526, 549, 572, 573, 574
Setting, Locale: *frontier*, 208, 378, 429, 455, 521,
    532; *rural*, 143, 183, 296, 297, 324, 330, 334,
    356, 382, 383, 435, 469, 485, 560; *small town*,
    140, 255, 258, 277, 282, 323, 367, 403, 436,
    472; *suburban*, 28; *urban*, 52, 114, 122, 151,
    152, 193, 207, 236, 244, 400, 420, 432;
    Period: *historical*, 4, 22, 37, 41, 51, 62, 69,
    75, 76, 95, 96, 120, 132, 139, 149, 195, 208,
    230, 234, 259, 280, 293, 301, 307, 353, 378,
    381, 401, 421, 429, 447, 480, 504, 521, 525,
    529, 532, 533, 543; *1900-1909*, 151, 209; *1910s*,
    560; *1920s*, 152, 277; *1930s*, 23, 85, 114, 126,
    253, 399, 403, 405, 441, 442, 476, 485; *1940s*,
    14, 103, 126, 163, 267, 380, 391, 408, 414;
    *1950s*, 52, 107, 130, 147, 227, 282, 286, 397,
    414, 468; *1960s*, 2, 13, 20, 27, 109, 190, 193,
    202, 211, 231, 299, 338, 368, 373, 388, 420,
    524, 539; *1970s*, 121, 240
Sexual Activity: Heterosexual, 1, 3, 4, 6, 7, 10, 14,
    16, 17, 19, 23, 24, 27, 30, 31, 32, 33, 36, 37,
    39, 41, 42, 48, 52, 53, 54, 58, 60, 61, 62, 64, 65
    66, 68, 69, 72, 73, 75, 76, 82, 84, 85, 86, 88,
    90, 92, 93, 95, 96, 97, 99, 103, 104, 112, 113,
    114, 119, 120, 121, 124, 126, 129, 136, 137, 139,
    140, 141, 142, 146, 148, 150, 153, 157, 158, 161,
    169, 170, 171, 176, 177, 179, 180, 182, 186,
    187, 188, 189, 195, 196, 198, 199, 203, 205,
    206, 211, 216, 217, 224, 227, 230, 234, 237,
    238, 239, 242, 245, 247, 248, 249, 250, 254,
    258, 259, 261, 262, 269, 270, 271, 272, 278,